Master Detective

The Life and Crimes of Ellis Parker, America's Real-Life Sherlock Holmes

(Updated and expanded with new information)

By John Reisinger

Glyphworks Publishing 2012

Copyright 2012 by John Reisinger
(www.johnreisinger.com)
ISBN 978-0-9838818-2-7

Contents

Author Note to the revised and updated edition

We tend to think that history is as fixed and unchanging as the stone monuments that commemorate it. After all, the past is over and done with; how can it be altered? Of course the past can't be changed, but our knowledge of the past is usually incomplete and is subject to revision and updating as new sources are discovered or old sources are discredited or supplemented in some way.

Since Master Detective was first published, I have met many people with an interest in both Ellis Parker and the Lindbergh kidnapping. Some of these are relatives of Ellis Parker, or are people whose parents or grandparents had some personal involvement in the case. I have also spoken and corresponded with several researchers who have done extensive independent work related to the Lindbergh case. As a result of these contacts, and more research on my own, the sometimes hazy picture of Ellis Parker he left behind has come into sharper focus in some areas and become murkier in others. One purpose of this edition is to incorporate this new information to clarify and expand what has already been written. While the whole truth about Ellis Parker will probably never be known with certainty, this book is an attempt to get as close as possible.

One surprise was that as more sources became available,

Ellis Parker's role in some of his cases became even less clear. In the Matilda Russo murder, for instance, Parker told author Fletcher Pratt that he had discovered the victim's body buried in the killer's dirt basement by pouring water on the floor and seeing what area was more absorbent due to newly dug earth. Contemporary newspaper accounts, however, report that the body was found by local police and that Parker, though fully involved in the investigation, was not present. Whether this was the result of a faulty memory or some self-serving exaggeration is impossible to say.

A second purpose of this edition is to include some up to date developments in the Ellis Parker story. One of Parker's grandsons has been researching on his own and working tirelessly on a pardon application for the Old Chief. He has turned up some medical information that may cast some light on Parker's state of mind when the Wendel affair unfolded.

The story of Ellis Parker, his amazing career, his involvement in the Lindbergh case, and his ultimate fate have been overshadowed by time and by the magnitude of the Lindbergh case itself. When Ellis Parker has been mentioned at all, it has usually been as a curious sidelight. But the story of this remarkable man is a mystery in itself and one that has never been satisfactorily explained.

In reconstructing his life, I have stuck to documented facts from primary sources as closely as possible. Since Ellis Parker's personal papers were destroyed, however, I have had to use many secondary sources, supplemented by interviews with some of the few people who had some connection with Parker. Ellis Parker's role in the Lindbergh investigation is still a matter of controversy. Some who have researched the case view Parker as a self-centered opportunist, and some as a selfless man who gallantly sacrificed his career to try to prevent a miscarriage of justice and thereby found the real kidnapper. In following this story, I have found neither of these extremes to be accurate. Ellis Parker was a flawed man, but a giant nevertheless. If his ego was big, his achievements were bigger. I hope the structure of this book will help paint a portrait of the real man behind the stories and put the tragedy of his final case into the much larger context of his long and distinguished career. Today Ellis Parker is remembered for how he died, when the real story is how he lived.

Although with Ellis Parker, it is often hard to tell where fact leaves off and myth begins, I have tried to be true to the people and events of this extraordinary story.

John Reisinger
January, 2012

To Barbara for all her help and support

Acknowledgments:

Discovering the story of Ellis Parker was a detective feat in its own right. I wish to thank the following people for their generous assistance that made it possible:

Herman Bading- Anna Bading's son

Mr. and Mrs. Conly D. Brooks, Jr- Who generously opened their Mt Holly home, and loaned the author a file of newspapers left behind by Ellis Parker

Elton A. Conda- County Surrogate, Burlington County, NJ- who remembered the Parker case and found Ellis Parker's will.

Robert Congleton, -Archivist of Rider University Library, who provided information on the "Cranberry King" murder

Walter Corter- Chief Detective, Burlington County, NJ- who discussed his predecessor and gave some new leads

James Dedman- Lindbergh case researcher-University of South Carolina

Mark Falzini- New Jersey State Police Museum Archivist, who guided the author through the Parker-Wendel-Hoffman files in the museum.

Robert Fisher- Who gave the author a tour of the Mt Holly Elks Club

William Fullerton,- Ellis Parker's Grandson- who maintains an Ellis Parker website and generously provided information about his grandfather as well as family photos.

Cindy Grassia- Camden Courier-Journal, who dug out the Courier Journal's extensive articles on the Parker-Wendel case.

Fred Kafes- Grandson of John H. Kafes, Paul Wendel's attorney

Kelvin Keraga- Lindbergh case researcher and author of the definitive study of the wood evidence.

Dave Kimball, Bill Reilly- Burlington County Prison Museum, who researched and provided records on Ellis Parker

Allen Koenigsburg- Lindbergh researcher and Lindbergh website manager, who compared notes and provided information

Harry McConnell- Chief Detective of Burlington County after Ellis Parker, who shared his files and personal reminiscences of Parker's secretary, Anna Bading.

Michael Melsky- Lindbergh case researcher and Lindbergh website manager who compared notes and provided information

Hope Nelson- Governor Hoffman's daughter, who shared memories of her father and Ellis Parker

Randall Parker- Ellis Parker's grandson, who provided some more pieces of the puzzle

Bill Reidy- Highfields Director, who gave a personal tour of the Lindbergh house and grounds

Steve Romeo- Lindbergh case researcher who compared notes and provided information

Andrew Sahol,- Ellis Parker's grandson who generously shared his files, photographs and memories.

Leon Sheer, M.D.- Who provided medical information on various medical questions including Parker's possible brain tumor, the condition of the corpse of the Lindbergh baby, and on the Situs Inversis condition described in the Washington Hunter murder.

And Dorothy Christopher, Jim Gentry, Shelly Greenberg, H.P. Ketterman, James Logan Jr., Paula Manzella, Stanley Schapiro, David Thaler, Phyliss at Bright Horizons Realty and many others who gave information and encouragement.

Master Detective

The Life and Crimes of Ellis Parker, America's Real-Life
Sherlock Holmes
(Updated and expanded with new information)

Also by John Reisinger:

Death of a Flapper
Death on a Golden Isle
Evasive Action
Nassau
The Duckworth Chronicles

www.johnreisinger.com

Chapter 1
A Crime in the Next County
1932

Cold gusty rain swept the rolling countryside near Hopewell, New Jersey, blowing dead leaves across bleak farm fields covered with stubble. Trees still bare from winter stood black and lonely against the low clouds in the night sky while gray stone walls marking property boundaries glistened darkly in the rain.

On a gentle rise at the end of a long curving driveway, a large whitewashed stone house stood alone, appearing gray in the darkness. Patches of light glowed warmly from several windows on the first floor. The second floor windows were dark. On one of those windows, a loose shutter rattled slightly in the wind.

Inside, the nursemaid put the baby to bed upstairs and pinned his blanket in place. She opened the widow a crack and placed a screen in front of the crib to deflect drafts. The baby went to sleep quickly.

The rain died away, but the cold wind still rose and fell, muffling the sound of soft footsteps as a shadow moved through the dark woods towards the house.

Around 9:00pm, someone downstairs heard a sharp cracking noise like wood breaking somewhere outside, but thought nothing of it. Finally, about 10:00pm, as everyone began preparing for bed, the nursemaid went in to check on the baby.

She didn't want to disturb him, so she only turned on the light in the adjoining bathroom. As she did, she noticed the room felt colder than she remembered, so she closed the window and turned on the electric heater in the fireplace. As she stood warming her hands in the dimly lit room, she was suddenly aware that she could not hear the baby breathing. Thinking the covers might have gotten over the baby's head, she walked over to the other side of the room, pushed the screen aside, and looked in the crib.

A few miles away, at the New Jersey State Police barracks at Wiburtha, in West Trenton, Trooper Bornmann pulled off his raincoat as he walked in out of the windy night. He greeted the duty officer, Lieutenant Dunn, commenting on the weather and the traffic accident he had investigated. The phone rang and Dunn answered.

"New Jersey State Police. Lieutenant Dunn speaking. Yes.... yes...."

Dunn frowned, picked up a pencil and began writing. "What time?..Yes."

He hung up the phone and sat with a bewildered look on his face.

"Who was that?" asked Bornmann, picking up a cup of coffee.

Dunn still looked confused, staring at the phone.

"Some guy who said he was Charles Lindbergh."

Bornmann's eyes widened. Everyone knew of the famous and reclusive Charles Lindbergh and his newly built estate just outside of nearby Hopewell.

"Lindbergh? No kidding? Well, what did he want?"

Dunn turned towards Bornmann.

"He said his baby's been kidnapped."

Hopewell Chief of Police Harry Wolfe and Constable Charles Williamson were the first investigators to arrive at the Lindbergh estate outside of town, pulling up at 10:40. They found Lindbergh and butler Oliver Whately searching the grounds. In the faint light, Lindbergh looked calm, businesslike, and in control, just as he always did in the newspapers. He led Wolfe and Williamson to the baby's second floor room where they found some small clumps of mud on a leather suitcase by the window. On the wide windowsill was a plain, unmarked envelope that the Lindberghs, in an effort to preserve any possible fingerprints, had not opened.

Outside they found footprints below the window and two rectangular indentations in the soft ground. Further away from the house they found a 3/4-inch chisel on the ground and still further away, a homemade ladder. The ladder had been made in three collapsible sections that nested together, apparently for easy transport. Only two sections had been used. The rungs on the ladder were unusually far apart, apparently to make the ladder lighter and more portable. Wooden dowels through the overlapping side rails had connected the two ladder sections, but the dowel holes had created a weak point. The lower part of the two upper side rails had split, the possible source of the cracking noise Lindbergh heard.

Ladder at the Lindbergh house
(Photo courtesy of the New Jersey State Police Museum)

By 11:00, checkpoints were set up in New Jersey and along the approaches to New York City. Corporal Joseph Wolf was the first of the state police to arrive and two more troopers arrived a few minutes later. One set up a checkpoint at the end of the long driveway to preserve any possible tire tracks, and the other stood watch over the area beneath the nursery window. By 11:15 over a dozen state police were on the scene, including their founder and superintendent, Colonel H. Norman Schwarzkopf. Like many others, Schwarzkopf was a great admirer of Lindbergh and regarded him with awe. He introduced himself to his hero and asked if he had any idea who could have done this. Lindbergh did not. Crime scene investigator Corporal Frank Kelly examined the envelope, but found no prints. Inside, on a single sheet of paper, was a message written in blue ink in an unsteady hand:

Dear Sir!

Have 50000$ redy with 2500$ in 20$ bills 1500$ in 10$ bills and 1000$ in 5$ bills. After 2-4 days we will inform you were to deliver the Mony. We warn you for making anyding public or for notify the polise the child is in gute care. Indication for all letters are singnature and 3 holes."

The last line referred to the curious way the writer of the note had signed it: a solid red circle in the center of two interlocking blue circles and pierced by three small holes. Schwarzkopf decided to keep the message confidential to make it easier to authenticate future notes.

Outside in the freezing darkness, reporters from the New York Times, the New York Daily News and other papers began to arrive, clamoring for details and lending the scene an air of hysteria and anxious confusion. The usually publicity-shy

Lindbergh invited the reporters, now over 20 strong, into the three-car garage where butler Oliver Whately served coffee. Because there was still so little to see in the darkness, most of the reporters soon departed to get their stories in before their morning deadlines. Those remaining at the house waited anxiously for word from the roadblocks.

By sunrise, the story was all over the nation, and hundreds of the curious public descended on the estate. Narrow local roads were soon jammed and visitors began to appear on foot, trudging through the woods from all directions, leaving trails of muddy footprints and trash in their wake.

About 30 police and other investigators were in the Lindbergh house by now, but Schwarzkopf knew more manpower would be needed, so various police were assigned to contact detectives around the state and enlist their help. Trooper William Horn left the Lindbergh house around 11:00 AM and headed to Mt. Holly to seek out Burlington County's chief detective.

By late in the day, the area was under control and police had set up a command post in the garage. The next morning, extra phone lines were laid along the Hopewell-Princeton Road. The police questioned local people and Lindbergh called upon a local tracker and hunter named Oscar Bush to follow the trail from beneath the window. Bush concluded that the footprints were from two different men who had been wearing covers over their shoes. He also found what appeared to be the tire tracks of two cars in the mud by the private dirt road that connected with the driveway.

To accommodate all the people assigned to the house, the police covered most of the first floor living room with mattresses. Meals were prepared and served almost continuously. The state police shared the command post/garage with the various reporters who surged in and out, and the library was used for conferences.

In addition to investigating, manning the 20 phone lines and providing security, several state police were assigned to review incoming mail. In the days to come, hundreds of letters would pour in from well-wishers, amateur detectives, psychics, and just plain kooks. People from all over the country wrote to relay their prophetic dreams, personal theories, astrology readings, or séances. The New York Times estimated more than 100,000 people coast to coast were involved in the search. The Commissioner of Public Safety in Pittsburgh announced he would send his entire force to visit every home in the city searching for the baby, even though there was no evidence the baby should actually be in Pittsburgh. The important thing was to do something, preferably something public.

Across the nation, everyone was talking about the case and everyone had an opinion. The most popular theory was that the kidnapping was the work of organized crime. The snatch racket as it was called was becoming more popular with professional criminals. Some said Detroit's Purple Gang was involved, or some New York crime boss, or the Touhey gang. There was even a rumor that Al Capone himself had arranged the kidnapping as a bargaining chip to get out of jail where he had recently been sent for tax evasion.

Lindbergh was convinced organized crime was to blame and wanted the investigation slanted in that direction. Schwarzkopf reluctantly went along, even though he didn't agree. The snatch racket targeted wealthy men, not babies, and certainly not the children of national icons. Schwarzkopf reasoned that the clumsy, broken English of the ransom notes, coupled with the modest ransom demand of $50,000, and the ladder left behind indicated the work of someone who was not an experienced kidnapper, and not involved in organized crime. But Lindbergh continued to influence the investigation, because he was more than a victimized parent, he was an American icon.

Only five years before, Charles Lindbergh, the Lone Eagle, had been the first man to fly solo across the Atlantic. From the moment he landed the Spirit of St. Louis in Paris, Charles Augustus Lindbergh became the most famous and admired man in America, if not the world. Brave, handsome, modest, Lindbergh was the perfect American hero. "Lucky Lindy" was celebrated in story and song everywhere.

In spite of his fame and popularity, Lindbergh valued his privacy. He and Anne Morrow Lindbergh divided their time between Anne's parents' house at Next Day Hill, near New York City, and their own nearly completed house near Hopewell. The Hopewell house was still under construction, so the Lindberghs spent only their weekends there. The kidnappers' timing had been suspiciously precise.

The investigators continued to mobilize and expand. On March 5, four days after the kidnapping, New Jersey Governor A. Harry Moore held a conference in Trenton of "all available municipal, federal, and private police forces throughout the country" to coordinate the efforts of all the many entities working on the case. One police commissioner, in an unfortunate choice of words said the conference would create "the greatest and smoothest working crime machine ever assembled." J. Edgar Hoover attended for the federal government, as well as police commissioners from around the country, local law enforcement people, and even private detectives representing the Burns Agency and the Pinkerton Agency. All told, there were 52 representatives from police departments as far away as St. Louis.

While the police met in Trenton, a second ransom note arrived at the Lindbergh estate. This note, written in the same hand and with the same fractured English-German word order and spelling, complained of the publicity and raised the ransom demand to $70,000. More ominously, it said that the kidnappers would have to keep the baby for a longer time than they had expected. The note gave no instructions for transfer of the money and no hint as to what Lindbergh should do next.

The noise and confusion surrounding the investigation continued. A bootlegger and con man named Mickey Rosner convinced Lindbergh's lawyer, Henry Breckenridge to make him and two of his "associates" intermediaries to deal with the kidnappers. The "associates", two mobsters named Salvatore Spitale and Irving Bitz promptly moved into the Lindbergh home and freeloaded without contributing anything to the case except more aggravation. One of Rosner's first actions was to circulate a copy of the ransom note Schwarzkopf wanted to keep secret. To add even further to the surreal atmosphere at the Lindbergh home, a private pilot began flying over the house every day taking people on sightseeing tours.

Amidst the constant din of publicity, false leads, hysterical speculation, second-guessing, interference, and intense public scrutiny, Schwarzkopf and his state police pushed ahead as best they could. The Lindbergh kidnapping had become the most discussed topic of the hour. All over the world, people followed each development with fascination, discussing and critiquing the performance of the state police. Suddenly, everyone was an amateur detective, like the heroes in the currently popular stories of Ellery Queen, Dashiell Hammett, Agatha Christie, and S.S. Van Dine. The theories, speculation, rumors, and outright gossip continued to swirl around the case like a swarm of angry bees. But of all those who were following the case, none followed more intently and with more interest than a certain individual a few miles to the south, in Burlington County.

Compared to the frantic, confused, and frustrated atmosphere at the Lindbergh house, the old Quaker town of Mt. Holly, the county seat of Burlington County seemed quiet and leisurely. In the crisp, cold air of March, the old colonial courthouse stood placidly on High Street amid bare trees and lifeless flowerbeds. Pedestrians bundled up against the chill strolled up and down the street as a few automobiles passed by. In the red brick Elks Club next to the courthouse, men in the second floor bar read the newspapers, played cards, and speculated about the Lindbergh baby. In the center of town, just a block away, people in the stores and small businesses along High Street and Rancocas Road shook their heads and talked excitedly about the kidnapping. Everyone had his own ideas on the case, each one heavy on speculation and light on facts. In short, Mt. Holly was pretty much like most other towns in America, and its citizens were pretty much like everyone else ... with one important exception.

In his small office on the second floor of the courthouse, Burlington County Chief of Detectives Ellis Howard Parker sat motionless behind a cluttered desk, slowly drawing on his pipe, occasionally refilling it from a can of Sir Walter Raleigh. He leaned back balancing on the rear legs of his chair, his back almost touching the radiator and the wall behind him, a fog of white smoke slowly rolled and spread through the room. He was a short stocky man, bald except for a fringe of white and a small mustache. No one would have called Parker "dapper". He was dressed in dark trousers, a mismatched vest, and an open neck white shirt that looked as if it had been worn during a wrestling match. Ellis Parker really didn't look much like a detective, more like the owner of the local hardware store. But his appearance was deceiving, as many criminals had found out the hard way. Behind the rumpled facade was a shrewd and calculating mind, coupled with a folksy manner that put suspects at their ease, and often coaxed them into a confession.

His secretary, Anna Bading, knew better than to disturb him when he sat staring at that spot on the wall. The Chief was thinking, and it didn't take a detective to figure out just what he was thinking about.

The Trenton Evening Times lay open on the desk in front of him. Like every other paper in the country, the front page was splashed with articles about the Lindbergh kidnapping. Of course there were other stories in the paper that day; stories about Hitler and Mussolini threatening Europe and the Japanese overrunning China.

The Burlington County Courthouse in Mt Holly
(Author photo)

Closer to home, the worldwide depression still had the nation in its grip, and the jobless sold apples on street corners. The doomed experiment of Prohibition was in its 12th unhappy year, and New York Governor Franklin Delano Roosevelt had just announced his candidacy for President in the fall election.

Spawned by both Prohibition and the Depression, organized crime was prospering, and men such as Dutch Schultz and Al Capone were household words. But even with all the turmoil elsewhere, the kidnapping of the Lindbergh baby was the one story that fascinated everyone, including Ellis Parker.

The kidnapping occurred in Mercer County, next door to Burlington County, and out of Parker's official jurisdiction. Five days had now passed since the crime. On the second day, State Trooper William Horn came by asking Parker to help out, but they expected him to work on routine tasks under the direction of the state police and Colonel H. Norman Schwarzkopf. Parker sent Horn away empty-handed.

Parker felt insulted by the request. He wasn't used to being just another detective because he wasn't just another detective. Ellis Parker was considered by many to be the greatest detective in America, possibly the world. The newspapers called him the "County Detective with the World Wide Reputation", and "The American Sherlock Holmes". He and his detectives handled hundreds of cases a year and nearly every one of them ended in an arrest and conviction. Around the office were battered old filing cabinets containing files on hundreds of cases he had solved. Asking him to be just one of the crowd was like expecting a racehorse to pull a plow. No, if Ellis Parker joined in the hunt for the Lindbergh kidnapper, it would not be as a lowly helper; it would be on his own terms.

Crumpled up in Parker's wastebasket was the newspaper report of Governor Moore's police conference in Trenton the day before. The governor had sent out an open invitation to police forces all over the nation to attend a conference and compare notes on the case. Police and private detectives answered the call, but not Parker. He didn't work as just a face in the crowd. He ran his investigations his own way, the way that got results.

Knowing his reputation, Parker's many contacts in the press asked him to comment on the case, but he remained silent. On March 5, however, Parker decided it was time to make a statement. In an article the New York Times placed on the same page as the report of the governor's conference, Parker told the press that the police were not any help in recovering the baby, and that things should be handled differently.

"If I were Colonel Lindbergh, I would clear out all the officers from his case and I would deal directly with the kidnappers. There is only one thing at issue in this case, and that is to get the baby back alive and restore it to its father and mother ... it's strictly a business proposition. The abductors are lying low awaiting immunity, and I believe they will delay any harm to the baby as long as possible."

The most important thing, he continued, was getting the baby back safely, not capturing the kidnappers. If the kidnapper would return the baby, he would personally do everything in his power to see that the kidnapper was treated fairly and with mercy. Parker reasoned that, with the hornet's nest they had stirred up, the kidnappers might be having second thoughts, and might welcome the chance to back out as gracefully as possible.

Later, Parker would claim he was concerned he ran the risk of being investigated for helping the kidnappers escape justice. After agonizing, he finally decided that the baby's life was worth more than the punishment of the kidnapper, and went ahead.

The statement annoyed the official investigators. They saw it as an attempt by Parker to insert himself into the investigation by making promises he could not possibly keep. However, Col A. J. McNabb, Jr., who had been military attaché to Anne Lindbergh's father in Mexico noted the article and decided to bring it to the attention of Charles Lindbergh himself. On March 9 McNabb wrote to Parker to say he had conferred with Lindbergh and that Lindbergh agreed with Parker's public statements. Even so, the state police remained at Hopewell.

Parker pushed back his chair and slowly stood up in the smoky gloom. He looked out the window to the park area behind the courthouse and spoke, partly to Anna Bading, and partly to himself.

"Too much time," he muttered. "Too much damn time. Every hour that goes by and the trail gets a little colder; especially now that Colonel Schwarzkopf and his pals have made a hash of the crime scene. They let every flatfoot, reporter, family member, and curiosity seeker stomp around there before anyone with a proper eye looked at it. They could have found the footprints of the kidnapper and maybe seen how he got there, and where he went afterwards. They could have matched up the prints with suspects, but not with that 'elephant's parade' they let through there. They were lucky they found the damn ladder."

The pipe had gone out. Parker scratched a wooden match on the windowsill to relight it. Fresh clouds of smoke arose as Parker continued.

"And every hour that goes by, the trail gets colder and the pressure for an arrest gets higher. They'll probably wind up arresting some poor Jasper who had nothing to do with it. I was against New Jersey having a state police force when they started it back in '21. I said it would just gum up real law enforcement. The way they're handling this case proves it."

Anna nodded in sympathy. She knew Ellis Parker had a low opinion of other detectives, and especially of the New Jersey State Police and their chief, H. Norman Schwarzkopf. Parker took a special joy on those occasions when he solved a crime that had the state police stumped.

Parker turned from the window, sighed, and addressed Anna directly.

"I'm going to get a bite of lunch. I'll be back in a half-hour or so."

"Over to the Elks?"

It was a good guess. Parker spent a lot of time at the Elks Club, though for lunch he often went into town just a block away. He could sometimes catch a comment or a bit of casual information that would fit in with a case he was investigating. Ellis Parker believed that there was no such thing as useless information, because you never knew when all the pieces would suddenly come together.

With his pipe still in his mouth, he got his overcoat off the coat rack in the corner.

"Oh, I may look in at the Elks, but I think I'll stroll into town and see what's doing. I'll eat at one of the places there, maybe the hotel." He grabbed his battered hat from the top of the rack and headed for the stairs. His footsteps caused the old wooden courthouse floors to creak and echo.

As he had done for so many years, he crossed the lawn behind the courthouse and make his way in the direction of the Elks Club just a few steps away. From there, he would continue down High Street into the center of Mt. Holly, greeting strollers and shopkeepers as he walked. Everyone knew the Chief, and everyone respected him. He encouraged people to call him Ellis, even children. Ellis Parker liked to bask in the attention of his admiring public. When Parker was immersed in a difficult case he often forgot to shave, and local people in Mt Holly claimed they could tell when Ellis was involved in a really tough case just by observing the thickness of his stubble.

With the world attention the Lindbergh case was attracting, everyone was feeling the pressure, but the official investigation made little progress. None of the roadblocks set up after the kidnapping yielded any suspects, and no one seemed to have seen or heard anything useful. License numbers of stolen cars were published, but with no results. Babies resembling the victim were reported in automobiles in Buffalo, Washington, Port Chester, Philadelphia, Nashua, New Hampshire, and a score of other towns. Neighbors reported hearing babies crying in unexpected places, and phony ransom notes continued to arrive at Hopewell.

The police questioned the members of the Lindbergh household but learned little. The kidnappers' knowledge of the location of the baby's room and the habits of the Lindberghs seemed to indicate the possibility of an "inside job", or at least some contact or leak within the house. But police soon learned that butler Oliver Whately had sometimes given the public guided tours of the house in the Lindberghs' absence. In fact, a number of the local people had dropped by to inspect the house while it was under construction. The maid, Violet Sharpe, was suspiciously nervous and evasive while interviewed, but this too led nowhere. In spite of all the intense investigation, there was still no suspect, and, most importantly, no baby.

A few days after the kidnapping, an obscure school principal and physical education teacher named John Condon took out an ad in a local Bronx newspaper offering a $1,000 reward for the return of the baby, and also offering his services as an intermediary. Condon had no connection with either the Lindberghs or the police, and there was no rational reason why his ad should have even been noticed, let alone taken seriously. (The Bronx Home News had a circulation of only 150,000.) Nevertheless, Condon received a letter from the kidnappers the very next day accepting him as an intermediary. Since the letter had been signed in the same distinctive way as the ransom notes, Lindbergh accepted Condon as intermediary. To avoid publicity when communicating with the kidnappers through ads in the newspapers, Condon was to be known as "Jafsie", a name derived from his initials, J.F.C.

So while the Lindbergh investigation went on with no results, America's greatest detective, just a few miles away, impatiently awaited his chance.

When Parker returned to his office after lunch, he received a phone call. The raspy voice on the other end sounded strained, distorted, and sinister, like someone disguising his real voice, but Parker could tell it was a man, probably middle aged, and with no accent.

"Did you mean what you said in that newspaper article?" the voice asked.

"Yes, I did," Parker replied. "If I had the money I'd pay it myself."

"Well, I trust you will interest yourself in the case without publicity, and I am sure you will have success."

The phone went dead.

Parker made a note of the time and substance of the call and returned to his other cases.

Soon, however, his mind came back to the Lindbergh case. What if the man on the phone was the kidnapper? Was it possible to get him to return the baby unharmed? Parker cursed to himself in frustration. If only he could get an official crack at the investigation. It would be the biggest case of his career. Solving the Lindbergh case would be his greatest challenge, the crown jewel of his remarkable 40-year career. Out the window he could see the old jail, with cells that had held so many of the people Parker had caught over the years. There was even a place where gallows once stood and where several of his more serious arrests had been hanged. In Burlington County, Parker was master of all he surveyed, but once across the county line, he had no official authority.

His eye fell on the newspaper on his desk once again and he shook his head in disbelief and frustration. Here, just a few miles away, was the greatest crime of the decade, maybe of the century, and he was being left out of it. Time was passing and the trail was growing cold, but without any access to the evidence he might as well be just a curious bystander with his nose up against the glass. Even if he somehow single-handedly found the kidnappers, he couldn't even arrest them unless they were in his county! If only he could be given the information and resources the state police had.

Now Parker was staring at the spot on the wall again, but this time he was not working out the trail of a criminal. He was reviewing his career; his mind drifting back over the years to all the cases he had cracked; all the criminals he had captured, and all the jaws that had dropped in disbelief when he had done it. His was a long, distinguished and remarkable career, and the one case that would top it off was out there in front of him, hovering in plain sight, but just out of his reach. To Ellis Parker, it almost seemed as if everything in his life had been leading him to this moment, to this one case ... to his destiny.

Chapter 2
A Fiddler Becomes a Detective
1871-1900

Ellis Parker did not set out to become a detective, or even a policeman. His entire career was almost accidental, the vocational equivalent of being struck by lightning.

Born near Wrightstown, New Jersey on September 12, 1871, on the site of what would later become Fort Dix, Ellis was a Quaker and attended the first Day School at Upper Springfield.

Ellis Parker was born into a rapidly changing America. When he was five years old, the country celebrated its Centennial with a fabulous exposition in Philadelphia that featured such exciting new inventions as the typewriter, linoleum, and the telephone. The completion of the Transcontinental Railroad seven years earlier connected the two coasts and unified the country. Ulysses S. Grant was president and another ex-Civil War General named George Armstrong Custer was chasing the Sioux and Cheyenne in the Black Hills of the Dakota Territory. In June, Custer caught up with them in a battle the Indians called the Greasy Grass, but history would call the Little Bighorn.

By the time he reached his teens in the mid-1880s, Ellis Parker was a skilled fiddler much in demand at barn dances. Ellis and his two friends Joe Raymond on the harp and Jake Walker on the banjo comprised the rather grandly named Brindletown Orchestra.

Parker traveled around the county to the dances in his father's horse and wagon. He didn't go to college; relatively few did in those days. The only hint of a future law enforcement career for Ellis was his insistence on posting each barn dance with signs prohibiting fighting within 100 feet of the event. With his outgoing disposition, he might have drifted towards politics, but everything changed one fateful night.

Parker fiddled at a barn dance and when it was over put his fiddle in its case and placed it in the wagon for the trip back home. Parker then made his way through the milling crowd to find the organizer of the dance and collect his fee; five dollars for the night's work. When he returned his horse and cart were gone.

For a moment Parker stood in silence, torn between disbelief and outrage. Losing his fiddle was bad enough, but losing his father's horse and cart was worse. Although he didn't know it, Ellis Parker was at the crossroads of his future. He could simply rage and curse his bad luck as many people would have done, or he could do something about it. He frowned, stuck out his jaw, and decided he would get the horse and wagon back. In that one decision, Parker set the course for the rest of his life.

Exactly how he found who had stolen the horse and wagon is not certain; maybe he systematically questioned people and scoured neighboring farms or maybe he found clues and traced them. However he did it, he was able to locate the farm where the horse and wagon had been taken. Burlington County was too scarcely populated and too crime-free to justify the expense of a full time sheriff, so Parker contacted the Monmouth, Ocean, and Burlington County Detecting and Pursuing Association, a private, vigilante type group formed during the Civil War to foil horse thieves. Parker found a local member of the association and went with him to the home of the suspect. In the barn was Parker's horse and wagon, with the fiddle still in the back. The man from the Association was impressed with the detective work. Not bad for a country fiddler, he thought, not bad at all. Someone like that could come in handy. He offered Ellis a part time job with the Association on the spot.

Thus Ellis Parker, the young country fiddler, started helping the Monmouth, Ocean, and Burlington County Detecting and Pursuing Association, and soon, in 1891, he was hired full time. Ellis Parker's career as a detective had begun. That same year, the J.B. Lippincott Company of New York published *A Study in Scarlet*, the first American appearance of Sherlock Holmes.

In 1890s America, policing varied considerably from place to place. In the west, law enforcement was in the hands of local sheriffs, local citizen's committees, and, occasionally, the local lynch mob. Six gun justice was the norm, and that justice was often swift and final. To supplement the often-spotty law enforcement protection of their commercial interests, private companies such as Wells Fargo had vigorous police forces of their own. Other private forces such as the Pinkerton National Detective Agency were running down outlaws such as Butch Cassidy and the Sundance Kid.

In the eastern cities, more organized uniformed police forces were the norm, and were expected to control the fast growing slums filled with immigrants. In 1890, one fourth of the population of Philadelphia was foreign born. But local police forces sometimes proved a fertile ground for corruption. In 1892, just as Ellis Parker was beginning his career a few miles to the south, a New York cleric went on a crusade to turn up corruption in the city. He found the police were extorting protection money from gambling parlors, bawdy houses, after hours saloons, and businesses of all types. Some police were even selling "licenses" for certain types of crime. As a result, every top police official in the city was forced to resign, including the superintendent. There was even talk of calling in the militia to police the city.

In contrast to some of the excesses of law enforcement elsewhere, the local Pursuing Associations in New Jersey were reasonably low key. There was not enough crime to generate any serious danger of corruption, and the very existence of the vigilante-type organization did much to keep the level of law breaking relatively low. Local people committed much of the local crime, so the association usually did more pursuing than detecting. Still, some crime proved more difficult to solve, so the Association needed someone with good detective abilities. Ellis Parker turned out to be just the man they were looking for.

Ellis Parker around 1910
(Photo courtesy of William Fullerton)

From traveling around playing at barn dances, Parker already knew Burlington County and many of its inhabitants well. As a result he could often track down a culprit by questioning people and comparing the answers. It was a technique that was to serve him well in later years. He also developed his remarkable deductive ability, reading hoof prints, scratches, broken twigs, and even trash for the secrets they contained.

In addition to his detective talents, Parker developed an instinct for publicity and self-promotion. He was soon on good terms with the local press and always made sure they were kept up to date on his exploits. Before long, articles began appearing in local papers and Parker's reputation grew. As a result, Parker caught the eye of Eckard P. Budd in the Burlington County Prosecutor's Office.

Then as now, Burlington County stretched across New Jersey from the Delaware River just above Philadelphia and Camden, all the way to the ocean. Along the way the county crosses the Pine Barrens in the center, and the farms and beaches in the east. Local government centered on the county seat, the quiet Quaker town of Mt. Holly. The Burlington County Prosecutor's Office was charged with prosecuting wrongdoers, but the actual apprehension of these criminals was in the hands of local constables and the private detecting associations. These law enforcement people varied greatly in ability, motivation, and honesty. Even when they managed to apprehend a suspect, they frequently did it in such a clumsy way as to leave the prosecutor without sufficient evidence for a conviction.

Although a casual and creaky system, it was tolerable for a sleepy rural area. But as the twentieth century approached, Burlington County was growing, both in population and in crime. Things were changing in New Jersey as they were all over the eastern United States. The west had been mostly settled, and with the industrial revolution, factories and industry grew in the cities. The population was growing and becoming more urbanized as immigrants who earlier would have headed west now filled the cities instead. The cities were not prepared for the growth and the population pressure, so people crowded into teeming and dangerous slums. In such conditions, crime flourished, and even spilled into the rural areas as criminals sought richer hunting grounds. The pursuing associations, structured for casual burglary and horse thieving couldn't keep up, so the various New Jersey counties began looking for better ways of providing law enforcement.

To deal with this need in Burlington County, Eckard P. Budd, the Prosecutor of Common Pleas for the County Prosecutor's Office decided the county needed its own law enforcement office headed by a full time county detective. By placing detection, apprehension, and prosecution under a single county office, he could centralize law enforcement. The county prosecutor would no longer have to wait for the Pursuing Association or town constables to apprehend criminals, and no longer have to face the prospect of losing cases due to sloppy police work that wouldn't hold up in court. After all, the prosecutor took the blame when a conviction wasn't obtained, even if it was really the result of bungling by a local constable.

Budd decided the detective had to be someone with a proven record of success apprehending criminals. For this high-profile job, a political hack or unemployed relative wouldn't do. This detective would have to be someone who knew his business and would make the prosecutor's office look good. Otherwise, Budd knew the whole arrangement would be a failure and he would get the blame.

As Budd surveyed the county for possible candidates, he remembered young Ellis Parker, and Parker's success in detective work. Thanks to both his competence and his publicity, Parker was highly regarded for his ability to solve the most tangled cases. Budd decided that Parker was exactly what he was looking for. After all, a man with Pursuing Association experience would know the area and have a working knowledge of law enforcement. He could take over the job right away without a lengthy and uncertain training period. And best of all, the pursuing association people would put up less of a fuss if the new county detective was one of their own rather than an unknown outsider. In 1894, the year *The Memoirs of Sherlock Holmes* was published, 23 year old Ellis Parker became the first Chief Detective of Burlington County, New Jersey.

Presented with this opportunity, Parker reported to Mt. Holly determined to make the most of it. Instead of a regular salary, he was paid on a fee basis for each crime he solved. If the criminal went free, the Chief Detective didn't get paid. This was additional incentive to find and convict the guilty parties, not that Parker needed more incentive. The thrill of the hunt, coupled with the excitement of outwitting criminals was really all the incentive Ellis Parker ever required.

The Burlington County Detective's Office was set up in Mt. Holly in the stately 18th century courthouse on High Street. Next to the courthouse stood the old jail, a massive, forbidding gray stone structure with its own gallows. The brick cells were small and damp and looked like something found in a medieval dungeon rather than in a pleasant town in New Jersey. An underground passageway connected the courthouse to the jail, reinforcing the impression.

The ominous presence of the prison did not dampen the overall pleasantness of the town. The tree-shaded streets were lined with large and comfortable Victorian, shingle, and stone houses with wide front porches shaded by oak trees. The automobile had not yet arrived, and horse-drawn carts, buggies, and carriages lent a romantic, if somewhat malodorous atmosphere to the place. The town centered on the courthouse, with stately homes located along High Street in both directions. Most people in town knew each other, and soon everyone knew young Ellis Parker. He was outgoing and friendly, even to people he arrested. Soon everyone was greeting him simply as "Ellis". Still a bachelor, Parker didn't live in Mt. Holly, but in nearby Columbus. Even in those early days, he had a few eccentric tendencies, such as keeping a pet raccoon.

The Burlington County Jail in Mt Holly
(Author photo)

There are few complete records of cases handled by Parker in the years before 1901. Old hand-written ledgers in the prison show arrest and conviction records for these years, and Parker's name shows up on many of them as arresting officer. The crimes became more varied than the horse thieving that was such a big part of the Burlington County scene a few years before.

There was a sprinkling of assaults, burglaries, and various larcenies. The more sensational cases of Parker's career were still to come.

One of Parker cases during this early period involved a career criminal and jail breaker who had eluded other detectives. Lorenzo Atkinson was born in Wrightstown, not far from Ellis himself, but there the resemblance ended. Atkinson was a sleepy looking little man with a sharp but expressionless face. His career predated Ellis Parker's. He was first arrested in 1877 for robbing a furrier's shop, and had been leading a life of crime ever since. When Parker was still fiddling at barn dances, Atkinson was locked up in the Mt. Holly jail and made his first escape. He eluded arrest for years while robbing stores from Mt. Holly to Freehold. Finally he was arrested again and imprisoned in Monmouth County.

One day the wife of one of his friends visited him. After the woman left and disappeared into the twilight, guards were amazed to discover she was still in Atkinson's cell ... alone. The woman and the prisoner had switched clothes, and the disguised Atkinson had escaped once again. Atkinson then moved his activities to Ocean County where he was again arrested and again escaped in 1892. He remained at large for several more years while unserved warrants piled up in three counties.

Ellis Parker was probably familiar with Atkinson from his time with the pursuing association, and saw him as a challenge. Through his growing network of contacts, Ellis Parker made inquiries and finally heard Atkinson was working in Tinton Falls, near Asbury Park. In 1899, using a bench warrant issued the year before for a grand larceny committed in 1892, Parker set out to capture the elusive Atkinson. By making some more inquiries in the area, Parker learned his quarry was using the assumed name of James Cummings. Soon, Parker located his man and snapped handcuffs on him. Atkinson claimed he was really James Cummings, but Parker was not fooled. Atkinson was placed in the Mt. Holly jail once again. This time, he did not escape.

In the Atkinson case, Ellis Parker relied mostly on his contacts and ability to follow a lead, but he continued to practice and hone other techniques during this time as well. Police work at this time, and for years afterwards mostly depended on informers, physical intimidation (the third degree), and the stupidity of the criminal. In an age when many police depended on the fear their authority enjoined to intimidate criminals, Parker was outwardly non-threatening. His appearance was usually rumpled, almost disheveled, and he often went without a tie, or even a coat. Once he had a suspect in custody, Parker used a variation on the "good cop-bad cop" technique. Parker played the good cop and cast the rest of the world as the bad cop. He was empathetic and helpful to suspects, engaging them in conversations that seemed harmless, but which established Parker as the suspect's one best hope against the terrible trouble he was in. Soon the suspect, sensing the stern but sympathetic detective was his only friend in a hostile and vengeful world, was confiding in Parker. Parker would listen and agree to do all he could to help the suspect, but only if an honest confession were made. Parker was sincere in this promise, and often went to great lengths to see that a suspect got a fair trial and a reasonable sentence. Other detectives made people confess. Ellis Parker made people *want* to confess. After a while, Parker's reputation became one of his greatest assets. Suspects caught by Ellis Parker felt it was hopeless to deny their guilt. Their best chance was to confess and hope to get Parker on their side.

Coupled with this down-home bedside manner was Parker's deductive ability. He was interested in every detail of a case, and asked numerous questions that other people sometimes thought were pointless. When Parker finally put all the pieces together, however, the result was usually an apprehension and a conviction.

Although he gave the impression of being old fashioned, Ellis Parker was always looking for more effective ways of doing things. One of his earliest innovations was probably inspired by his experience with the Pursuing Association. He set up an ingenious system of quickly notifying farmers when a horse theft had been reported so they could help head off the culprit before he got too far. In 1898, he began a program of photographing those he arrested, and started a Rogue's Gallery in the County Jail to aid with prisoner identification. He was not the first detective to use this technique (Wells Fargo agents had used it for several years) but he was certainly among the first. Thanks to Parker, law enforcement in Burlington County had come a long way in just a few short years.

Although the records don't show any really sensational cases during this period, something happened to Ellis Parker that had as profound an effect on the course of his life as when his horse and cart were stolen. As the century neared its end, the dashing young bachelor detective met a young lady named Cora Giberson. Cora was quiet and reserved, almost the opposite of the outgoing Ellis, but she was steadying, sympathetic, and loyal. Around the turn of the century, these were the ideal qualities for a prospective wife. On February 10, 1900, Ellis Parker and Cora Giberson were married, and started on a road that did not end until 40 years and 15 children later.

Cora was the homemaker and the helpmate, but never interfered, or even discussed "business" matters. She was a retiring and somewhat nervous woman, very much focused on her home, her children, and domestic matters.

In later years, Ellis often said his success was due to a "good wife and a contented mind", and there is no doubt that Cora Giberson became the most important source of long term stability and support of his life.

The horse was still king of local transportation. Ellis Parker himself used a horse and buggy on his investigations. The big musical craze was ragtime, as played by Scott Joplin. A young magician named Eric Weiss was becoming the sensation of vaudeville as the Handcuff King because of his ability to escape from locks. He was better known by his stage name; the Great Houdini. In Kansas, Carrie Nation began a crusade to fight the evils of alcohol and encourage temperance. She advanced this cause by joining with several dozen like-minded ladies and invading saloons armed with axes. Although she succeeded mostly in smashing private property, she planted the seeds of

Prohibition, which was to become a big part of Ellis Parker's life 20 years later.

New Jersey was still mostly a farming state, although industries were growing in the more urban areas. In the state capitol at Trenton, horse-drawn carriages and wagons clopped down dirt or cobblestone streets that smelled of manure in the summer and coal fires in the winter. In the middle of the state were the mysterious Pine Barrens, a wild wooded area that gave rise to rumors of monsters and strange happenings.

During the sweltering New Jersey summers, those who could escaped to the Atlantic beaches. Families of well to do men often spent the entire summer there and took their servants with them to places like Asbury Park, Margate, the Wildwoods, Cape May, Sea Isle City, and Avalon. But for the really well off, only Atlantic City would do. There the rich could be pushed along the boardwalk in wheeled wicker sedan chairs with the Atlantic Ocean on one side and genteel hotels such as the Dennis, the Brighton, the Garden, the Rudolf, and Craig Hall on the other.

Like the new century, Ellis Parker's star was rising, and his years of dazzling success were only beginning. New cases lay ahead; difficult and dangerous cases. Soon Ellis Parker's abilities would be tested as they had never been before. The seemingly simple county lawman was now on his way to becoming one of the shrewdest and most successful detectives in American history.

Chapter 3
Bloody Murder and Burning Barns
1901-1919

Snow pelted the town of Mt. Holly one winter's night in 1901, sending residents scurrying for shelter. Ellis Parker was relaxing at his new home, the large three story Victorian house at 215 High Street he and Cora bought shortly after their marriage the year before. The house was across from the jail and only a block from the courthouse and the Elks Club. When he wasn't in his office, hunting ducks with the Egg Island Gun Club or pursuing a case, Ellis Parker could usually be found at the Elks Club, but on this particular night, Ellis was in his parlor.

About 9:00, there was a knock on the front door and a neighbor came in to warm up on his way home. People often dropped by at all hours, and Ellis liked both the company and the occasional bit of useful information such visitors provided. The neighbor had come from New York City, and he remarked that the weather up there was unseasonably warm, almost spring like.

After the neighbor left, Parker went to bed but there would be no rest this night. Several hours later, two of his detectives, Dean and another man, pulled up in a sleigh and banged on the door with the news that there had been a murder in Riverdale. A local farmer named Washington Hunter had been bludgeoned and stabbed to death, and the house robbed of several thousand dollars. Hunter's wife had seen the murderer leave. Parker, of course, knew the 70 year old Hunter, just as he knew most of the local residents.

Parker's house at 215 High Street today
(Author photo)

When they arrived at the Hunters' house after a drive through the snowy night, Parker carefully examined all the footprints in the snow. Although there had been a lot of trampling by neighbors and the police, Parker spotted one set of prints heading south into the woods. He set out with Dean to see where they led.

"The assailants split up when they left the house," Parker remarked. "This fellow went off on his own and was running hard. You can tell by the deep toe prints. What's more, he isn't familiar with the area. The trail wanders and doubles back all over the place. This fellow was feeling his way."

The trail of footprints ended at railroad tracks by a junction. A watchman reported seeing a coatless and hatless man about the time in question. A train bound for Camden had come through about the same time.

"Well, that settles where he went," said Parker. "Now let's look in the house."

The body of Washington Hunter lay crumpled face down on the floor, stabbed numerous times on the right side and beaten with an iron bar. His wife reported she heard a loud struggle and saw a man running out the back. The man had no hat or coat.

Parker examined the body, lit his pipe, and declared the killer knew the victim because the wounds were mostly on the victim's right side.

"Washington Hunter was a left-sided man," said Parker. "He had a medical condition where his vital organs were transposed from where they usually are. That means the heart is on his right side. The killer struck Hunter mostly on the right side where the heart is. And don't say the killer was just left handed; the killer had to reach across Washington's body to stab him like that. And there's more than one killer, too. Washington Hunter was too strong to be overpowered by only one man."

A search of the house turned up another clue: a new fedora hat that Mrs. Hunter said she had not seen before. Parker noted it was a different size from Washington's hats as well, indicating it belonged to one of the killers.

From the brakeman on the train the killer jumped, Parker learned the killer was a blond-haired man with no overcoat, no hat, and walked with a limp. The man Mrs. Hunter saw and the man the brakeman saw were not wearing overcoats. Even if they had been the same man, why go out without an overcoat in a blizzard? They must have come from some place with spring-like weather that day. Then Parker remembered what the neighbor told him the night of the murder; it had been warm in New York City! That's where the killers must have come from. And if the killers had come from New York City, they most likely came by train.

Parker went to Riverside train station and asked the stationmaster about trains from New York and if he had noticed anyone getting off. The stationmaster's information enabled Parker to deduce the 11:40 train was the most likely, but the stationmaster hadn't noticed who had gotten off.

"You could check with the auditor's office in Philadelphia," the stationmaster suggested. "All the tickets go there after they're collected. They can separate out the ones with Riverside as a destination"

Parker set off in his horse and buggy for the auditor's office in Philadelphia where he was given a bundle of punched Riverside tickets from the 11:40 train from New York. Four of the tickets to Riverside originated in New York and had been punched by conductor Thomas Dennison.

When Parker told Dennison he was interested in the night of the blizzard, Dennison remembered the four men from New York. They were all well dressed, spoke with German accents, and one was drunk. Dennison gave good descriptions of each man and said another conductor named Owens had just arrived and he had worked the 11:40 and a return train the next morning.

"Yes, I remember them," Owens said, after examining the tickets. "They got on at Perkins the next morning and paid in cash, but the one in the brown suit wasn't with them."

Parker smiled. The drunk in the brown suit then must be the one who ran through the woods and hopped the train for Camden. It was all fitting together.

"Now, Mrs. Hunter," Parker asked the next day, "can you give me the names of any recently hired hand who wasn't local and who spoke with a German accent; someone who might have overheard you or Washington mention his left-sided condition?"

She named three men. Two of them lived in New York City. Parker contacted the New York police, who were familiar with Young, one of the men. Young was arrested, along with two friends who were with him. Parker then brought the two conductors to Tombs prison where they identified all three as the men who had been on the train. One, named Keller, was the blond haired drunk who had split off and run across county.

Parker got an extradition order and brought the three to New Jersey, but none of them would talk and Mrs. Hunter could not make a positive identification. Parker could now prove they were in the area the night of the murder and departed the next day, but still couldn't prove any of them were involved.

"We'll get them to talk by using the unnatural detail," Parker told Dean. "Do you remember how Keller split off from the others the night we tracked them? Keller was in unfamiliar territory in the dark, yet he went on his own. The most likely reason he split off is that he wanted to get away from the others."

"But he was with them when he was picked up in New York afterwards," Dean pointed out.

"Yes. Whatever the problem was, it somehow got fixed later, and didn't exist before the murder. The only change in the status of the gang was that when they came down Keller was drunk. But by the time they ran from Hunter's house several hours later, he would have had time to sober up. Maybe he hadn't bargained for a murder. Maybe he thought it was more dangerous to be around the others than to go it alone, or maybe he realized he had something on him he had to get rid of or conceal in case he was caught. Keller talks like an educated man, so I'm going to check with authorities in Washington and see if they have any information on him."

The State Department reported back that Otto Keller was the missing son of the mayor of Stuttgart, Germany and came from a noble family. He had come to America several months before and disappeared.

Parker took Keller aside and showed him a picture of Washington Hunter.

"Do you see that?" he asked. "That's the man you murdered. You are in something very serious. We need to let the people back in Stuttgart know about it so they can arrange for your defense."

Keller went pale. "No. Don't do that! It wasn't me. Young killed him. I didn't even want to come with them. They got me drunk in a bar in the Bowery and got me on the train. I thought it was a prank at first, but when they killed the old man I just wanted to get away. I was afraid they'd blackmail my father back in Germany."

Parker nodded. "And that is why you ran in a different direction? To get away from them?"

"Yes. Also I wanted to have a chance to tear the labels out of my suit in case I was caught. They had my family crest on them."

Parker patted Keller on the shoulder.

"Now you need to write it all down," he said.

With Keller's confession, the case broke open. The murderers, Young and Braun, were sentenced to be hanged in the courtyard of the prison in Mt. Holly. The fourth member of the gang was killed in a barroom brawl before he could be arrested.

When Parker went to the yard of the Burlington County Jail to witness the execution, Charles Braun decided to make a break for it. A few minutes before he was to be executed Braun struck at two guards with a bludgeon he fashioned from lead pipe he took from his cell. The guards were able to knock the weapon from his hands as he fled into the prison courtyard. As he got closer to freedom, Braun found an ax and raised it to strike at the remaining guards. Parker, who had been standing in the rear, ran up behind Braun and knocked the ax from his hands. Braun was recaptured and then executed under heavy guard. In an unusual example of modesty, Ellis Parker's diary for that day simply noted that he had attended the execution, with no mention of his derring-do.

Ellis Parker around 1915
(Photo courtesy of William Fullerton)

Although the Washington Hunter case was one of a number of sensational murders Ellis Parker successfully closed during this period, the predominant crime continued to be horse thievery. Today, so many years removed from that era, people tend to think of horse thievery as a less serious, almost humorous type of crime; and horse thieves seem more like rascals than real criminals. In New Jersey, though, as in much of America during the early part of the century, the theft of a horse was a very serious crime indeed. New Jersey was mostly rural, and consisted of numerous small family farms. A farmer's horse represented a large part of both his wealth, and his ability to produce food and income. Since the automobile was still in its infancy, a horse was usually the farmer's only means of transportation and only means of getting to market. If someone stole a man's horse, he might very possibly be stealing his livelihood and endangering the victim's family as well.

Much of the horse thieving could be traced to ex-hired hands that were easily caught, but some of the crimes presented more of a challenge.

In one case, Parker followed the hoof prints of the stolen horse (horse thieves usually rode the stolen horses away). The prints led into a wild, wooded area called Cream Ridge. Within Cream Ridge was a tangled area of chopped-up dirt roads and scattered houses known as the Maze. Parker noted that the man on the stolen horse never doubled back and never made a false move in the huge, confusing tangle. From this, Parker surmised the man was born and raised in the area. Now he could narrow his search down to hired hands born and raised locally.

Only two men fit, and one of them was eliminated. The other, a man named Joe Thomas, had just quit his job saying he had become a horse trader, then disappeared. Parker gathered all the information he could about Thomas and found that his mother lived in a nearby town. He had her place watched and soon got a report that she had sent her son a package to be picked up at the baggage room at the train station in Trenton. Thomas was arrested when he went to pick up the package, and Parker, using the disarming psychology that served him so well, casually questioned him. When Parker pounced on an inconsistency in Thomas's story, Thomas confessed. Parker remarked that he had seldom had as much trouble from a single horse thief, but did not realize just how much trouble he would get from Joe Thomas until years later.

These early cases clearly show Ellis Parker's uncanny ability to reconstruct not only the crime, but the probable events that led up to it, including the thought processes of those involved. As he followed each thread, he eliminated possibilities until his chain of reasoning led him to the solution. Using a friendly disarming manner, Parker instinctively sought the key that would coax a suspect into revealing all.

STOLEN
Horse, Buggy and Harness

On Thursday, February 23, 1922, a woman known as Lillie Shaffer, alias Diano, age about 35 years, about 5 ft.-6 in. in height, weight about 135 lbs., medium complexion, dark hair, and wore a black coat and hat, and she speaks broken, hired a horse from T. Harry Bowker, of Mount Holly, N. J., and got away with it. It was a bay horse, 15 hands high, about 12 years old, weighs about 950 lbs., has mane clipped and carries head low. Horse had nickle mounted harness. Buggy was painted black with new light on left hand side. Had gray striped blanket in buggy.

This woman's husband, Willis Diano, left at the same time.

They are both wanted, also, for defranding a boarding house.

Should you gain any information concerning either of these two parties, or the horse and buggy, please hold them and notify me by telegraph.

ELLIS H. PARKER, County Detective.
Mount Holly, N. J.

Telephone 144 Mount Holly. (Reverse call).

"All points bulletin" post card from 1922
(Author photo of post card provided by Harry McConnell)

In those days of relatively primitive technology, Parker would sometimes put out an "All Points Bulletin" to surrounding states using penny postcards. Fingerprinting was not often a factor in these cases. Although fingerprinting had been known since the early 1800s, there was still a lack of good techniques for recovering prints, and the lack of any comprehensive central file of criminal fingerprint records. Instead, the favored method of criminal identification was the Bertillion System, a complicated method of physical measurements that was supposed to yield a unique profile for each individual. In 1903, however, officials at Leavenworth Penitentiary found they had two prisoners with almost identical Bertillion measurements. What's more, the prisoners, though not related, had the same name, Will West. The only way to distinguish between the men was by fingerprints.

Two years later, in 1905, the U.S. Department of Justice created a Bureau of Criminal Identification to set up a centralized collection of fingerprint cards for reference. When the collection was moved to Leavenworth Penitentiary two years after that, local police forces decided to set up their own identification bureau maintained by the International Association of Chiefs of Police. The two collections were finally merged and put under the FBI (Then called the Bureau of Investigation) in 1924 by an act of Congress.

But the crafty Parker, at least in his early days, was not just a thinking machine. He could be a man of action as well, often making arrests on his own. Occasionally, he faced real danger, such as when he foiled the armed escape of Charles Braun. In 1908, Parker single-handedly tracked and apprehended Henry Willis, who had attempted to murder an Allentown farmer named John Borden and his wife. In the fight, Borden had inflicted severe injuries on Willis, enabling Parker to stay ahead of a lynch mob and get his man by following a blood trail. On another occasion in 1916, a wanted criminal named

John Kairey pulled a gun and fired at Parker on a crowded trolley. No one was hurt. Kairey eluded the law until 1930, when he was arrested at Riverside on a weapons charge. Parker remembered Kairey, however, and the gunman was sentenced to 15 years in prison.

During the early part of the century, as Parker was pursuing murderers and horse thieves, most of the Parkers' 15 children were born, although only eight ultimately survived to adulthood. In 1901, Anthony was born. Mildred and Charlotte followed in 1903, and Ellis Jr. in 1910. Lillian was born in 1915, Jane in 1917, and Edward in 1919. Like their mother, Parker's children went about their business quietly for the most part, leaving the limelight to Ellis. Only Ellis Jr. would one day become almost as well-known as his father.

As the Parker household was filling up with children, it was also a place for Ellis's work. Ellis Parker was one of the first in Mt. Holly to have a telephone, and he published his home number (Mt Holly 145) on the Prosecutor's office letterhead as a number where he could be reached after office hours. Ellis seldom discussed his cases at home, but the family learned to accept the late night calls and visits from assorted characters as part of the routine in the Parker household. The house on High Street was large, and the Parker family shared it with several boarders who helped defray the expenses. Two other families lived with the Parkers during this time, including a child. What these tenants thought of the constant stream of odd-hour visitors is not recorded.

Parker handled an amazing variety of crime in those early days. In addition to murder, robbery and theft, Parker investigated such crimes as rape, indecent exposure, throwing rocks at train windows, stealing cabbage, stealing a barrel of flowers, stealing an overcoat, blowing a safe, incest, and the attempted derailment of a Pennsylvania Railroad train.

In 1906, a spinster named Florence Allison was found beaten to death in her barn in Moorestown. The victim's four-year-old niece was in the main house at the time. Gently coaxing information from the child, Parker learned the culprits were two black men who had also stolen an heirloom watch. By obtaining a description of the watch and picking up subtle clues on the scene, he was able to deduce where the men were probably headed. Based on this deduction, he alerted pawnshops in Baltimore and Washington. Once again, he had reasoned correctly and a man was caught trying to pawn the watch in Baltimore. This was a remarkable bit of reasoning, an example of Parker's ability to reconstruct the crime backwards.

The case wasn't over yet. Parker, along with several other men, picked up the suspect, Rufus Johnson, in Baltimore to transport him back to Mt. Holly by train. When they arrived at Wilmington Station, word had leaked out and a curious crowd waited to see the suspect. By the time they reached Philadelphia, people waited as well, but this crowd was an angry mob, yelling and threatening to lynch Rufus Johnson. Ellis Parker, handcuffed to Johnson, escorted him through the mob along with local police. The crowd pressed in on all sides howling and threatening as the party pushed their way down the steps towards a waiting car. Johnson was in a panic by this time, and the escorting police barely were able to keep the crowd at bay. Slowly the crowd gave way, and Parker managed to get himself and his prisoner into the back seat of the car, only to find the driver wasn't there! He had been delayed by the crowd and was still slowly pushing his way towards them. The crowd pressed in on the car, and the escorting police prepared to draw their pistols. Finally, the sweating driver appeared through the threatening crowd, jumped in the car and was able to pull away from the mob. The drive to Mt. Holly was one Parker would long remember.

"I never rode so fast in my life," he said later, "and I don't want to go as fast again unless I'm compelled to."

After the harrowing ride through the back roads, expecting to encounter another lynch mob at every turn, the party arrived in Mt. Holly. Johnson was relieved to be in the relative safety of the jail. When later confronted with the little girl witness, he named the other man, George Small. After a sensational trial, the men were hanged at the prison in Mt. Holly. On the way to the gallows, Johnson told Parker he had treated him fairly.

Murder, of course, is the part of detective work that most interests the public, but one of Parker's most famous cases of this time did not involve murder at all. In 1911, he was called on to find a firebug. For several years, a series of catastrophic barn fires had plagued the surrounding counties. In one hour's time in the middle of the night a farmer could be wiped out. By the time a bucket brigade could be organized, the barn and everything in it was gone. Farmers for miles around talked darkly of the mad firebug and even set up vigilante committees to stop him, but to no avail. Parker was aware of the fires, and the hunt for the mad firebug, but no fires occurred in Burlington County, so he remained occupied with other matters. Finally, after 14 barn fires, a barn burned down in his county and Parker was on the case at last.

Arson, especially when committed by a madman would seem to be a random crime that would be almost immune to Parker's logic-based methods. Even so, Parker visited the barn fire and started to look around.

The ground around the burned-out barn was a quagmire from being trampled by the bucket brigade, so no footprints were of any use. Still, Parker walked in ever-widening circles investigating the surrounding area. Finally, he noticed a section of fence with the rails removed. The farmer said that the rails were in place the day before.

Looking closer, Parker saw two sets of hoof prints: one heading towards the barn and the other heading away.

"The person who did this is not a madman," he said. "He's not even a firebug. He did it to cover up another crime. Look carefully at these prints. Notice the horseshoes? They don't match. I need to talk to the blacksmith that does your shoeing."

When the blacksmith arrived, he recognized the shoe prints heading away from the barn as ones he had done, but did not recognize the prints heading towards the barn. Parker then took him to the still smoldering remains of the barn. The horses were only mounds of ash, but Parker asked the farmer to point out which stall held his best horse. When the place was identified, Parker poked around until he found a horseshoe and held it up for the blacksmith.

"That looks like the shoe that made one set of those prints at the fence," the blacksmith said, "but that's not one of my shoes. I shoed that horse just a few months ago, but I'm sure that's a different shoe."

The farmer scratched his head. "But I never changed that horse's shoes. What does this all mean, anyway?"

"That's the other crime the fire was meant to cover up; horse thievery."

"But none of my horses are missing," the farmer protested. "I had eight horses and now there are eight piles of ash."

"There were eight horses in the barn all right," said Parker, "but one of them wasn't yours. The thief brought an old nag to your barn and substituted it for your prize horse, which he stole. Then he burned the barn down so you'd think the horse had been destroyed. That way, no one would be looking for it."

"My God," said the farmer. "You mean a man would destroy a barn full of horses just to steal one?"

Parker nodded. "It's cruel and ruthless act," he said, "but this man has been doing it all over the state. I think it's time to put a stop to it."

Meeting with police from the surrounding counties and working from detailed maps, Parker helped set up a telephone early warning system to quickly cut off all the escape routes once a barn fire was reported. The next time the pyromaniac/horse thief struck, they would be ready.

A few months later, during a sleet storm, another barn went up in flames, this time over the line in Monmouth County, near Prospertown. The farmer was Elisha Jones, an old friend. Parker drove to the farm and started on the trail. Once again, he saw the trademark two tracks; one for the old horse being brought in and one for the thoroughbred being taken away.

"The pursuing association tracked him," Jones said, "but he headed north towards Cream Ridge and they lost him in the Maze."

Parker frowned. The Maze in the Cream Ridge. Just like that case a few years before. Could another horse thief have come up with a similar scheme? Maybe, but to Ellis Parker, there was a more likely explanation: Joe Thomas was out of jail and back in action.

"I know why the firebug hasn't been caught by the roadblocks," Parker said. "He's still in the district!"

Parker had the roads leading out of the Cream Ridge watched and then began the tedious job of checking the farms in the area. He reasoned that Joe Thomas was working quietly as a hired hand on one of those farms and selling his stolen horses out of the area when he got the chance. Acting on his theory, Parker had copies of Joe Thomas's old jail photo made and sent to the local farmers. About a week later, he got a call from a farmer who said there was a hired hand named Joe Williams on his farm who closely resembled the photo.

When Parker arrived at the farm, the farmer pointed out a man working in the field. Parker approached him, and saw it was Joe Thomas.

Parker handcuffed Thomas and drove him towards Mt. Holly. (Parker had traded in his horse and buggy for an automobile by this time.) In spite of his deductions, Parker realized he really had no evidence to connect Thomas with the barn fires. It was time to use psychology once again.

The drive back was a long one, but the usually garrulous Parker kept quiet, knowing the suspense would be eating away at Thomas, who had no idea how much evidence Parker had. Finally Thomas spoke up.

"What do you want me for, Mr. Parker?" he said.

"All I want to know is where you stashed the last horse, Joe. The rest can keep."

Thomas swallowed hard. Apparently Parker knew everything but this one detail.Thinking he was sunk for sure, Thomas blurted out the whole story and agreed to sign a confession.

But this wasn't the end of Slippery Joe Thomas. Some time later, Parker took him around to the barns where he had stashed the stolen horses, barely avoiding an angry lynch mob of farmers in the process. On the way back to Mt. Holly, Thomas slipped out of the car and disappeared. Following footprints, Parker tracked him until he found a break in a hedge along the side of the road. Sure enough, Thomas had ducked in the gap and was hiding in the hay in a nearby barn. A few probes with a pitchfork and Parker had his prisoner once more.

Thomas received a 59 year sentence, but escaped from Trenton State Prison three years later and once again, Ellis Parker got the call.

"We think he's headed back towards your area, Ellis," said the Warden.

Figuring Thomas would head for the Cream Ridge once again, Parker went that way too. He remembered Thomas's mother lived at Lakehurst, and figured he'd go there, since it was late October and Thomas would not be able to get hired on another farm so easily.

There was a heavy frost on the ground and Parker soon found footprints leading into the woods. Knowing it wasn't hunting season, and no one else would have any reason to plunge into the woods, Parker followed the tracks, broken twigs, and displaced leaves until he came to an abandoned farmhouse. There were no tracks coming out. Parker wedged the front door with a piece of timber then went in the back with his gun drawn. He found Slippery Joe Thomas hiding in a closet. Soon he had him back in prison, where he would stay until Thomas was taken to an asylum several years later.

Yet another of Parker's famous murder cases began on October 5, 1916, when Henry Rider, the highway commissioner of Genoa, New Jersey accompanied his brother Andrew, Andrew's daughter Elsie, and a mechanic named J.M. Ridgely on a motor trip to Andrew's cranberry bogs near Atison, New Jersey. In addition to being a cranberry entrepreneur, Andrew was the president of the Trenton Business School, later to become Rider University. The outing was to deliver the $4500 payroll to the cranberry workers. Somehow word of the payroll must have gotten out because the group, with Elsie at the wheel came upon a band of a dozen armed men and women blocking the road. (Some accounts say they were all men, some disguised as women.) Instead of stopping, Elsie drove through the group in a hail of bullets. Elsie was wounded and the car stalled a few hundred feet down the road. The robbers rushed the car as Ridgely pulled a gun from under the seat and returned fire. Ridgely, Elsie and both Rider brothers were wounded before Elsie was able to restart the car and drive off to safety.

Although everyone in the group had been shot, only Henry Rider died from his wounds. Some later accounts, mixing up the victim and his brother, refer to the case as the murder of the "Cranberry King". Ellis Parker was soon on the trail and found the murder-robbery was the work of an Italian gang led by a man named Luigi Pinto. Although the criminals scattered and some even left the country, they were rounded up by both Parker and other local authorities. Luigi Pinto, however, became an international fugitive and was to elude Parker for another 15 years.

In 1917, America entered the Great War that had been raging in Europe since 1914. Eldest son Anthony was a little too young and Ellis himself was a little too old, so the war did not greatly affect the Parker family directly, but did spill over into Ellis's duties with reports of saboteurs, spies, and suspicious people with German accents. New Jersey had been a prime settlement area for German immigrants ever since the American Revolution, so there was no shortage of potential suspects. In addition to the hunt for spies there were other changes during the war; food and gasoline were voluntarily rationed and women began to appear in the workplace in greater numbers. When the war finally ended in 1918, everyone was anxious to return to "Normalcy." An outbreak of Spanish Flu in that year caused thousands of deaths nationwide, but crowded New York City was especially hard hit.

In December of 1919, another incident changed Ellis Parker's life, and it came in the unlikely form of a new secretary. Parker's previous secretary, Robert Peacock retired, leaving Parker in need of a replacement. Parker hired Anna Yoos, who had worked at the Camp Dix Separation Center, processing American servicemen leaving the Army now that the Great War in Europe was over. Realizing her job would last only as long as the diminishing supply of returning Doughboys, Yoos was seeking other employment. She was a bright, good-natured person with a calm disposition and a ready smile. As with her boss, however, looks could be deceiving. Parker may have expected a girl Friday, but what he got was a Dr. Watson. Anna Yoos turned out to be the final piece to fall into place to make Ellis Parker the "local detective with the world-wide reputation." She became Parker's indispensable right hand, and he probably confided in her more than in anyone else. While taking shorthand notes, she became a teammate in Parker's interrogations, complementing his sly questioning with motherly sympathy and advice that "confession is good for the soul." Many times a suspect who could not quite bring himself to open up to Parker, would tell all to that nice Miss Yoos afterwards. She was perceptive, smart, thorough, and unflappable. No amount of murder, mayhem or outrage could shake her. It was all in a day's work.

Anna Yoos (Later Anna Bading)
(Photo courtesy of William Fullerton)

With his sharp eye for people, Ellis Parker quickly recognized the value of his new secretary and took her into his confidence. He became protective of Anna Yoos, trying to leave her out of the more sordid aspects of his cases when he could. When questioning suspects, he became highly indignant if anyone used bad language in front of her, ignoring the fact that he often turned the air blue himself. Ellis Parker had found the perfect crime-fighting partner. Between Ellis Parker and Anna Yoos, no criminal was safe in Burlington County.

Chapter 4
Bootleggers, a Pickled Corpse,
and 175 Suspects
1920- 1922

As the 1920s began, Ellis Parker's world was about to change once again, Temperance societies, concerned about the effect of alcohol on people's lives and dedicated to discouraging alcohol in all its forms had been growing in power. Moderation was not enough; only total abstinence would do. To these activists, alcohol was more than just a problem; it was an evil to be eradicated. As Mark Twain wryly put it, "Nothing so needs reforming as other people's habits."

As is the way with so many reformers, The Dries as they were sometimes called, started out with friendly persuasion, but soon started pushing for laws to coerce people into doing things their way. Laws prohibiting the manufacture or use of alcohol appeared here and there, but mostly the matter was left to the states until the First World War. Taking advantage of the war effort, prohibitionists argued that grain used to make liquor was needed for the war, neatly painting distillers as unpatriotic as well as corrupters of the public. Mostly on the strength of this argument, Congress passed national laws prohibiting the manufacture and sale of alcoholic beverages. In 1917, Congress passed the 18th amendment to the constitution, making the ban nationwide and permanent. By the time the war ended, the states had ratified the amendment, and in 1920, Prohibition came to America.

Like many well-intentioned attempts to regulate human behavior, Prohibition soon ran up against a far stronger law; the law of unintended consequences. Most people didn't see alcohol as the big problem the reformers did, and resented being told what to do. Middle class "social drinkers" who did not abuse liquor felt that prohibition was all well and good for the poor and the criminal classes, but certainly shouldn't apply to them. The result was an instant market for illegal booze and a flouting of Prohibition by people who were normally law-abiding. Although touted as a way of decreasing crime, Prohibition actually brought about an explosion in crime, with gangsters, bootlegging, speakeasies, smuggling, bribery, and even murder flourishing. Criminals rushed to fill the public demand for liquor and illegal suppliers fought over territory. Former petty criminals now became heads of criminal empires. The most famous of these crime figures was Al Capone in Chicago, who was nationally known, but there were powerful crime figures on the East Coast as well. In New York, underworld figures such as Arnold Rothstein, Vito Genovese, Carlo Gambino, Frank Costello, Dutch Schultz, and Lucky Luciano all got on the Prohibition bandwagon. To their established activities of gambling, prostitution, and extortion, they now added bootlegging, rum running, and operating speakeasies. Prohibition caused widespread disrespect for the law since so many people routinely tried to circumvent it. Al Capone put it best;

"When I sell liquor they call it bootlegging; when my customers serve it on silver trays along Lake Shore Drive, they call it hospitality."

The huge profits from this illicit trade made corruption of Prohibition agents a constant concern. One New York supervisor, tired of seeing his agents arrive in expensive new cars each morning ordered the men to place their hands on a table. Everyone wearing a diamond ring was immediately fired. Prohibition encouraged crime in more unexpected ways as well. Bars and taverns were closed down almost overnight, but such establishments had long been hangouts for criminals. By placing informants in the bars, the police had always had a cheap and effective low-tech method of gathering information. Now it was gone. Of course, these people now could be found in speakeasies, but these establishments were much harder for the police to infiltrate.

Like the crime bosses, a few of the law enforcement agents became famous as well. In New York, a pair of Prohibition Agents named Isidore Einstein and Moe Smith became legendary for the successful and highly colorful way they pursued illegal alcohol. Using scams, disguises, play-acting, and various outrageous deceptions, Izzy and Moe, as the newspapers called them, seized more than five million bottles of illicit booze and arrested more than 5,000 bartenders and bootleggers. The unlikely duo personally accounted for over one fifth of all the federal liquor shutdowns in New York during their five-year career. Their standard announcement: "Dere's sad news here. Yer pinched!" became a New York catch phrase.

Meanwhile, the federal government, reacting to a national fear and mistrust of foreigners and a series of mail bombs sent to prominent people, began a campaign to crack down on Anarchists and Bolsheviks, who were presumed to be behind it. A series of raids, arrests, and deportations were made under the direction of Attorney General A. Mitchell Palmer. The "Palmer Raids" as they were called would continue well into the 1920s, creating an atmosphere of fear and paranoia among immigrant communities in the cities. Now it was no longer necessary to be a criminal to run afoul of the law; a person could be arrested for pamphleteering, giving a critical speech, or any of the activities that were covered under a greatly expanded definition of sedition. Since taking a drink had just been made illegal as well, being a law-abiding citizen had gotten much harder.

While Prohibition and the Palmer Raids were stirring the criminal pot, the nature of crime was changing for other reasons. With improved police communications, better security, and improved local police, hit and run robberies of the Jesse James variety had become rare by the early part of the century, but the automobile, combined with better roads began to make such activity tempting for criminals once again. Prior to 1920, most cars were open to the weather, unreliable, and could only be started by a hand crank. As the 1920s wore on, however, both cars and roads improved dramatically. Criminals, quick to take advantage of technology, found the automobile an ideal accomplice. Motorized bandits in Packards or Cadillacs could easily outrun the horse-and-buggy police and quickly be safe across state lines. Even motorized police forces usually had the much slower Model T Ford. This imbalance prevailed throughout the 1920s. Just how poorly police forces were equipped with motor vehicles could be seen after the infamous St. Valentine's Day Massacre in Chicago in 1929. The neighborhood police station had only two vehicles and they were both out. Radios had not yet been installed, so the officer on duty had to hitch a ride with a civilian to get to the scene of the crime. The advent of motorized criminals combined with Prohibition portended bad years for law enforcement.

New Jersey was affected by the crime explosion as well, especially around Newark, Jersey City, and other areas just across the Hudson from New York. Further south, in the more rural areas such as Burlington County, illegal stills sprouted up to supply thirsty customers in New York City, and back roads became bootlegger highways to transport the product to market.

As the effects of Prohibition spread, Ellis Parker was forced to devote more of his energies to chasing bootleggers. The temptation to make some easy money breaking a law that was unpopular and considered victimless had drawn more than a few lawmen to collect payoffs or even participate. Some people claimed Ellis Parker dabbled in the business himself on occasion, in spite of his zealousness in pursuing bootleggers. In Parker's case, nothing was ever proven, but the rumors persisted and were to come back to haunt him later.

Few of the big name criminals turned up in Burlington County, but the moonshiners and bootleggers who did business with them did. Parker, with his network of informers, friends, fellow lawmen, and ordinary citizens managed to keep his finger on the pulse of crime as well as anyone could. Chasing all the thousands of violators of Prohibition was a Herculean task, but in the early part of the 1920s, Burlington County still had plenty of more traditional crime for Parker as well.

During this period, Parker solved his most famous cases and also the one case, outside of the Lindbergh kidnapping, for which his name still appears in criminology and forensic textbooks; the Case of the Pickled Corpse. It was this case that probably best exemplifies Ellis Parker's methods and his command of deduction, forensics, psychology, human nature, and persistent detective work. It was also another case he deftly solved when others were stumped, a favorite trick he would later try, but fail to pull off on the Lindbergh case.

On October 5, 1920, a bank messenger named William Paul set out from the Broadway Trust Bank in Camden, bound for the Girard National Bank in Philadelphia. He carried a leather pouch containing $42,000 in checks, and $40,000 in cash. When he failed to arrive, the Broadway Trust Bank called Chief Detective Larry Doran of the Camden police.

In Paul's locker at the bank, Doran found a thick pack of letters from over a dozen different women over a period of three years. The letters told of a round of dances, drunken parties, and general carousing, much of it taking place at a spot referred to as the Lollipop Inn in Clementon. Frank James, a local well-to-do auto salesman, was also involved. Neither the police nor the bank employees knew of any place called the Lollipop Inn.

When Doran questioned James's wife, she had the disgusted and resigned look of a wife who knew her husband was habitually unfaithful, and had somehow learned to live with it. She said he had been away several days, probably at the Lollipop Inn. She explained that the Lollipop Inn was a bungalow James owned and used for parties with women and several other men, including the missing bank messenger, William Paul. Doran tracked down the other Lollipop Inn men, who acknowledged their activities, but all denied seeing Paul since well before his disappearance.

The case had struck a dead end, and there it stayed until October 16. On that day the duck hunting season opened and four hunters stumbled on a recently dug shallow grave in the woods north of Camden and just over the line into Burlington County. Ellis Parker was now on the case.

Parker knew the body was the missing William Paul as soon as it was unearthed. Paul was originally from Mt. Holly, and Parker had known him for years. In the grave, Parker found the leather pouch with the $42,000 in checks, but no cash. The checks were wet and the ink had run. He also found a thin, oddly shaped piece of leather that appeared to have been part of the interior trim of an automobile. On the ground were marks of the body being dragged up the slope from the direction of a causeway that crossed the steam below. Parker theorized that Paul had been killed eleven days earlier, when he disappeared, but two doctors who arrived on the scene disagreed. After examining the body, they assured Parker and Doran that Paul had been dead for less than 48 hours due to the amount of deterioration and the fact that bruises could still be seen. That would mean the murder had occurred on October 14th or 15th. Doran, who had come up from Camden with the two doctors, scratched his head.

"Well, Ellis, what do you think? Did he run out with an accomplice and then get killed in a quarrel a week later?"

"No," said Parker. "Look at the checks. If Paul wanted to run away with the money, why did he keep the pouch and the checks with him for eleven days? Why not destroy them or plant them somewhere? Even better, he could have delivered the checks to the Girard Bank, telling them the cash was coming later. That way no one would suspect anything was wrong for at least another day. Besides, if he planned to run away, he would have destroyed or hidden the letters you found in his locker so there would be no trail. No, running away was not his idea."

Doran nodded. It was simple when Ellis explained it.

"And then there's the matter of the ink running on the checks," Parker continued. "The checks were in a sealed, heavy leather pouch. It was almost waterproof. It would have taken days for ground water to seep through to the checks the way it did. Even then, only the checks on the outside would have been damp enough for the ink to run. No sir, that body has been submerged, and then it was fished out and buried."

"All that in the last two days?"

"No. He was killed over a week ago, soon after he disappeared," said Parker. "And I'll tell you something else; the killers were local men. The body was dumped in Bread and Cheese Creek soon after the murder, probably from the nearby causeway. But the killers got nervous later when they remembered that duck season started on October 18, and would bring hunters into the woods and streams where they might find the body. So they fished Paul out and dragged him to the shallow grave. That would account for the marks on the ground, the timing, the condition of the checks, and the missing money."

"That makes sense, Ellis," replied Doran, "but the doctors say Paul has been dead less than 48 hours."

Without replying, Parker walked over to Bread and Cheese Creek, and with a bottle borrowed from one of the doctors, carefully took a sample of the water.

"I'll have this checked," he said. "Meanwhile, what route would you say Paul took when he left the bank?"

"Probably down Main Street to the ferry to cross to Philadelphia," Doran answered.

Parker nodded. "Well, I doubt he was murdered at midday on Main Street in Camden. He must have been killed someplace else, and since he was diverted on a main thoroughfare, he must have gone with someone he knew well, especially since he still had the money on him at the time. So question the Lollipop Inn crowd again; especially any of them with a car. I think someone offered Paul a lift to the ferry, then drove off and killed him the same day."

Doran questioned the Lollipop Inn men again, but all of them had strong alibis for the time the medical examiner said the murder occurred. The same day, however, Parker received a phone call from the chemist that had analyzed the water sample from the creek. The water was full of Tannic acid. (Some accounts attribute the presence of the acid to an upstream tannery, while others claim it was from nearby oak or walnut trees.) Tannic acid is a preservative. The body could be in that water for a month and only look as if it had only been a couple of days. Parker decided to test a sample of water from the clothes as well.

The water from the clothes matched the first sample. Now Parker knew that the murderers had killed Paul the first day, probably in their car, and thrown the body off the causeway into the creek, where the acidic water helped preserve it. Later, realizing duck hunting season would soon bring hunters to the causeway, where they might notice the body in the water below, the murderers had moved the body to where it was finally found. The duck hunting tie-in suggested a local man familiar with both the area and with duck hunting. Parker was a duck hunter himself, and knew when the season began and how many hunters it attracted.

Now that the time of death was corrected, the most likely suspect seemed to be Frank James. He had been in Detroit for the past two days, but had no alibi for a week earlier, the time Parker had now established as the real time of death. He also had a car, but otherwise there was not much hard evidence tying him in with the crime. Parker was in his office staring at the spot on the wall and contemplating this problem when Doran called.

"Ellis," Doran said, "I arrested Frank James. Someone saw him on Main Street with his car with the window curtains down the day Paul disappeared. On top of that, James is a duck hunter. It all fits. He denies everything and says he was at a party with some women he won't name; says he's too much of a gentleman. That's a laugh."

As Parker refilled his pipe after the call, he suddenly remembered the piece of leather he found at the grave. He took it to several automobile dealers in town. They told him the piece came from the inner door of a Ford.

Frank James
(Photo from The Cunning Mulatto)

On Parker's advice, Doran examined James's car and found a tear that matched the piece of leather. In addition, the windshield was cracked and there was a new back seat. Once again, Frank James shrugged it off as the result of a wild party. The investigation was stuck once again.

Doran then questioned people who lived along the road between Camden and the causeway. He found a man who saw Frank James and another Lollipop Inn man named Ray Shuck riding towards the bridge with someone he didn't know in the back. (Some newspaper accounts give the spelling of the man's name as Schuck.) Ray Shuck, the manager of the local telephone company, was another prominent citizen. Parker decided that Shuck was the man they would get to talk.

For the next few weeks, Parker, Doran, and the Philadelphia Police painstakingly reconstructed the movements of James and Shuck during the critical weeks. Doran turned up a girl friend of Shuck's named Mary. From talking to Mary's friends, he found out she had been seeing Shuck for a year and thought that the married man was actually single. When Parker found that out, he chuckled to himself. He had found the lever to pry loose a conviction.

Parker contacted Mary and arranged to meet her to talk about the case. As if by accident, he let it slip that Shuck was married. He saw Mary stiffen up, but pretended he hadn't noticed and continued on for a few minutes to let her digest the information. Finally, he asked her what he really wanted to know. By that time, she was in no mood to protect the two-timing Mr. Shuck.

"Did you see him the night of October 5th?" (This was the day of the murder.)

"No, but I saw him the next day."

"Did he have any money with him when you saw him?"

"Oh, yes. He had a roll of twenties."

Parker made a mental note. Most of the stolen bank money had been twenties!

"And how about Tuesday, October 13th; did you see him that night?" (This was the day the body was moved.)

"No," she replied, obviously annoyed. "The double-crosser made a date with me then stood me up!"

Parker thanked Mary for her help. He now had what he wanted. That afternoon, he arrested Shuck.

Shuck was more nervous than James had been, just as Parker had figured. He stared to question him about his movements each day during the critical time between Paul's disappearance and the reburial of his body. Since Parker already knew most of the answers, he questioned Shuck on so many details that Shuck began to get more and more nervous about how much Parker already knew. Finally, Parker dropped the bomb.

"What did you tell Mary about all the money you had with you the night of October 6th, Raymond?"

Shuck gasped. Now he knew that Mary had talked.

"I...I told her I won it at the World Series." He said finally.

"So where did you really get it?"

"I can't say." Shuck looked as if he was about to go silent, so Parker shifted gears.

"Never mind," he said. "Let me ask you something else. Where did you buy the shovels you had in the car on the 13th, the day you drove down to Irick's causeway.

Shuck turned white, and refused to answer, but as Parker passed his cell the next morning, Shuck grabbed his arm.

"I didn't do it," he blurted out. "James killed Paul. It was only supposed to be a robbery, but James just seemed to go crazy and beat Paul until he was dead. Then he said he'd shoot me if I said anything!"

Confronted with Shuck's confession, James finally broke as well, except he blamed Shuck. In fact, they each blamed each other up until the very end ... in the electric chair. At the trial, Parker arranged to have Mary seated close to Shuck, just to keep his testimony honest.

Around the time Parker was investigating the Pickled Corpse Case, he became involved in a more minor matter in the state capitol. Parker was widely known as a man to turn to for help, especially if you were in trouble with the law. This may seem a strange reputation for a lawman to have, but it suited Ellis Parker. He liked being in charge; the man who could make things happen, the arbiter of justice and court of last appeal. As with many things he did, Parker had a more practical reason for this legal social work; it produced a steady supply of people who owed him favors. Such people often came in handy for some of Parker's more creative efforts at crime detection.

One such case came to his attention in 1920 when he learned the Reverend Hugo Wendel's son Paul was in trouble in

Trenton. Reverend Hugo Wendel was an old acquaintance of Parker's. Trained as a pharmacist, then as a lawyer in Germany, he started off as a county attorney in Oenringen and Nurtigen, Germany, then, in an abrupt change of course, became a Lutheran minister in a field mission in Pennsylvania. He was currently minister of the German Evangelical Lutheran Trinity Church on South Broad Street in Trenton.

Although not noticeably religious, Paul Wendel followed in his father's footsteps in other ways; he too was both a pharmacist and a lawyer. He received a degree in pharmacy, and worked in that profession for a while. Then, for reasons that are not entirely clear, he began studying law in 1913 under prominent Trenton attorney and councilman John H. Kafes of the law firm of Bayard Stockton. Kafes was to represent his former pupil later. Wendel was admitted to the Bar in 1918 and was currently practicing law in Trenton.

Paul Wendel used his pharmaceutical background to conduct chemical experiments at home, apparently intending to come up with some commercially viable product. Wendel was an obviously intelligent person but he had a strong streak of instability and dishonesty. He seemed to be one of those who often got in trouble and blamed circumstances or other people. In the 1907 yearbook of the Philadelphia School of Pharmacy, there is an entry for Paul Wendel that would prove prophetic; "...he is happiest when most in trouble."

In December of 1919, Wendel represented a client before the New Jersey Court of Chancery. During the trial the judge became suspicious of the authenticity of some of the documents in the case and questioned both Wendel and his stenographer about them. The result was Wendel's suspension from the bar and his arrest for perjury. Wendel was convicted and sentenced to nine months in the Mercer County Work House in 1922. After he served his term, he sought reinstatement, and restoration of his rights of citizenship. After a period selling real estate and insurance, Wendel received a pardon in 1924 and was reinstated to the Bar in 1925. At some point between 1920 and 1924, Parker took an interest in his case and signed a petition for Wendel's pardon and reinstatement.

What other actions Parker may have taken on Wendel's behalf are not recorded, and Parker's contribution appears to have been marginal at best. Even so, Paul Wendel was grateful for Parker's efforts and became his friend from that time on. Wendel kept in touch with Parker on an irregular basis, and even became friends with Parker's family and associates. On several occasions, the Parkers and the Wendels had dinner together. Although used to dealing with the wide spectrum of her boss's contacts and friends, Anna Yoos was wary of Wendel and mistrusted him. Parker's relationship with Wendel was similar to his relationship with many people whose cases he espoused, but was to have dire consequences for him years later.

While Parker was solving some of his greatest cases, crime was on the minds of the state legislature in Trenton as well. For years, the New Jersey State government had realized that no matter how competent local police might be, criminals who increasingly operated across county and state lines were getting bolder and more elusive. Pressured by the New Jersey Grange and the Chamber of Commerce, the state of New Jersey created the New Jersey State Police in 1921. The decision only came after several years of debate and controversy. Opposing the argument for statewide control and coordination to fight crime crossing jurisdictional borders was the argument that the added expense and the usurpation of local control would cause more harm than good.

Much of the most fervid opposition came from the county sheriffs and county detectives who thought that they could handle things just fine if they were only given the resources. Resources, of course, were an important issue. The local chiefs feared the state police would get all the newest equipment and most lavish budgets. This fear was not unfounded. Ellis Parker was particularly opposed to the creation of a state police force and said so on more than one occasion. In Parker's view, a centralized police bureaucracy could never have the local presence and local knowledge that the county people brought to the task. He also feared that the presence of a powerful state agency with overlapping jurisdiction meant he would lose the freedom he had always enjoyed to conduct his business as he saw fit.

Once the decision to create the state police was made, Governor Edward "Teddy" Edwards had to appoint a head of the new agency. Political bosses statewide, seeing how powerful the new agency would be, demanded a voice in who would be appointed. Two contenders were the strongest. The first was Frank Hague, mayor of Jersey City and head of the Hudson

County Democratic Party. The other was the head of the state's Department of Motor Vehicles, Harold Giles Hoffman. Hoffman's claim was strengthened by the fact that the Department of Motor Vehicles already had a small, motorized criminal investigation force operating on a statewide basis. Harold Hoffman also happened to be a friend of Ellis Parker.

Faced with contending claims from politicians, and not wishing to create a powerful new position beholden to someone who might be a rival, Governor Edwards decided his best option was to appoint a head who was not political at all. He felt he needed someone who had strong administrative experience in a military type organization, yet would not be encumbered by his political background. One night, Edwards's son Irving suggested H. Norman Schwarzkopf, an ex-classmate of his at West Point and a fellow artillery officer in France during the Great War (World War II had not yet occurred, so World War I was still called the Great War.). According to Irving Edwards, Schwarzkopf was so non-political he wasn't even registered to vote.

Seeing a possible way out of his dilemma, the governor decided to check up on H. Norman Schwarzkopf. After the war, Schwarzkopf became a Provost Marshall with the Army of Occupation. Later, he returned to the Seventh Cavalry at Fort Bliss, Texas, and again served as Provost Marshal for the El Paso area. Upon leaving the army, he worked as a floorwalker at a local department store for a time, but otherwise had the solid administrative background Governor Edwards had been looking for. When the governor interviewed him, he decided Colonel H. Norman Schwarzkopf was the man he wanted.

H. Norman Schwarzkopf
(Photo courtesy of the New Jersey State Police Museum)

The newly appointed head of the New Jersey State Police was not really a crime detection expert like Parker or the other county detectives. Parker was especially contemptuous of Schwarzkopf, seeing him as not only a rival, but a man lacking in deductive skills or experience. What Parker refused to accept, however, was that the head of the state police had to be more a commanding officer and general manager, relying on specialized subordinates for the details of detection work. In short, Schwarzkopf wasn't an expert detective, but he didn't have to be. He was a manager.

In keeping with his background, Schwarzkopf organized the state police like a military operation, with strict discipline, high standards, and rigid routines. He achieved high morale and a relatively efficient operation, but his force was never as good at finding and arresting bootleggers as Parker with his deductive skills, extensive contacts, and local knowledge.

Some sources have speculated that much of Parker's bitterness was sour grapes, and that he wanted to head up the new agency himself. In view of Parker's prestige and the almost complete autonomy he already enjoyed in his county, however, it seems unlikely he would be eager to trade it all for the scrutiny, political infighting, and bureaucratic routines that the state police job would have entailed. On another occasion, much later, Parker said he wouldn't have the job if it were "offered on a silver platter." It seems clear he viewed the state police as a politically protected rival to his own law enforcement efforts, one that could interfere and cause him a great deal of trouble in the future. In this, Ellis Parker was absolutely correct.

In the same year the state police were established, Ellis Parker solved two more of his most famous murder cases. The first was the murder of 12 year old Matilda Russo of Moorestown. The case started off as a missing person complaint, but as days passed without the girl appearing, Parker knew there was foul play. By this time, detectives from Moorestown, Camden, and even Philadelphia were involved, so it is difficult to say just how independent Parker's investigation really was. At any rate, there was no body, no leads, no witnesses, and absolutely nothing to go on, but such minor problems seldom stopped Ellis Parker for long. If he didn't have evidence, he used psychology. Since Matilda Russo had disappeared on her way home from school, Parker started off by questioning people who lived along the route. To bluff the killer into thinking the law was hot on the trail, he accused each person he questioned of having been seen talking to Matilda Russo the day she disappeared. By now Parker knew Matilda Russo had probably been murdered since the Russos did not have enough money to be targets of robbery or kidnapping.

After letting a few days pass, he questioned the people again. At one house, he found the resident, a mixed race Philadelphia street sweeper named Louis Lively had left suddenly on a trip. Parker searched his house, apparently without a warrant, and found Lively had taken almost all his clothes, indicating he was not returning. His wife did not know where he was or when he would be back. Satisfied he had flushed the killer out, Parker arrested Lively's wife as an accessory, then looked over the scene to try to determine where the murder had taken place. There was no secluded place outside, so it had to be in the house. Although the house was ill kept and cluttered, the floor of one room had been recently scrubbed clean.

What happened next is unclear because different sources do not agree. Parker later claimed he explored the basement, a gloomy room with a dirt floor. He noticed a dusting of ashes covered the floor, possibly to conceal any surface signs of recent digging. To test his theory, Parker poured water over the floor. As he expected, the water stood in puddles over most of the hard packed floor. In one small rectangular area, however, the water was quickly absorbed, indicating the soil was loose from recent digging. Parker dug in the area and found the body of Matilda Russo. Her throat had been cut. Contemporary accounts in the New York Times, however, say the body was actually discovered by Chief Bradshaw of the Moorestown force, along with one of his patrolmen. No water was used and Ellis Parker was not even present at the time.

A check of Lively's criminal record showed he had served time for stabbing a man, and had lived in Morris County the year before when another young girl had been found murdered in identical circumstances. Now that Parker had his man, he had to find him. Lively's sister lived nearby, so Parker had her watched in case Lively made contact. Knowing Lively had been a brush maker, and that most brush makers were in New England, Parker contacted brush making factories to be on the alert for any new job applicants matching Lively's description. Sure enough, one New England plant had just turned Lively down for a job. There were no openings as the industry was experiencing a slump. Lively would have to look elsewhere.

But Lively then made a fatal error; he started to write threatening letters to both Ellis Parker and Detective Frank Lore of Cumberland. The first letter, threatening to cut out Parker's liver if he didn't drop the case, came from Three Rivers, Ontario, and the second came from Windsor, Ontario, opposite Detroit. This told Parker that Lively was working his way back through Canada and Michigan. Parker believed the letters were intended to provoke a response in the papers that would tell Lively, through his sister, if it was safe to return yet. Parker immediately had Lively's wife released and made sure the papers carried the story. This would signal to Lively that the case was dying down and it was safe for him to come home. This was exactly what Parker wanted.

From questioning Lively's friends Parker claims he learned Lively had a tremendous appetite, so he decided to use this information to set a trap. He contacted small hotels, restaurants, and hash houses in several counties he expected Lively to pass through and told them to be on the alert for a man of Lively's description ordering a large meal. Sure enough, a lunch wagon near Vineland soon reported a man of Lively's description eating a huge meal that included a double order of pork chops and three orders of custard. Contemporary newspaper accounts say nothing of a lunch wagon, only that Lively was spotted.

He was captured after a gun battle in Landis Park in Vineland and spirited away by both the local police and Ellis Parker before he could be lynched. He was locked in the Burlington County Jail in Mt Holly, where he confirmed he had been in New England and Canada before returning to New Jersey. He claimed the killing had been an accident he was afraid to report. His wife was indicted for aiding and abetting, since she had tried to mislead the police. Louis Lively was never lynched, but was tried and executed at the Trenton State Prison a few months later, along with George Washington Knight, the killer of the organist of a Perth Amboy church.

Louis Lively under arrest
(Photo from The Cunning Mulatto)

Ellis Parker later claimed Louis Lively was the most thoroughly evil man he had ever dealt with. Considering the people Parker ran up against in his career, that is saying a lot.

About the time Louis Lively was executed, Parker embarked on another of his legendary cases; a murder in which he had 175 suspects! The case began when Captain Quinlan, the Intelligence Officer at Camp Dix, near Wrightstown contacted Parker for help. Sergeant Michael Gregor had gone AWOL in September and his body was discovered three months later on the outskirts of the camp near the artillery range. He had been shot twice in the head.

Before he even visited the camp, Parker sought and found what didn't fit. Questioning Quinlan, he discovered that two of Sgt. Gregor's tunic pockets were unbuttoned and empty, indicating the killer took the contents with him. He also determined that Sgt. Gregor's wallet was missing, as well as his watch and his pistol, an army-issue .45 with serial number 399274. He then came up with another deduction.

"From where you told me the bullets entered," he said, "there is no way he could have been on his feet when he was shot. The killer must have struck him on the head unexpectedly, then shot him while he was on the ground."

"On the ground?"

"Yes. A head shot at night at a moving target is damned difficult. Even if the killer hit him with the first shot, he wouldn't have been able to get off the second. Either of the two shots would have been instantly fatal, so if he was shot standing up, Gregor would have fallen right away, making the second shot miss, especially in the dark. You have the body exhumed and see if there isn't a mark from a blow to the head. And also dig up at the spot where the body was found. The bullets are probably in the ground. We'll need to find them. And I'll have to question everyone in the company."

So Ellis Parker began the tedious task of interviewing 175 suspects; the sort of thing he referred to as "spade work". He asked each soldier about his background and what he knew about Sgt. Gregor. From these questions, he learned that Sgt. Gregor had been in the habit of loaning money until payday at high interest rates. When payday came, then, everyone knew Gregor would be carrying a lot of cash around. It seemed like a strong motive, but didn't narrow down the suspects at all.

After asking these initial questions, Parker asked each man what he had been doing on the day of the murder. For almost anyone else, getting anything useful from all this questioning would have been doubtful, but the sly Parker fell back on one of his pet theories: the suspect with the best alibi is usually guilty.

His reasoning was based on his knowledge of human nature. Most people, when asked about their activities on a specific date months in the past, would have only the vaguest idea what they were doing that day. The only person who would know, Parker reasoned, was someone who had made it his business to have a carefully constructed story ready in case he was questioned later. Parker quickly eliminated anyone who was unsure of where he had been and narrowed his list down to 10 men who had given detailed accounts of their actions. He then called each of them back and questioned them in detail about their answers. Nine of the men got confused and finally admitted they had been a little more imaginative then they should have been, and really didn't remember everything they had said. Only one man, a soldier named Duncan, stuck to his story and kept every detail consistent. He even knew what he had done the day before and the day after!

Parker knew he probably had his killer.

Meanwhile, a further examination of the body confirmed there had been a blow on the head in addition to the gunshots, just as Parker had deduced. Even more important, a search of the ground turned up the two .45 caliber bullets. Parker had

Duncan's army .45 tested, but the bullets didn't come from that gun.

"He must have used Gregor's gun," Parker said to Quinlan. "Now we've got to find out what he did with it. Monitor who Duncan communicates with. Maybe some other clue will turn up."

Another search of the grounds failed to turn up the gun, but Parker did find a sawed off pool cue, which makes an excellent club. A short time later, the army intercepted a letter from Duncan to a fingerprint expert in Chicago asking if fingerprints were distinctive to each individual, and if fingerprints could be taken from clothing. In the letter, Duncan explained that he was interested because a man had been shot nearby after being clubbed on the head. Parker was delighted. Not only was the letter suspicious in itself, but the fact that Gregor had been clubbed was not public information. Duncan had to be the killer.

As more letters were intercepted and read, it became apparent that Duncan was writing frequently to a woman in West Virginia. On the chance Duncan sent the gun to her, Parker went to West Virginia and talked to her. Parker spent a long time talking to her in a non-threatening way to put her at her ease. Finally he asked whether her friend in the army ever sent her any presents.

"Why yes," she said. "He sent me a gun."

The gun was an Army .45. Parker checked the serial number and smiled. Clearly stamped into the cold metal of the gun were the numbers 399274.

When Duncan was confronted with the pool cue and the gun, he readily confessed. Parker had found the killer out of 175 suspects.

The case had a bizarre footnote. Sergeant Gregor's sister traveled all the way from St Louis to the Mt Holly jail to confront Duncan. She claimed she had been having dreams of the man who killed her brother, but he had always had his back to her. When she saw Duncan and persuaded him to turn around with his back to her, she claimed she then recognized that he was the man in her dream.

Chapter 5
Two Weddings and a Scandal
1922- 1929

The Roaring Twenties continued on their brash course with gangsters, religious revivals, bathtub gin, and the occasional lynching. Two immigrant Italian anarchists, Sacco and Vanzetti were found guilty of the murder of a paymaster and guard during a Massachusetts shoe factory robbery. The controversial case was nationwide news and revealed widespread uneasiness with immigrants who were seen as hostile to America's values and customs. Another sign of this anti-foreigner sentiment was the renewed strength of the Ku Klux Klan and the Palmer Raids.

Prohibition was still in full swing, and still being circumvented by everyone from gangsters to respectable old ladies. Young women were adopting the "flapper" look and dancing the Charleston with wild abandon. Writers such as F. Scott Fitzgerald, Sinclair Lewis and H.L. Mencken chronicled the decadence. Perhaps to help combat the rising tide of lawlessness and questionable morality, the Lutheran Church voted to drop the word Hell from the Apostles Creed and substitute the word

Hades. If America was going to Hell (or Hades) in a hand basket, as some claimed, a lot of people seemed to be enjoying the ride.

Ellis Parker was also doing well. He was the champion detective in America, king of the hill in New Jersey, and an institution in Mt. Holly. In spite of his initial misgivings, Parker found the state police were not a serious problem to him. In fact, he enjoyed the competition to catch bootleggers, since with his contacts and local knowledge, he usually left the state police in the dust. In his usual style, Parker soon developed contacts within the state police ranks, and used these as a source of information to add to his already formidable network.

Financially, he was doing just fine. In 1922, his $2,500 salary was raised to $3,500, and he began buying properties at auction as an investment. He also bought a two-story summer house at Brant Beach on the Jersey Atlantic shore about twenty miles north of Atlantic City. Although it was not directly on the ocean, the house was a typical wood shingle New Jersey beach house with sand dunes drifting across the yard, and tufts of sea grass bending in the wind. Cora and the children spent much of their summers at the Brant Beach house, escaping the heat of Mt. Holly. Ellis joined them on weekends when he could. When grandchildren started to come along, they came to the house as well.

Parker had always valued his acquaintances and contacts, but now he became more active in Republican politics, actively supporting several candidates. As before, he was the darling of newspaper reporters. His self-described exploits were the stuff of dime novels, and were being carried not only in newspapers, but in such places as New Age Magazine. In a 1927 article titled "A County Detective with a World-Wide Reputation", the sub-title of the article identified the detective as Ellis Parker and called him the "Most Borrowed Detective in International Police History", a reference to Parker's work for other jurisdictions and countries. Accompanying the article was a large photo of Parker with a bent collar, crooked tie, and his ever-present pipe. Under the photo is a quote.

"I don't believe there is a person living, but what if he had witnessed some of the crimes I have, would champion capital punishment."

This confusing statement would seem to oppose capital punishment, but is really just a case of Parker having trouble with using the proper number of negatives in a sentence. In the article, his position is much clearer.

"In my judgment, some murderers are such animals that it is the only mode of punishment which fits their cases, because society would be far better off completely rid of them."

He acquired nicknames such as "the Bald Eagle of the Pines", or "the American Sherlock Holmes". Parker, of course, enjoyed the attention and used his reputation to advance his career. He used psychology on reporters as effectively as he did on suspects. He was usually vague when working on a case, preferring to present the reporters with a completed success story rather than a work in progress. Parker relished explaining every hair-raising detail of how he caught the perpetrators once they were safely behind bars. Like a magician, Parker kept his secrets until he could dazzle his audience with a final, spectacular effect that left then gasping. This was usually Sherlock Holmes's method as well.

Since 1920 Anna Yoos had been his steady right-hand woman. She provided counsel, support, and an uncanny way of encouraging suspects to tell all. But there were changes coming for the indispensable Miss Yoos. During the Pickled Corpse case in 1920, she struck up a friendship with Herman Bading, a big man who kept fit and looked like a football player. Bading later became a member of the newly formed state police. Their courtship proceeded slowly, but they saw more of each other as time went on. Parker's reaction to this development isn't recorded, but he probably welcomed having another acquaintance with contacts in the state police. On the other hand, he probably deduced where the courtship was heading and he must have been somewhat uneasy with the prospect of perhaps losing his dependable partner in fighting crime.

At the beginning of 1922, however, the possible divided loyalty or departure of Anna Yoos was only a remote threat to Parker's comfortable world. She was still by his side and helping him fight the good fight.

And there was plenty of crime to fight. Motorized robbers were still creating havoc as they swooped down on banks or other targets, then disappeared in a cloud of dust. Bank robberies had become so frequent that the Pennsylvania

Banker's Association advocated making bank robbery a capital offense.

Murders, too, were still going strong, and not just in New Jersey. In a Chicago suburb, 14 year-old Bobby Franks was murdered in cold blood by two privileged boys who did it mostly for the thrill, although they intended to get ransom as well. The Leopold and Loeb case made nationwide headlines, and the two boy killers only escaped the electric chair because they were defended by Clarence Darrow, who was later to defend science itself in the infamous Scopes Monkey Trail in Tennessee.

During the 1920s, the way the police detected and pursued crime changed. The automobile became standard for police forces, as did the teletype and radio communication. Most importantly, fingerprinting came into its own as the standard method of identification of criminals and suspects, finally replacing the clumsy and complicated Bertillion Method. Individual police departments had used fingerprints for years, but in 1924, the FBI (at that time simply called the Bureau of Investigations) started its Identification Division with 810,000 fingerprints on file from across the country, the first centralized fingerprint database. Now prints could be cross-referenced with the federal files.

Prohibition continued to make demands on Ellis Parker's time and attention. Parker was not the only lawman compelled to chase bootleggers. By the middle of the decade, 90% of the cases brought to federal court in New Jersey were liquor law violations.

Still, there were other cases that tested Parker's now famous detecting ability. The 1922 murder of William Giberson was one of the cases when the police in another jurisdiction, this time Lakehurst in Ocean County, borrowed Ellis Parker. Giberson, who had become quite well off by operating a fleet of taxis between Lakehurst and Camp Dix during the war, was found in the second floor apartment of a building he owned at 8 Union Avenue, lying dead in his bed with a single gunshot to the head. According to Ivy Giberson, William's wife, two burglars awakened her while her husband was still asleep. They took her into the adjoining kitchen of their apartment where one intruder tied her up as the other searched the bedroom. Suddenly a shot rang out from the bedroom.

Scene of the Giberson murder (Upper right windows)
(Photo courtesy of Bernadette Dugan)

"What the hell did you go and shoot him for?" the kitchen intruder demanded of the unseen man in the next room.

"He was waking up. I had to," came the reply.

Parker was already suspicious of Ivy Giberson's story and this clinched it for Parker. He knew she was lying. Wilfred Jayne, the Ocean County prosecutor who was working with Parker agreed.

"Mrs. Giberson was on the side of the bed against the wall," Parker observed. "I don't care how good a sleeper Mr. Giberson was, there is no way she could have climbed over him to get out of bed without waking him up. Secondly, the way the place is laid out, you can't see the bed from the kitchen. So if the burglar heard a shot and couldn't see what had happened, why would he assume his partner had shot Giberson? Wasn't it just as likely Giberson had awakened and shot his partner? The natural reaction would have been to run to see what had happened or to get out of the house."

Both Parker and Jayne noted, too, that the twine Mrs. Giberson claimed was used to tie her up was too thin for the purpose and that the scissors supposedly used to cut the twine had been unnecessary. The twine could be easily broken by hand.

Acting on his suspicions, Parker came up with a plan to lure Ivy Giberson into giving him the evidence he needed for a conviction. He carefully noted her description of the men she said were responsible and sent alerts to police in the surrounding areas asking them to be on the lookout, all the while assuring Mrs. Giberson that a manhunt was under way. Now that he had convinced her she was not a suspect, and thus encouraged her to let her guard down, Parker had Ivy Giberson followed. Noticing she made a number of trips to an outbuilding, he got a warrant and searched it. Under a pile of debris, he found the murder weapon. The fingerprints matched Ivy Giberson's. Also in the outbuilding was a pile of love letters from several men.

Ivy Giberson and her husband
(Photo from The Cunning Mullato)

Mr. Giberson had been very successful in his business endeavors, so Mrs. Giberson was able to hire several private detectives to dig up evidence to support her story and fight the charges. The trial was full of sensational testimony about altered bank books, multiple love letters, chloroformed pads hidden in a coffee pot, a feuding stepson, previous robberies, and shadowy bootleggers. In the end, however, Ivy Giberson was convicted of murder and received a life sentence. Some newspaper accounts indicate that prosecutor Jayne did most of the detective work and Parker just helped. This is hard to believe. Apart from the unlikelihood of someone like Parker simply "helping out", prosecutors generally do not get involved in sifting evidence until a suspect is under lock and key. A measure of the accuracy of one of the articles is the fact that Ellis Parker is referred to as Ellis Butler. The writer apparently confused Parker with contemporary humorist Ellis Parker Butler.

The same year, Parker tackled another of his unusual and long-remembered murder cases; a case that held a hint of troubles to come much later. On a cold night in March, Parker investigated the apparent suicide of John Brunen, shot through the head in his home. Parker saw at once that Brunen had not killed himself. He had been shot in the lower part of the head while sitting in front of a window. There was a hole in the window and shards of glass blown inward. Brunen's wife had reported the incident as a suicide, but Parker saw that the shot had been fired from outside. John Brunen had been murdered. Parker soon found out that, in addition to his unusual death, Brunen had had an unusual occupation. Brunen was owner of a circus, the Colonel Ferrari and Mighty Doris Combined Shows. The Doris part was named after his wife.

In addition to reporting the apparent suicide, Doris Brunen told Parker the New York gambling crowd knew her husband as "Honest John Brunen", and she suspected them in the murder. Parker became suspicious Mrs. Brunen was trying to lead him in the wrong direction. His suspicions were reinforced when he noticed a pet parrot in a cage in the basement. Mrs. Brunen said the parrot was usually kept in the room where her husband was murdered, but had been ailing. Parker believed the parrot had been moved from the room on the off chance he might blurt out the murderer's name; more evidence of an inside job. When he noticed mud on Mrs. Brunen's shoes, she became defensive and said she had only gone out to check on the dog. Parker examined the footprints in the yard from which the shot had been fired and saw two sets of male prints, one considerably larger than the other. These prints overlapped those of Mrs. Brunen, indicating they were made after she was outside. The killers' footprints led to a lane nearby and to a set of tire tracks.

When he examined Brunen's pockets, he found a letter from Brunen to his sister expressing concern that his wife intended to kill him.

Parker spoke with the neighbors and learned no one heard the dog bark. To Parker, this indicated the killer was someone who knew Brunen well enough to be recognized by his dog and well enough to know he sat by the window at night. From the neighbors, he also learned Brunen was a quarrelsome man with a number of enemies. What's more, he and Doris had had a fierce fight on Christmas, a fight that ended with shots being fired in the house!

The next morning, one of Parker's detectives brought him a piece of a broken shotgun he had found along the lane where a car had been parked. Parker was beginning to get a picture of the killers. One was a big man, but the actual gunman was a small nervous man. Parker deduced this from the size and placement of the footprints and the fact that a shotgun was used at extremely close range, a sign that the killer was unsure of his marksmanship. The fact he had broken up the shotgun and dropped part of it seemed to confirm the theory. Parker arranged for local police to investigate people who lived along the road to see if any of them had seen anything. He then asked one of his detectives a strange question.

"Find out if Brunen took his dog with him when he traveled with his circus. We know the dog didn't bark because he knew the killers," Parker explained. "If Brunen took the dog with him, everyone in the circus becomes a suspect, because the dog would have known them too. If not, we only have relatives or people in the neighborhood."

The detective later reported back that Brunen had indeed taken the dog with him.

Parker then got a copy of The Billboard, a directory that carried addresses and personal information about people in the entertainment field. Using this, he started going through the names of everyone connected with the circus to see where they spent their winter months. He had to work quickly because the circus was due to leave in a few weeks.

Meanwhile, someone living along the road turned in another discarded piece of the shotgun. To his delight, Parker found that this piece had the manufacturer and serial number stamped on it. And even better, the shotgun was a relatively rare Belgian make. Now it was time for some of Parker's "spade work". From the Belgian consulate he learned only ten shotguns of that particular brand had been sold in the area to a company in Philadelphia. Using the serial number, he traced the shotgun through two owners to a pawnshop in Philadelphia. The pawnbroker remembered selling the shotgun just after Christmas to a stocky man with a red face.

Checking back with The Billboard, Parker was able to eliminate most of the circus people, but was left with two men: Charles Powell and Harry Mohr. Mohr had strong motive: he was part owner of the circus and stood to gain it all if anything happened to Brunen. In addition, there was one more significant fact about Harry Mohr: he was Doris Brunen's brother. As for Charles Powell, he was a longtime friend and hanger-on of Mohr's. Their descriptions, Parker found, matched the men he was looking for. Mohr was stocky and Powell was small and nervous.

Parker questioned Mohr and found him gruff and cool. He had an alibi, but it had enough flexible time in it to still allow the murder. Parker did not have conclusive evidence on Mohr and Mohr knew it. Even later, when the pawnbroker identified Mohr's photograph as that of the man who bought the Belgian shotgun, Parker knew he still did not have enough for a conviction. Mohr stood to gain the circus and had no reason to crack.

Powell, however, was a different story. He was already nervous, and did not apparently have much to gain from the crime. He had probably only done it at the urging of Mohr, and would be a lot easier to crack. To break the case, Parker felt he would have to take Powell into custody and get him to confess. The problem was, Powell was in Camden, outside of Parker's jurisdiction, so he had no clear power to arrest him.

Parker decided to have him kidnapped, at least that was the term Parker used, although the exact nature of the arrest is somewhat hazy. (Other sources indicate the arrest was done properly with a warrant, and that there was no hint of a kidnapping.)

In light of what came later, this claim was revealing. Parker could have asked the Camden Police to make the arrest, but he claims he didn't. Was this merely a reflection of a lawless era, or an early sign Ellis Parker was sometimes willing to circumvent the law in an effort to enforce it? Parker himself refers to his action matter-of-factly as a kidnapping in his account of the story in The Cunning Mulatto, a book of his cases written some years later. Perhaps when he was interviewed for the book in 1934, Parker was already toying with the idea.

Charles Powell
(Photo from The Cunning Mulatto)

The kidnapping/arrest went badly according to Parker's account. Powell's wife saw the men coming and called the Camden Police. Everyone was taken into custody. When the dust settled, however, Parker was finally able to question Powell. As Parker expected, Powell went to pieces and confessed almost immediately. He had been paid $1,000 to kill Brunen, and Mohr had come with him because he was afraid the job would be bungled again. It was Powell's fourth attempt. Powell's confession led to the arrests of Doris Brunen and Harry Mohr. Unlike Powell, however, they had no intention of confessing to anything.

The trial of Doris Brunen and Harry Mohr in Mt Holly was a sensation. Doris Brunen's 18 year old stepdaughter Hazel testified bitterly about Doris Brunen and the Christmas showdown that resulted in shooting, while Harry Mohr shouted "You lie!", and Mohr's wife shouted "Hazel, don't talk like that you little tramp, or I'll smack you dead!". Even Mohr's attorney became hysterical and had to seek medical help while the judge cleared the court. Later, Parker told a reporter that there was a danger of Mohr shooting John Brunen's daughter in the courtroom and that extra security precautions had been taken. The final verdict was a curious one; Harry Mohr was convicted while Doris Brunen was acquitted.

The Honest John Brunen Case became another part of Parker's legend. The newspapers ran stories with artist's renderings of the killer's position on the lawn and Parker pointing it out. The citizens of New Jersey shook their heads in admiration; the American Sherlock Holmes had done it again. Almost no one noticed, however, that he claimed he did it by attempting to kidnap his suspect. The fact that the supposed kidnapping paid off in the confession of the suspect and solving the case overshadowed the questionable methods that may have been employed by the forces of law and order. This lesson was not lost on Parker.

One of the most thrilling chapters in the exciting life of Ellis Parker was the murder of "Honest John" Brunen, circus owner, at Riverside. Here is "Chief" Parker standing beside the Brunen home, pointing to the window where the victim sat when slain. An artist's outline depicts how the killer knelt and fired the fatal shot.

Newspaper account of the John Brunen murder

(Photo courtesy of William Fullerton)

The fall of 1922 also brought a sensational case in which Parker's role was limited, but which would affect his life years later. On September 16, an Episcopal minister, the Reverend Edward Wheeler Hall was found shot to death along with a singer in the church choir, Eleanor Mills, in a local lover's lane in New Brunswick. Around their bodies were scattered dozens of love letters that made it clear the two had been carrying on an affair for four years. In addition to being shot, Eleanor Mills's throat was cut and a later autopsy revealed her tongue had been cut out. Hall's wife and two of Mills's relatives were suspected of the crime, but things went wrong for the police. The crime scene was overrun by the curious and thoroughly contaminated while police from Middlesex County and Somerset County were settling the question of jurisdiction. The Reverend Hall's calling card, an important piece of evidence found at the scene, was passed around among the spectators, ruining any value it may have had.

The police arrested several people, including the woman who discovered the bodies, but had little real evidence against any of them. Early in the case, Mrs. Mills's daughter requested that Ellis Parker be assigned to the case, but was refused, since Somerset County was out of his jurisdiction. After some more police problems with witnesses and conflicting stories, the state took over the investigation in October to get the case back on track. Although the newly formed state police were part of the investigating team, Detective James Mason of Essex County was appointed chief investigator, and he asked Ellis Parker's help as well. Parker was cautious when questioned by the press, warning that the investigation could be slow and time consuming because of the extensive interviews required. The new blood did little to stem the confusion since the crime scene was now over a month old and trampled by the curious. The police work was so sloppy at the crime scene that two cartridges left at the scene did not turn up until the end of October, and they were found by a sightseer! A new witness did turn up, however, a local farm woman dubbed the "pig woman" by the press because she raised hogs. Her story kept changing, however, and so her testimony was thought to be less than credible. Her own mother contradicted her.

And so, in this chaotic and compromised case, Ellis Parker went to work. In January of 1923 Eleanor Mills's husband told Parker that she had had the love letters found at the murder scene with her a few nights before. Apparently she intended to deliver the letters to Reverend Hall the night the two were murdered.

The investigation plodded on. Finally, in November, a grand jury was convened to consider proceeding against Mrs. Hall and her two brothers, but found there was not enough evidence. The case did not go to trial until 1926, where, after a flurry of sensational claims and contradictory testimony, the three were acquitted. The state police received a black eye and a reputation for bungling the frustrated Schwarzkopf was anxious to rectify. Stung by the criticism, Schwarzkopf longed for another high profile case his people could crack to silence the critics.

Ellis Parker's role in the Hall-Mills case was unusually low keyed for him. Here was a sensational case that almost cried out for bold action and clever police work, but Parker stayed in the background and displayed little of his famous crime-solving ability. He made almost no statements to the press, came up with little new information, and seemed content to let others take the spotlight...and the blame. Perhaps he knew a fiasco when he saw one since the trail was so cold and the evidence so compromised by the time he got involved, so he just kept his head down. Then again, he may have been reluctant to do anything extraordinary when it was likely that others would get the credit, including his rival H. Norman Schwarzkopf and the state police. A cynical person in Parker's position might have actually wanted the case to fall through to give Schwarzkopf a black eye. When the case was unsuccessfully retried several years later, in fact, Parker was accused of helping and advising the defense. Parker denied the charge and it was never substantiated.

The same year as the ill-fated Hall-Mills trial, Anna Yoos and Herman Bading were married. In the Chief Detective's Office, that nice Miss Yoos would now become that nice Mrs. Bading. Despite Parker's fears, Anna Bading continued in her job and remained the indispensable right hand woman. Now that she had two men in her life, she was determined to do justice to both.

Anna Yoos marries Herman Bading
(Photo courtesy of Herman Bading)

Herman Bading soon left the state police and became one of Parker's detectives for a few months before returning to the state police once again. Possibly to avoid confusion, and possibly out of force of habit, Parker continued to frequently refer to Anna Bading as Miss Yoos.

In 1925, the state of New Jersey looked for a new way of dealing with a rising crime rate and criminals crossing city and county lines. The New Jersey State Police, created over Parker's objections four years earlier, was providing statewide law enforcement, but a more sophisticated state-of-the art entity was needed to do the intricate and exhaustive investigation that more complex crimes required. State officials considered establishing a New Jersey Criminal Investigation Division. In spite of his opposition to the establishment of the state police, Parker supported the proposed CID enthusiastically. The reason might have been because he was rumored to be in line for the directorship at a salary of $8,000 a year. Whatever the reason, it was not to be. The state police, perhaps recognizing a threat, became more of a service agency for local police departments with the establishment of the Criminal Records, Fingerprint, and Auto Theft Bureaus. The CID became a function of the established state police, and Ellis Parker continued as Chief of Detectives of Burlington County knowing that the state police was now more competition than ever. The simmering feud between Schwarzkopf and Parker continued.

A few miles away in the state capitol, Paul Wendel, the erratic lawyer/pharmacist Parker had tried to get reinstated several years earlier was making a comeback. Although, still in debt from his earlier troubles, his legal career had recovered to the extent he was hired as counsel to represent Clark Hendrickson, former warden of the Mercer County Work House charged with blackmail and perjury. Wendel was certainly familiar with the Mercer County Workhouse, since he served a nine-month sentence for perjury there just three years before! An associate of Hendrickson, Mark Dries, was also involved, and Wendel represented him as well. This was an extremely high profile case involving fraud and abuse of public office by a high official. Wendel's selection as counsel was announced in the front-page headline of the October 30, 1925 Trenton Evening Times. Incredibly, just a year after his reinstatement, Wendel had become something of a celebrity attorney, and in a case involving the place he had once been incarcerated. It was like going to a high school reunion and finding a student who had been expelled was now the school principal.

But while Wendel's star seemed to be temporarily rising, trouble was brewing for Ellis Parker. Just a few weeks before Wendel's selection as counsel to the beleaguered Clark Henderson was announced, the New Jersey State Police observed a suspicious looking sand barge tied up Adam's Wharf on Rancocas Creek near Bridgeboro. They had been tipped off by Charles Carslake, a private detective and former revenue agent, that rumrunners were using the creek to land illegal liquor. Rancocas Creek is only a few miles from Mt. Holly and because it connects with the Delaware River and Philadelphia, was often used by bootleggers for transporting their wares. The barge, named the *A.B.Blaters*, had all its hatches closed, and seemed to be receiving visitors from all over. Something about the barge was attracting a lot of interest and the police were betting it wasn't sand. Four state police, along with Carslake, finally raided the barge and found it loaded with 20,000 cases of illegal liquor, worth an estimated $300,000. The police theorized the *Blaters* had been loaded from a boat out at sea beyond the twelve-mile limit, then towed up the Delaware and into Rancocas Creek for distribution.

Fifty-five men, many of them heavily armed, were arrested both on the wharf and on the barge. The men offered Carslake and the four police $15,000 each to forget about it, but were arrested anyway. Thirty of the men were packed in a waiting truck and sent off to Burlington to be arraigned, while the rest were locked in the barge's cabin. Someone set fire to the cabin and the suspects tried to escape. When they were finally rounded up, they too were taken to Burlington. There, however, the whole affair took a sour turn. New Jersey Supreme Court Commissioner Claude Palmer and Prosecutor George Hillman released the men on low bails ranging from $200 to $500 each. The total bail of $14,500 was considerably less than the $75,000 in bribes that had been offered, and it was promptly paid in cash. After the men vanished, authorities discovered that most had given false names and addresses. No one could even establish the identity of the man who paid the bail.

As the investigation unfolded, some of the remaining men offered to turn state's evidence and tell all they knew. A few weeks later, several officers of the Burlington Industrial Alcohol Company were arrested, suspected of using their company's frontage and wharves to ship some of its product out without undergoing the denaturing process as required by the Prohibition law. The whole business was now being called the Rancocas Creek Rumrunning Scandal, and a Burlington County grand jury was called upon to investigate. Justice Frank Lloyd charged the jury to get to the bottom of the case and to investigate the possibility of official corruption in the Burlington County Prosecutor's Office. This office, of course, included Ellis Parker. Justice Lloyd charged that two detectives from Parker's office had been sent to the scene earlier and had done nothing.

"Such a situation suggests more than mere neglect of duty," the judge said solemnly, "I need not say that corruption in office is offense of the first magnitude..."

The jury, he went on to say, was to determine if the low bail was the result of "corrupt motives, or merely a stupid blunder."

Several of the state's witnesses told of Burlington County being an especially hospitable place to smuggle liquor, and Ellis Parker's boss, Burlington County Prosecutor George H. Hillman was beginning to feel the heat. After all, he had been instrumental in setting the low bails the night of the raid and people were looking at him with suspicion. On November 10, in an admitted effort to defuse mounting public criticism, Hillman relieved Ellis Parker of his duties. Detectives Cliff Cain and

Arthur Carabine, the two detectives sent from Parker's office to investigate the barge but did nothing were suspended as well. To keep Parker's office running, Hillman requested the state assign Trooper Herman Bading to take over. Bading had recently returned to the state police but knew the Burlington County office procedures well from his time there.

The fact that the suspensions were merely a ploy by Hillman to deflect public suspicion and criticism became obvious when Parker continued to report for duty and work as if nothing had happened. Herman Bading also reported for duty but found he had little to do. Bading would later testify he didn't believe Parker had been suspended at all. Although Hillman's problem was solved, the state police resented being used as props for a local public relations shell game. Three days after Bading reported, it was apparent Parker was still running the office. Lieutenant William Nichols, head of the state police in Burlington County demanded a "showdown" with Hillman to determine Parker's status and threatened to withdraw Herman Bading if things weren't clarified.

"I don't intend to permit anyone to make a joke out of the state police," Nichols was quoted as saying.

Herman Bading was eventually withdrawn, but the scandal wasn't over yet.

By the end of the year, the grand jury had handed down 95 indictments, but citing lack of time, had not gotten around to investigating Parker. No indictments were ever returned for Parker, but Arthur Carrabine and Clifford Cain were brought to trial in April of 1926 on charges of Malfeasance in Office for not trying to stop the barge before the state police did. The charge was lowered to misfeasance during the trial. The trial was a minor sensation. On day, 150 women from the Women's Christian Temperance Union showed up in court after praying at several local churches. In the end, however, the evidence was insufficient to convict. Paul Wendel took an interest in the troubles of his friend, and would later claim he was instrumental in getting Parker's suspension rescinded, but Parker was never actually suspended in any real sense of the word, and the matter was quietly dropped. To Parker, the situation must have encouraged cynicism. He had possibly kidnapped a man in the John Brunen case (at least that is what he later claimed) and been praised, but had done nothing wrong in the rum running case and had been suspended.

Kidnapping was still an unusual crime in the 1920s, but not unknown, especially if a wealthy person was the subject. An odd case occurred in 1926 when Aimee Semple McPherson was kidnapped in California. McPherson was the most famous and spellbinding evangelist of the day. Dressed in flowing white robes, she whipped her audiences into frenzy, and raised phenomenal amounts of money from her efforts. In 1926, she disappeared while swimming near Venice Beach, and the public anxiously awaited the ransom demands. Thirty-two days later, she stumbled out of the Arizona desert with a tale of being kidnapped, held in a desert shack in Mexico, drugged and tortured. Ellis Parker was not involved in the case, but even without his help, local police noticed quite a few things that didn't fit. After walking over thirty miles through the desert, her shoes still looked almost new, the desert hut was never found, and, though she disappeared wearing a bathing suit, she reappeared fully clothed, including her corset! Police never did determine what happened. Later witnesses reported seeing her at several hotels with a man, but she stuck with the kidnapping story. Although the case was never solved, it was the most publicized kidnapping the nation had ever seen.... so far. The case was an object lesson in the publicity potential of a celebrity kidnapping and might well have been on the mind of whoever contemplated kidnapping the Lindbergh baby four years later.

In the same year as the McPherson kidnapping, Ellis Parker became involved in a mystery a little closer to home. His daughter Charlotte had been seeing William Fullerton of Camden for some time. They announced their engagement and Ellis Parker said he would set the wedding date for that fall. Not wishing to wait, Charlotte and William Fullerton casually announced they were going off to Camden for a visit, and got married in secret on June 24. The secret wasn't revealed to Ellis Parker until well into July.

The newspapers found the idea of the master detective being outwitted by his own daughter to be irresistible, and gleefully reported the story with headlines such as "PARKER OUTWITTED", or "CHIEF BAFFLED", or "PARKER FAILED TO SEE CUPID" One such article was typical.

"County Detective Chief Ellis Parker may be wise to all kinds of deduction in chasing lawbreakers and have an X-ray eye in digging out bootleggers, but he appears to be quite blind to nuptial symptoms around home sweet home. In fact, Dan Cupid has been hanging around the Parker homestead for some time, and the esteemed Ellis Parker failed to notice a single clue......Parker reflected a moment then mentally remarked that if he hadn't been so keen on stills and politics and other things, he might have observed Dan Cupid breaking into his home."

.

Parker just smiled, lit his pipe, and took it all in stride; at least he was in the headlines. Besides, he had an excuse. During the period when the elopement was being plotted, Parker was involved in another of his sensational and baffling murders; the Wilson –Roberts case.

On the night of June 1, two wealthy young Philadelphia socialites, Ruth Wilson and her former fiancée Horace "Red" Roberts, were found dying of gunshot wounds to the head in Wilson's bedroom in her parents' home in Moorestown. Wilson and Roberts had been engaged a year earlier, but Ruth Wilson had broken it several months later and returned the ring. Even so, they still saw each other and appeared to be on good terms. In fact, they had just returned from a trip to Ocean City with friends. Wilson's parents had gone to a neighbor's house to play cards and returned after midnight to find Robert's hat on a chair and the door to Ruth's bedroom locked. Repeated calls and knocks on the door brought no response, so Mr. Wilson climbed across an adjoining porch roof to look in the window. To his horror he saw the couple lying motionless and bleeding, his daughter on the bed clad only in her stockings and a light coat, and Roberts partly on the bed and partly on the floor. Roberts was completely nude.

Though both were still alive, Wilson died a few minutes later and Roberts lived for several more hours before dying at the local hospital. Neither regained consciousness. The case was a classic "locked room" mystery so beloved by writers of detective fiction. To make things even more baffling, investigators found that Wilson had been shot twice in the head and Roberts had been shot three times in the head, apparently ruling out suicide, even though a .22 pistol was found under Roberts's hand.

Police theorized a murder had taken place, but Ellis Parker, after a one day investigation, concluded that Roberts had shot Wilson, then killed himself. Parker learned that Roberts had been depressed at his rejection and had been sullen and withdrawn on the trip to Ocean City, even refusing to eat.

"Love will bring havoc or happiness into human lives," Parker declared. "Horace Roberts had all the evidence of a disturbed mentality before this happened. ….Young Roberts was in an insane fury caused by the girl's refusal to marry him. He left the house, undressed, then came back and fired the shots. The bullets were small; the third bullet made him unconscious."

The circumstances of the deaths, coupled with the families' high profile in the community led to rampant public speculation about what had really happened. Finally, Burlington County Prosecutor Hillman and the coroner bowed to public pressure and had the bodies exhumed and an autopsy performed to "still the rumors and innuendoes." Local police opposed such a move, believing it unnecessary. The autopsy and coroner's inquest revealed that Roberts had actually been shot FOUR times in the head! Ruth Wilson's mother Orellia had been sedated and confined to her bed since the killing, and was only given a notice to testify ten minutes before she was scheduled to appear. Despite all the public talk of conspiracies and outside killers, a coroner's jury agreed with Parker's murder-suicide theory and the case was officially closed.

Parker (lower right) with other detectives at the Mt Holly jail around 1930.
(Photo courtesy of the Burlington County Board of Chosen Freeholders)

The authorities may have been through with the case, but the public wasn't. People still talked about the mysterious circumstances and were skeptical about the inquiry's conclusions. Why would Roberts wait over two months after the engagement was broken to experience an "insane fury" at his rejection? And regardless of how small the caliber of the bullets, how could anyone shoot himself four times in the head? Bradway Brown, a neighbor who was a friend of both Wilson and Roberts and had testified at the inquest hinted that there was more to the story, but the inquest was complete and the case was closed. Parker had not heard the last of Bradway Brown.

By 1929, Parker's friend Paul Wendel was having problems again. He still contacted Parker from time to time, but he was constantly drawn towards trouble elsewhere. Wendel still had a strong interest in chemistry and continued to experiment with various compounds and processes in his spare time, seeking some moneymaking product or process. One such process involved producing alcohol from other compounds. During Prohibition, this would be the answer to a bootlegger's prayer, and was pursued as fervently as alchemists in the Middle Ages pursued turning base metals into gold.

According to some sources, Wendel once claimed he had perfected such a process, and approached several underworld figures about it. One such contact, Frank Cristano, was associated with Al Capone himself. Wendel approached Cristano with what he claimed was a way to convert ordinary tar into alcohol, and asked him to help sell it to Al Capone. If successful, this would have made everyone associated with it rich, but the process Wendel was touting was worthless. To demonstrate his discovery to Cristano, Wendel added some powder to a container of tar, then asked Cristano to return in an hour. While Cristano was out, Wendel secretly switched a container of alcohol for the container of tar. When Cristano returned, he was impressed. On the basis of Cristano's report, Capone became interested and arranged for Wendel to come to Chicago. Capone put Wendel up in the Lexington Hotel in Cicero and advanced him $700 to start the process going. Not being a fool, however, Capone assigned some of his people to investigate Wendel at the same time. How Wendel expected to keep up the ruse is anyone's guess, but soon the inevitable happened, and Capone discovered he was being conned. By some miracle, Wendel escaped the St. Valentine's Day treatment by returning Capone's money and leaving town.

As the decade approached its end, prosperity appeared to be a permanent thing. Everyone, it seemed, was a stock market investor and considered Wall Street to be the foolproof road to riches, investing all the money they had. Some people even invested money they didn't have, borrowing heavily to buy the latest high-flying stocks. This practice, called buying on margin was not limited to a small percentage of the value of the stock as it is today, and many people became dangerously overextended. Still, the bigger the risk the bigger the potential reward, and as long as the stocks kept going up, there was nothing to worry about.

Chapter 6
Depression Crimes
1930 - 1932

On October 29, 1929, the good times ended. After a decade of inflated stock prices fueled by frenzied speculation, the Dow Jones average lost a third of its value in a single day. It would lose 90% of its value within the next two years.

With the crash of the stock market, America entered the thirties and fell into the grip of the Great Depression. The collapse was slow at first, a few banks failed and unemployment started to creep upward, but within a few years, armies of the unemployed would be selling apples on street corners, or standing in bread lines for food. There was a domino effect as the momentum of the Depression picked up. A few banks failed, leading people to take their money out of the remaining banks, which led to more bank failures. At the same time, Congress managed to make a bad situation worse by passing the Smoot-Hawley bill setting an array of tariffs on foreign goods to protect American industry. Other countries, also in the grips of the depression, levied their own tariffs in retaliation, and foreign trade dried up. Later, Congress tried to stimulate foreign trade by lowering tariffs, but it wasn't enough.

Crime adapted to hard times. Organized crime was still going strong and speakeasies were still thriving, but a new type of criminal arose. The hard times combined with the widespread availability of the automobile and improved roads gave rise to the motorized outlaw. Motorized bank robbers, of course, were nothing new; they had appeared in the 1920s. But the old criminals had often been associated with organized crime and had foreign sounding names. The new breed was mostly home grown and independent of any organized crime affiliations. Often armed with machine guns, they were wild and reckless. John Dillinger complained the new ones were "giving armed robbery a bad name."

As the depression deepened, armed criminals roamed the country holding up banks and creating mayhem. The most famous were Bonnie and Clyde, Pretty Boy Floyd and the Ma Barker Gang. The increasing number of bank foreclosures on farms made the banks unpopular and gave many outlaws folk-hero status. Outlaws claimed they were just stealing from banks what banks had stolen from the people. The fact that "the people" never got to see any of the money the outlaws stole back was seldom mentioned as the public came to regard armed robbers as Robin Hoods. In an effort to counter this wholly unjustified image, law enforcement people began referring to criminals as "Public Enemies", and began rating the more famous ones.

One reason for the glamorization of crime was the radio. In the 1920s, radio was a novelty, but by the 1930s almost half of all families had one, and it was their window on the world. Formerly disconnected people gathered around their sets and listened to shows like Amos and Andy, Gene Autry, or music and news broadcasts. Radio was dramatic, immediate, and cheap entertainment. Accounts of bank hold ups and high profile outlaws spread quickly over the airways, and help spread the fame of the big name crooks. Not everyone read newspapers, and many people only read local ones, but radio became what television would two decades later. An excited announcer could give a sense of importance and immediacy to crime that no newspaper could match.

Detectives, too, were becoming glamorous figures, at least fictional private detectives. Crime fiction and true crime stories were popular entertainment. Dashiell Hammett's *The Maltese Falcon* was published, featuring the hard-bitten American private eye. For those who preferred the more genteel and cerebral type of detective, there was always Agatha Christie's Hercule Poirot, or S.S. Van Dyne's Philo Vance.

As always, crime in New Jersey had a few twists of its own, including a celebrity who was a convicted criminal. Robert Burns, a Great War veteran down on his luck, robbed a grocery store in Atlanta in 1922. Although the robbery netted him only $5.80, Burns was sentenced to six to ten years on a Georgia chain gang. After enduring hellish and inhuman conditions, Burns escaped, running through a swamp with bloodhounds baying at his heels. He found his way to Chicago where he got married, and became a successful magazine publisher and respected member of the community. Then his wife, suspecting him of being unfaithful, reported his identity to the police and Burns was soon back on the chain gang. Finally, in 1930, he escaped again and came to New Jersey where he wrote an expose book, *I Was a Fugitive from a Chain Gang*. The book became a sensation and was made into a popular movie. With his newfound fame, Burns, who had been living under an alias, went public. The Georgia authorities, smarting from the barrage of criticism *Chain Gang* had caused, issued a warrant for Burns's arrest.

But Burns had become a popular figure in New Jersey by this time and Governor Moore himself conducted the extradition hearing. Burns was cheered as he entered the hall and a parade of witnesses, including the grocer he held up in 1922 testified to his good character. Extradition was denied and Burns was eventually pardoned by the state of Georgia, though not until 1945. The governor's denial of extradition was to be used as a precedent years later to Ellis Parker's benefit.

Unlike most of the country in the 1930s, Ellis Parker's business was still going strong. Crime knew no Depression. Parker's reputation insured that in addition to whatever law breaking he handled in Burlington County, he had a constant stream of requests for his assistance in dealing with mayhem elsewhere. One such case occurred in May of 1930, when James Mercer Davis, the prosecutor of Ocean County asked for Parker's help. Davis would return the favor seven years later when he represented Parker at his trial. A double murder, or a murder-suicide occurred near the Lakehurst Naval Air Station, the main East Coast headquarters for America's fleet of airships. Because of its facilities for handling lighter-than–air craft, Lakehurst was often host to foreign dirigibles as well. Seven years later, it would be the scene of the disastrous explosion and burning of the Hindenburg.

The two dead sailors, Robert Evans and Albert Duffy, had been drinking in the bungalow where Evans lived with his wife. She left early in the evening and stayed with neighbors named Danes overnight. When she returned in the morning, both men had been shot dead.

The bodies were found in a bloody and wrecked living room near a Colt automatic pistol that had obviously been fired recently. Both men died from gunshot wounds to the chest, but they were both beaten about the head as well. There were no good fingerprints to be found, but Parker found a bullet in the wall and one in a doorjamb. There were also bullet holes in two windows on different sides of the house. Parker measured the height of the bullet holes above the floor and found considerable differences between them. Finally, he examined the rug and found three fresh green clover leaves.

At the Danes house, where Mrs. Evans was staying, Parker found a woman named Marion Leary who said Hattie Evans had come to the door the night before and said that her husband had hit Duffy with a blackjack. Parker questioned her about this since he had not found a blackjack at the murder scene, but Marion Leary stuck to her story, as did the Danes.

Neither one heard any shots and no one investigated what they thought was just a brawl. The next morning Hattie woke up and said she was afraid her husband was dead. She said she had heard a shot the night before.

Outside again, Parker spoke to Davis. "Those men were both murdered. Hattie Davis didn't say a word about a shot until this morning, yet she knew her husband was dead. And she said she only heard one shot when we know there were several. She didn't shoot them but she knows who did."

"But why couldn't she have shot them?"

"Because the murderer shot them from outside the house, and they were shot by a man considerably taller than Hattie Evans. The shot that came in the bedroom window was traveling inward; you can tell from the glass fragments on the floor. It was also traveling slightly upward, as you can see from the fact that the hole in the window is slightly higher than the hole in the screen. What's more, the shots came from a rifle. The Colt was fired and left there as a blind because there were only four shells in the house but there were at least five bullets accounted for. Besides, the angle of the shot through the screen indicates it came from outside. The one that broke the window will tell us where the killer was standing."

They were back at the bungalow now and Parker pointed out the bullet hole in the window with the screen. By lining up the holes in the windows, walls and screens, Parker was able to establish the bullets' trajectories and trace them back to a point of origin.

"Just as I thought," said, "It's that patch of clover over there. That would fit the angle, and I found some fresh clover on the rug inside. The killer tracked them in when he went to finish the job. We know the killer was a good shot because he fired at least five bullets in quick succession, killed two men, and only made a small hole in the glass."

"And you don't think Hattie Evans did it?"

"No," said Parker. "She was wearing slippers with smooth soles. There were no laces or ridges to catch the clover and track it inside."

Davis still wanted to arrest Hattie Evans, since she was obviously involved, but Parker talked him out of it.

"If we arrest her now," he explained, "it'll put her on alert and give her time to think up a story. Don't worry, we'll come back to her. Besides, we can do more good at the Naval Air Station."

Lakehurst Naval Air Station was a big, sprawling place. The cavernous airship hangers were so big, they actually made their own weather when moist air rose to the underside of the high roofs sometimes condensed and caused a sort of drizzling rain inside the buildings. Parker and Davis went to see Commander Muller, the base commander, and asked him to have everyone's rifles inspected for evidence of recent shooting and for marks on the butts that might have been left from the beatings. He also asked for a list of men who had been off base the night before, and personnel records of Evans and Duffy

Both men had clean records and were not known for fighting or drinking. Evans was due to be discharged in a month or so. There was no apparent motive for the killing, since neither man had a lot of money and neither seemed high enough in rank to know any guilty secrets. Thinking the crime might involve jealousy, Parker gathered what gossip was available on the two men and especially on Hattie Evans. He found that Hattie Evans was frequently seen in the company of other men, but no one could provide any names. Now Parker had found a possible motive.

The ballistics test came back and showed that, just as Parker had deduced, the bullets that killed the two men were from a 30-30 rifle not from the Colt pistol. Commander Muller told Parker that the 30-30 rifle was the Enfield, an English rifle licensed for manufacture in the United States during the Great War and now used only by the Marines. The Navy men used the .30 caliber Springfield M1903. What's more, all the rifles on the base had been accounted for; either in the armory or issued to individuals. None had been reported stolen."

"How long has your security system for the rifles been in place?"

"Only a month or so," the commander replied. "Before that, it would have been possible to take a rifle away without anyone knowing it."

"So if someone had planned far enough in advance, and was stationed on the base for over a month, he might have gotten a rifle away for future use?"

The commander nodded.

"Can you give me a list of marines who were on leave last night?" Parker asked.

The commander frowned. "Of course, but it's a funny thing; two of them have not returned and are AWOL: Leon Bagwell and Madison Chappell. They're young and have good records. I can't imagine them mixed up with Mrs. Evans."

"Can you tell me who Bagwell and Chappell were friends with and where they each come from? If they've flown the coop, it's likely that they each headed for home."

"Leon Bagwell is from South Carolina and Madison Chappell is from New York. I have their home addresses here."

"Good. I'll get the local police looking for them right away. But I'm still bothered by what happened to the rifle. If it was taken away before the new security system was put in place, wouldn't it be hard to return the rifle afterwards? Isn't it more likely that the rifle has not been brought back to the base?"

"It's entirely possible," the commander replied, "I don't know how anyone could return a rifle that was not in the new inventory system."

The next day Parker had Ocean County Police searching the area around the bungalow and between the bungalow and the base for the missing rifle. They found it buried in the mud of a dam sluiceway, along with two other weapons. Both were .30-30 rifles of the type used by the Marines at Lakeland, and one of the weapons was scarred and splintered at the butt, as if it had been pounded against something; something like a victim's head.

Since it was now certain more than two men were involved, Parker got the names of everyone who had been off the base the night in question. He then methodically eliminated all who had been on the base for less than a year, since they would not have had time to smuggle the rifles out before the new inventory system was implemented. He was left with six names, two of which were the AWOL men, Bagwell and Chappell. That left four men to question. One had an alibi that checked out, two men, Lester Underdown and Claude Carmichael said they were at the movies with the fourth man, a sailor who had been sent to sea that morning on the destroyer *Overton*. Parker requested that the fourth man be sent back for questioning.

About this time, the detectives who had been sent to the homes of the two AWOL men reported back that a month before, two Marines had called at the Brooklyn Navy yard asking when Evans was scheduled to be discharged. The two men were Bagwell and Underdown! Parker now suspected that Underdown was probably the killer, but he needed corroborating evidence. So he talked to the neighbor, Marion Leary, once again. He only asked her one question.

"Mrs. Leary, did you ever hear Hattie Evans speak of a man named Leon Bagwell, or Madison Chappell, or Claude Carmichael, or Lester Underdown?"

"Well, I never knew his last name," she replied, "but I often heard Hattie speak of someone named Lester."

The sailor from the destroyer finally arrived back at Lakewood and firmly denied that he had been at the movies with Underdown and Carmichael on the night of the murders. Now Parker had not one, but four possible murderers; Bagwell, Chappell, Underdown, and Carmichael. But he needed more proof. Now it was time to bring in Hattie Evans and try a little Parker psychology on her. First he called Mt. Holly and asked

Anna Bading to come down the next day to transcribe what promised to be an interesting interview.

The next day, he had Underdown and Carmichael handcuffed and brought to the police station at Toms River, then had them wait in the outer office with two police, so that Hattie Evans had to pass them on her way in. When she got to his office, Parker could see she was unsettled from seeing the men in custody. Without mentioning the men, Parker asked her is she had seen anyone when she left the house the night of the murders. She trembled slightly, and Parker could see she was trying to come up with a story. Before she could, he asked another question.

"You didn't see Lester Underdown by any chance?"

She hesitated. Finally she said she had heard several shots after she left her house, then saw Lester Underdown on the road and asked him to walk with her to the neighbor's. Parker nodded. Her testimony placed Underdown at the crime scene. Along with the rest of the evidence, it should be enough to convict. But Parker had one more trick up his sleeve. He brought in Mrs. Leary and Mrs. Duffy, the wife of the other murdered man. Mrs. Duffy wasted no time in accusing Hattie Evans of having her husband murdered, and a fierce argument ensued with Anna Bading taking it all down. Finally, Hattie Evans broke down and admitted everything.

She had been having an affair with Underdown for months and was afraid it would end when her husband left the service. She arranged for Underdown to kill her husband. Duffy was only shot because he happened to be there at the time.

Although they tried to make it look like a fight, Underdown got carried away and bashed in the victims' heads with his rifle butt. Carmichael and Chappell had gone along, but Underdown did all the actual shooting. It turned out that Bagwell, who was later found in South Carolina, had run away out of fear when the murder was proposed. He turned state's evidence against the others and Underdown was convicted along with Hattie Evans. Underdown got life imprisonment and Hattie Evans got the death sentence. Her sentence was later reduced to life after several women's groups presented a petition for leniency.

During this period, Paul Wendel's legal career had another setback. Accused by a client of wrongfully endorsing a check connected with an estate, Wendel resigned from the New Jersey Bar under pressure from the Bar Association Ethics Committee in 1930. This set off a string of complaints from former clients and between October 1930 and May of 1931, Paul Wendel accumulated nine separate charges of embezzlement, false pretenses, and writing bad checks in Mercer County. He posted bail to six of these charges, but eluded the rest. Wendel managed to avoid the remaining warrants by making frequent trips away from home. He contacted Parker in 1931 to tell him about the several outstanding warrants against him. Since the warrants were in Mercer County, Parker was not responsible for apprehending his old friend. He advised Wendel to lie low for a while so he could investigate and see what could be done. Just what action Parker took is not known, but the warrants remained, and Wendel tried to keep a low profile.

That same year, Parker successfully closed a case that was 15 years old, the murder of Henry Rider, erroneously referred to as the "Cranberry King". (The real "Cranberry King" was the victim's brother, Andrew Rider, founder of Rider University.)

Luigi Pinto, ringleader of the gang that had ambushed and killed Rider in a botched robbery attempt in 1916 had been hopping around the world ever since. By sending descriptions to police agencies around the world, Parker had tracked Pinto through India, China, and Africa before the trail went cold in California just a few months before. Finally, the Los Angeles police reported they had just arrested a man matching Pinto's description for passing bad checks. Parker sent one of his detectives to California to identify the man and bring him back for trial. Ellis Parker had lost none of his stubborn determination.

As the Depression wore on, organized crime began looking for new sources of income. One was kidnapping, also known as the "snatch racket." Kidnapping had been relatively rare in America, but now was on the upswing. In the 1930s, more well-known criminals turned to kidnapping. The most famous was probably George "Machine Gun" Kelly. In January of 1932, just a little over a month before the Lindbergh kidnapping, Kelly kidnapped a South Bend Indiana banker named Henry Woolverton. A ransom of $50,000 was demanded. After driving Woolverton around Indiana for two days, Kelly and his partner were convinced that Woolverton would need more time to raise the money. They released him and made him promise to raise the ransom. Needless to say, he never did. Kelly and his wife planned other kidnappings, but were equally inept until Kelly and another man kidnapped millionaire Oklahoma oil man Charles Urshel from his home in 1934. Although Kelly successfully collected the ransom money this time, the kidnapping started a series of events that led to Kelly's arrest and conviction. He died in Alcatraz in 1954.

More competent kidnappers were at work in the 30s as well. Organized gangs carefully planned the kidnapping of wealthy men for ransom. In 1931 alone, almost 300 kidnappings were reported and probably more that went unreported after the ransom was quietly paid. Wealthy businessmen were the favored targets. They could pay large sums but were not well known enough to stir up a public outcry.

Although he didn't have to deal with any kidnappings in Burlington County, Parker continued to tackle baffling cases, including one where nothing made sense and all the evidence was contradictory. In this case, Ellis Parker came as close to being stumped as he ever had.

In December of 1931, he got a call from McKinley Hospital in Trenton about a man who had been found badly injured by a friend. The man, Robert Brewer, lived on the third floor of a rooming house and the man who discovered him, a man named Lawyer, lived on the second floor. Lawyer had discovered his friend lying across his bed unconscious with a bloody head. At the hospital, X-rays revealed a small hole at the back of Brewer's skull, just behind his ear. Brewer, going in and out of consciousness, said he had been hit in the head with a bottle.

To Parker, this sounded like a routine brawl, so he sent Clint Zeller and William Horn to deal with it. They reported back that Brewer worked on a farm for Lawyer and was only paid every six months. On payday, Brewer would get roaring drunk, and it was after one of these occasions that Brewer was found. The doctors said there was a small object that looked like glass in the skull and that Brewer had been drunk at the time.

"That backs up the story of getting hit with a bottle,' said Parker. "Does it look like Lawyer did it?"

"I don't think so, Chief," Horn replied. "These two have been together for years and have never quarreled. What's more, Lawyer was in Trenton when it happened."

"On the other hand," added Zeller, "Brewer's room was a mess when we saw it. The place looked like there had been quite a struggle."

"Any other suspects?" said Parker.

"Well, seems that when Brewer went off on one of his payday toots, he was in the habit of getting the booze from some Negro bootleggers over in Bordentown. He might have flashed his pay and gotten a bottle to the head for his trouble."

"Well," said Parker. "I'll come down tomorrow."

When Parker arrived at the hospital, Brewer was talking freely. He said he had been drinking with a black bootlegger named Newton Ashbey and that Ashbey had hit him with the bottle. Parker knew Ashbey and knew he wasn't always on the right side of the law, so he brought him to the hospital. Brewer complained of seeing and hearing only in flashes as if an electric light was being switched on and off. During one of his lucid moments, he saw Ashbey and repeated his accusation.

Ashbey denied it and told Parker he had been at a pool hall on the night in question, and his family backed him up. A few days later, the hospital reported that Brewer had gotten well enough to sit up in bed and have his dinner, but then suddenly had a relapse and was fading fast. The next night, Brewer died.

"Well, it's a murder case now," said Parker. "And what's more, we've got a deathbed identification of Newton Ashbey."

"So it looks like Newton Ashbey is our man," said Horn.

"No, I don't think so," replied Parker.

"But Chief, it's a deathbed identification. A dying man has nothing to gain by naming the wrong person. "

"Yes, but there are some things that don't add up," replied Parker, slowly lighting his pipe. Horn knew the Chief enjoyed these Sherlock Holmes moments when he could confound everyone.

"Brewer said he was struck by the bridge, but the nearest bridge is over a mile from where Brewer lived. Would Ashbey, or anyone for that matter, bludgeon a man then drag him a mile uphill back to his house? He'd have to get through town and up three flights of stairs without anyone noticing. If that part of his story is false, what about the rest?"

The doctors at the hospital could not account for Brewers "flashes" and told Parker they were sure he did not have any signs of choking on his neck when he was brought in. A doctor came out of the autopsy room with amazement on his face.

"Mr. Parker, that man died from a bullet. He was never hit with a bottle at all. The earlier X-rays missed the bullet altogether because of where it was lodged. A large section of brain was destroyed. It's unbelievable he lived as long as he did. That would also explain the flashes of light and the episodes of blindness."

"Could he have shot himself?" asked Parker.

The doctor shook his head. "I don't see how he could have. From the position of the bullet and the position of the entrance wound, it would have been impossible for Brewer to hold the gun at that angle and still fire it."

A ballistic analysis determined that the bullet was a .32, but without a gun, that wasn't much help.

Everything in the case seemed to be falling apart. The more Parker found out, the less it made sense. The deathbed identification was now pretty much destroyed, but what did happen? Parker decided to visit Brewer's room and try to reconstruct the crime.

Brewer occupied two third floor rooms and Parker could see that there had been a disturbance. Horn had inspected the room before Brewer died and had reported that the place looked as if there had been a struggle. Drawers were pulled out, clothes were strewn about, the bed had been pulled out from the wall, and several floorboards had been pried up. On a table by the bed was a glass partly filled with bootleg gin. The covers were pulled back on the bed, and Parker noticed a blood stain. The stain soaked through to the fold beneath, indicating that Brewer had been shot and fallen on the bed after the covers were disturbed. Parker sent for Lawyer and asked him about Brewer's habits.

"Why did Brewer do his drinking with the Negro bootleggers in Bordentown?"

"Well," said Lawyer, "he didn't really drink with them, he just got his liquor from them. He did his drinking up in his rooms. I liked Bob Brewer. We were friends for years, and I don't want to speak ill of the dead, but the fact is Bob Brewer was as tight as the bark on a tree. He must have saved 95 cents out of every dollar he made. He bought from the Negroes because they were cheapest."

"So he had a lot of money in the bank?"

Lawyer shook his head. "Bob didn't trust the banks. He hid his money, and he changed hiding places every so often."

Now there was a new angle to this ever-changing and baffling case. Parker called Horn and Zeller back to Brewer's rooms.

"Now you said there had been a struggle, but look again," said Parker. "This chair is broken, but the break is old; it has dust in it. And who stops during a fight to pull drawers out?"

"You're right, Chief," said Horn. "Someone was looking for something."

"And from what we now know of Brewer, it was probably his money. So Brewer was shot by a robber. Either he was shot first, or he interrupted the robber, and then he was shot. Now, I want you to put everything back in its place. When you find something that doesn't belong, something like a bag or box that once held Brewer's money, bring it to me."

As the two detectives researched the rooms, Parker lit his pipe, sat down, and thought some more. Things just didn't feel right. There was something that still bothered him. The bloodstains on the bed indicated that the covers had been pulled back *before* Brewer was shot and fell on it, but that raised even more questions. If the intruder had shot Brewer before he searched the rooms, the covers under the body on the bed would not have been pulled back first, as they obviously were. On the other hand, if Brewer had walked in on the robber in the act, he would have been shot from the front, not the back. Of course, Brewer could have discovered the thief, started to run, and been shot in the back of the head. But then why wasn't his body on the floor rather than the bed? The intruder would hardly have taken the time or trouble to move the body from the floor to the bed. In any event, there were no bloodstains on the floor.

Zeller came in from the other room to report that he had dusted the gin glass for prints and found only Brewer's. Parker frowned. Now he had another piece that didn't fit. Just when did Brewer drink the gin? He certainly didn't sit drinking while his place was being ransacked, and he was in no condition to drink afterward. But if he was drinking when the intruder arrived, how did he wind up on the bed *after* the bed was searched? The sequence of events seemed to be that the room was searched, *then* Brewer sat drinking, *then* he was shot. But then when did the intruder show up? Nothing made sense. As Parker wrestled with these questions, Horn and Zeller came to him.

` "No sack or box, Chief. And no sign of any money, but look at what we found under a drawer."

Horn held out seven .32 caliber cartridges. Parker, for once, was at a loss for words as he stared at the bullets. Finally, Horn offered a theory.

"Maybe the killer dropped them?"

Parker finally found his tongue. "No. There are too many. A killer doesn't go around with a handful of cartridges, dropping them all over the place, and he sure as hell doesn't drop them under a bureau drawer. They must have been here before, but why? And where is the gun?"

"Well," said Zeller, "it looks like whoever killed Brewer was after his money, and it looks like he found it because it sure isn't here."

Parker started pacing the room with his pipe jutting out defiantly. "But the bullets... There are just too many of them. Everything indicates that Brewer had a gun of his own in the house and the robber used it to shoot him."

"Maybe one intruder ransacked the place and a second one came and killed Brewer," said Horn, thinking out loud.

Parker snorted. "And Brewer sat drinking quietly after finding the place turned upside down? Absolutely not!"

Parker sent the bullets to Trenton to see if they matched the murder bullet and decided to question Newton Ashbey again. Since he was still a suspect, and couldn't raise bail, Ashbey was still in the Burlington County jail.

"Newton, how did Bob Brewer act when he was drunk? Did he talk about his money?"

Ashbey smiled slightly. "He never had no money to talk about. Mr. Parker, that man, he used to sponge on everybody for drinks. He was so stingy, why, I swear he used to hide his money from hisself before startin' on one of his parties so he wouldn't spend none of it while he was drunk."

Another new angle had just appeared.

Parker returned to Crosswicks, the farm where Brewer had worked, and questioned Lawyer once more.

"Do you know where Brewer kept his money?"

"No, I don't. He was always hiding it some new place. It could be anywhere."

"Well, we know it's not in the house. Where is the next most likely place?"

"Probably around the farm. There are several outbuildings that would be suitable. I'll show you."

After searching several buildings, Parker found a sack with $4,000 sewed up inside. Bob Brewer's money had been found.

"Well, that clears up one thing," said Parker. "The intruder didn't find the money after all. But I still don't know what happened. Is there anything you forgot to tell me about that room when you found Brewer? You didn't remove anything from the room?"

Lawyer shook his head. "No......well, just my gun."

"Your what?" Parker found himself amazed and annoyed at the same time. "It was *your* gun?"

"Well, I found it lying there, so I took it back. Bob used to borrow it from time to time. I have it in the house now. Do you want to see it?"

The gun was a small .32 caliber with four cartridges and one empty shell in the cylinder. Parker frowned at it, then smiled. The pieces finally fell into place. He knew exactly what had happened the night Brewer was shot. Parker took the gun back to Mt. Holly and showed it to Horn and Zeller.

"You can send it to Trenton for analysis," he told them, "but I know what they'll find. This is Lawyer's gun; and it's the gun that killed Brewer."

Horn took out his handcuffs. "So then Lawyer is our killer after all."

Parker shook his head. "No, he isn't, and put those damned things away."

"But if Ashbey wasn't the murderer and Lawyer wasn't the murderer, then who killed Brewer?"

Parker paused for dramatic effect. He enjoyed moments like these.

"Nobody killed Brewer," he said finally. "*Brewer shot himself.*"

"But the doctor said he couldn't have shot himself."

"No, the doctor said he didn't see how he could have shot himself based on the angle of the bullet. He assumed that where they found the bullet was where the bullet lodged in Brewer's head, but remember that Brewer was talking and sitting up in bed before he took a turn for the worse. Remember too that the doctor said that a large chunk of Brewer's brain was destroyed.

The answer is obvious. The bullet shifted and settled lower in Brewer's skull when he sat up in bed. The shift of the bullet is why he got so much worse so quickly. When the doctors found the bullet during the autopsy, they assumed that was where it had been all along and the apparent trajectory looked like it was too flat for Brewer to have shot himself. But the bullet was originally much higher up and the real bullet trajectory was steeper, so Brewer could easily have managed it."

"All right, Chief," said Zeller. "Brewer certainly could have shot himself, but it doesn't explain why he would want to? And if he shot himself, then who ransacked his rooms?"

"He did. Look, we have been assuming there were two men in that room, but the evidence kept staring us in the face that there was only one. In fact the only evidence that there might have been two men was the missing revolver, and now that has been cleared up. In addition to the lack of anyone else's fingerprints is the strange sequence of events in which the room is ransacked, Brewer sits drinking, then he is shot in the back of the head while sitting on the bed. All that is impossible if there is another man in the picture, but perfectly logical if there is only one. Ashbey said Brewer hid his money from himself when he was going on a toot. He was afraid he'd get drunk and wake up to find he'd spent all his money, and that was the one thing he could never bear. So he hid the money where he couldn't find it when he was drunk. But his precautions backfired on him. The night of December 20, he got drunk and started looking for his pile, but he couldn't remember where he had put it. He apparently thought it was somewhere in the house, so he took the place apart looking for it. When he couldn't find it, he sat on the bed drinking and thinking with his gin-soaked brain. He decided his money was gone and his life was no longer worth living so he reached for the gun. But he didn't die right away. By a near miracle, the bullet severely damaged the brain, but Brewer remained alive for a few days. The damage the bullet did to his brain caused him to imagine that Newton Ashbey had hit him with a bottle down by the bridge. So we wound up with a case where a deathbed identification was worthless."

"So what do we do now, Chief?"

"Get over to the jail and let Newton Ashbey out. If you hurry, you can get him back home in time for dinner."

Ellis Parker at a crime scene around 1930
(Photo courtesy of William Fullerton)

In spite of his spectacular success in detecting and apprehending wrongdoers in so many complex and baffling cases, there is no record of Ellis Parker ever dealing with the well-known "celebrity" criminals and gangsters of the time. He never arrested Lucky Luciano, or Mad Dog Koll, or Dutch Schultz or any of a hundred other criminals whose names had become household words. Parker may well have felt left out by his lack of opportunity to apprehend big-name, nationally known criminals. In spite of his abilities and his knack for publicity, he was beginning to find himself upstaged by events and people elsewhere. In Chicago, federal and local agents had taken down the infamous Al Capone. Only a few months earlier, the House Judiciary Committee heard exciting testimony about crime from a Sergeant Stevens, who was described as the "ace detective" in the Al Capone case. In nearby New York, Mayor Walker and federal agents were in the midst of a highly publicized "war on crime" that had netted over 200 arrests already. Parker knew he was nearing the end of his career and possibly felt his chance for lasting fame was slipping away because Burlington County did not provide the kind of criminals people were reading about in the papers and hearing about on the radio.

In 1931, the Wickersham Commission, appointed by President Herbert Hoover, released the results of their study of Prohibition and law enforcement. The commission reported widespread police brutality and illegal methods used to enforce the law. To Parker, who never used the "third degree" or mistreated suspects, the police who were getting all the favorable publicity in these highly publicized crime wars were little better than the criminals they mistreated. None of them could hope to match Parker in pure detecting ability.

The same year the Wickersham Commission published its report, Parker was invited to address the thirty-seventh annual convention of the New Jersey State Federation of Women's Clubs in Atlantic City, where he told the audience that a "...stiffening of the parental spinal column and a resolution of women to safeguard their children..." was the answer to preventing crime. To Parker, speaking to women's clubs while other detectives were praised in the national media must have been galling. Lesser men were overshadowing him.

By 1932, Ellis Parker, with his ego and his thirst for publicity and recognition, may have been looking for his chance to make his mark nationally with a case so big and so important it would command the attention of the entire country. If so, it would help to explain Parker's actions and lapses in judgment when such a case finally did come along, a case that commanded the attention of the entire world.

The stage was set and the actors had taken their places. Ellis Parker was seeking to outshine the rival state police and gain the nationwide recognition only the successful pursuit of a sensational crime or criminal could provide. Schwarzkopf and the state police were looking for a big crime to crack to make people forget the Hall-Mills case. Paul Wendel was looking for a way to avoid his warrants and gain income. A nation anxious about the Depression and war clouds overseas warily watched out for more signs of insecurity and danger while seeking a diversion from their troubles.

For Ellis Parker, it started with a phone call early in the morning of March 2, 1932. Above the sound of the cold wind whistling outside, an insistent telephone bell suddenly echoed through the darkened Parker house like a cry for help. Ellis was awake instantly and glanced at the clock as he reached for the phone. It was well past midnight. He lifted up the receiver to find one of his old reporter friends on the other end. Reporters often called Ellis Parker when there was a crime to write about. Parker usually had an insight or some pithy quote to liven up the story. This time, however, the reporter caught Parker unaware.

"Ellis, have you heard the news?" the reporter asked breathlessly.

"No; I was in bed. What's going on?" came the scratchy voice of the Old Chief.

"It's the Lindbergh's baby, Charles Jr. Somebody's gone and kidnapped him!"

John Reisinger

Chapter 7
The Crime of the Century-
The Case of a Lifetime
1932- 1933

When Ellis Parker received the reporter's phone call in the early morning of March 2, 1932, he realized he faced the biggest case of his career. If he had been seeking a high profile case that would make news nationwide, this was it. Like everyone else, Parker realized that cases don't come any bigger than the kidnapping of the Lindbergh baby. He also realized that he might not get his chance. The fact that he heard about the crime through a reporter rather than any official sources warned him he might be frozen out of the case.

On the surface, the exclusion of Ellis Parker seems to make no sense, and many have wondered why the New Jersey authorities would fail to use such a valuable resource in such a critical case. The answer lies in the atmosphere and the politics of Lindbergh investigation.

The news of the kidnapping of Charles Lindbergh, Jr. set off a scramble of over a dozen police agencies vying to take part in the investigation. Within a week of the crime, the New York Times estimated there were more than 100,000 people investigating or searching in some way. The public was mesmerized by the case. For the police, however, the crime was a great opportunity.

The child of an American hero cruelly kidnapped in the night was a story everyone would be watching. Public interest and sympathy were going to be intense, and whoever got the baby returned safely would be a national hero. For many in law enforcement it wasn't just the crime of the century, it was the case of a lifetime.

New Jersey Governor A. Harry Moore, realizing the nationwide attention the case would attract, was determined to keep the investigation firmly under his state's control. He placed the New Jersey State Police, under Colonel H. Norman Schwarzkopf in charge of heading up the investigation and coordinating the efforts of any other agencies involved. The state police also had custody of the evidence, and controlled access to the crime scene and the witnesses, a circumstance that automatically placed any contending investigators at a considerable disadvantage.

Much of this law enforcement competition was due to a genuine outrage and desire to help among the various law enforcement agencies, but there was an element of self-serving grandstanding as well. Some multi-jurisdictional confusion was inevitable, since the Lindbergh estate was split by the Mercer/Hunterdon County line; there were many aspects to the crime; and, the potential areas of investigation were so extensive.

In Washington, J. Edgar Hoover, head of the Bureau of Investigation held an emergency meeting in his office only a few hours after the kidnapping was reported. (The FBI was called the Bureau of Investigation at this time. In July the name was changed to the United States Bureau of Investigation, then the Division of Investigation, and finally the Federal Bureau of Investigation in 1935.) Hoover set up a special "Lindbergh Squad" of twenty agents headed by Agent Thomas Sisk. His plan was to offer the Bureau's help and then take over the case. Hoover had more incentive than most: Senator Dwight Morrow, who had resisted Hoover's attempts to expand the agency's power, was the baby's grandfather. Morrow had died the year before, but if Hoover could get the baby back it would be a dramatic demonstration of how the vital the Bureau could be, even to its critics.

Unfortunately for Hoover, kidnapping was not a federal offense; that would come in a few months with the passage of the Lindbergh Law. Even so, Hoover had justification for his attempts to take charge of the case. His Bureau of Investigation had far more experience dealing with kidnappings than the New Jersey State Police, who didn't even have a proper crime lab at the time. Though regarded as a local matter, kidnapping often involved transporting the victim across state lines, making it difficult for a single state agency to coordinate an investigation that was broad enough to be effective. In spite of Hoover's efforts, which included personally appearing at the Lindbergh estate a few days after the kidnapping, the state and local police wanted no part of the "federal glory hunters". Lindbergh refused to meet with Hoover, satisfied to leave everything to local authorities. Hoover could not even get copies of the ransom notes until weeks later, and had to be content to work on the sidelines.

Other federal agencies worked around the fringes of the case as well. Immigration inspectors from the Federal Department of Labor investigated aliens living in the area and the Treasury Department, the Bureau of Standards, the U.S. Coast Guard, and even the Post Office made contributions. In spite of all the agencies and police departments involved, Governor Moore and New Jersey State Police Superintendent Schwarzkopf saw to it that the New Jersey State Police remained firmly in charge, jealously guarding their position against all comers. Even when the Newark and Jersey City police were involved, they reported to the state police.

Under these circumstances, the sidetracking of Ellis Parker was inevitable. With national attention focused on the case, and police agencies fighting a high profile turf war, the last thing any of the investigators wanted was for someone else to show them up, especially a homespun county detective. On March 2, the state police did ask for Parker to help as one of many detectives working statewide under state police direction, but drew the line at giving him any independent authority. Everyone knew Ellis Parker had a reputation for pulling criminal rabbits out of a hat, and that he enjoyed taking bows to the cheers of a sympathetic press. Turning Parker loose on a case to do things his own way was acceptable to local police when they were stumped on a particularly difficult case the public would soon forget. In the Lindbergh case, Parker was competition. If he should be successful, Ellis Parker would get the glory and everyone else would get the criticism.

For Schwarzkopf, there were personal reasons as well. The state police was only a few years old, and Schwarzkopf had not forgotten Parker's criticism of him and the force. Parker said with some justification that the state police was a military organization with no real skill in crime detection. J. Edgar Hoover had the same opinion, remarking privately that the New Jersey State Police spent its budget on fancy uniforms rather than crime detection. Because of Parker's criticism and his reputation, Schwarzkopf was not going to give the Old Chief a forum to show him up. Schwarzkopf was also determined to redeem the reputation of the state police after the Hall-Mills case a few years before. In that highly publicized case, the state police had failed to gain a conviction and the case was still regarded as unsolved. No, the state police would remain firmly in charge on this case and they would bring the kidnappers to justice. Then the world would see just who was the real backbone of serious law enforcement in New Jersey.

For the first few days after the kidnapping, Parker made some inquiries, and followed the case closely, but with no official authority, his ability to act was severely limited. Governor Moore's March 5 law enforcement summit conference in Trenton came and went. Fifty two representatives attended, including the chief of police of Atlantic City but Ellis Parker stayed away.

In addition to his informal inquiries, Parker received a number of telephone calls from various sources offering information. Some of these were clearly hoaxes or cranks, but a few seemed promising, especially the ones from a man who was obviously disguising his voice. The caller was always brief, but gave enough information to convince Parker he knew a lot more about the kidnapping than the public.

"He was pretty brief that time," said Parker after one call. "But I think I know who he is."

Anna came into his office and sat down. "So do I. It sounds like Paul Wendel!"

Parker agreed. Paul Wendel, the bright but unstable man Parker had tried to help get reinstated from his disbarment in 1920 seemed to be the caller. Wendel was now almost a fugitive due to his outstanding warrants for embezzlement and writing bad checks. Could Paul Wendel be making the phone calls? And if so, why?

Several accounts written later, including one by Governor Hoffman, claimed Parker traced the calls to Paul Wendel, but this is unlikely. The technology of the time made tracing phone calls a fairly slow business, and the calls were all brief. In addition, Wendel was moving around quite a bit at the time to stay one step ahead of the law. Even if Parker had been able to trace the calls, he would not necessarily have known who had made them.

Parker wondered if Wendel be the caller and if he knew something about the Lindbergh kidnapping. Wendel had no record of violence, but he did have a propensity for getting mixed up with unsavory people and questionable enterprises. Wendel had stayed in touch with Ellis Parker irregularly for years so Parker felt he knew him pretty well. If Wendel did have some special knowledge, Parker thought, it wouldn't be long before he would have to let people know. Like Parker himself, Paul Wendel was not one to downplay his accomplishments.

On March 8, Wendel appeared at Parker's office. He was 46, a little on the heavy side with a pale, puffy looking face, thinning gray hair, and a somewhat bulbous nose that might indicate a drinking problem. In his double-breasted suit and fedora, however, Paul Wendel looked pretty much like what he was; an attorney fallen on hard times. Parker said nothing about the phone calls.

Paul Wendel
(Photo courtesy of William Fullerton)

"Good morning, Doc." (Parker usually called him "Doc" due to his pharmaceutical background.) "I haven't seen you for a while. What brings you to Mt. Holly?"

"I saw your piece in the paper, Ellis," Wendel said, "You know; about the kidnapping, and I thought I could help you."

Parker lit his pipe and eyed Wendel thoughtfully. "Oh? And how can you do that?"

"Look, I know I've gotten into some trouble from time to time, and you've helped me get out of it."

Parker shrugged. He had helped a lot of people, but none of them offered assistance in finding kidnappers.

"Well, as a result, I have a few underworld contacts," Wendel continued, "I think some of them may know where the baby is and may be able to get him back."

"Who?" asked Parker.

Wendel pulled up a chair. "I don't know exactly who just yet. But if the mob took the baby, maybe I can find out and get it back."

Parker puffed on his pipe and looked at Wendel. "Well Doc, I can certainly use any help I can get. Where would you start?"

"I'm meeting with a New York contact tomorrow. I'll see what I can do, but I have to be able to assure him everything will be confidential. They won't help if they think it's a trap."

"All right. I'll give you a letter you can show them."

The letter Parker dictated requested Wendel's help through his contacts. Then he assured anyone who helped of secrecy.

March 8, 1932

Dear Doc:

Knowing that you have a good many friends in New York, Chicago, and other places and since you are a person who can be trusted to secrecy, may I call upon you to use your influence with your friends, or whatever way you may choose, to ascertain, if possible, to return Charles Lindbergh, Jr., who was taken from his parents' home about a week ago.

Now, Doc, you have my word that there will be no information as to who returns this child, nor will there be any information as to where obtained, nor what happened between any of your friends and you.

If they do not want to deal with me personally, they can deal with you and you can turn the baby over to me............

Please act promptly, because I myself was a personal friend of Senator Dwight W. Morrow, now deceased and desire to help his daughter in any way I can.

Rest assured no harm will come to you, or to anyone associated with you.....I would be very glad to aid you in any way possible and I will go the limit.

And so Paul H. Wendel, former pharmacist, former attorney and presently a fugitive from justice became an unofficial investigator for Ellis Parker's unofficial investigation of the Lindbergh kidnapping.

While it might seem strange he would suddenly volunteer as a part time detective, Wendel had much to gain by involving himself in the Lindbergh case at this point. For one thing, he saw an opportunity to associate himself in the case that was the talk of the nation, something many people desired. His involvement also gave him a chance to show off for his old friend Ellis Parker, and act as an investigator on an equal footing, which appealed to his ego. Most importantly, working with Ellis Parker was Wendel's insurance policy. How could he be arrested on those relatively petty outstanding warrants when he was engaged in such important work for such a famous detective on such a vital matter? He may even have thought he could use some of his shady acquaintances to actually get the baby back. If so, he would be famous and his future would be assured. He would be a rich man, and no one would dare bring up the outstanding warrants. Wendel had nothing to lose and much to gain by investigating for Ellis Parker.

Parker too saw advantages in having Wendel do some investigating for him. If Wendel really did have inside knowledge or organized crime connections that could help in the case, why not use them? Using organized crime to help recover the baby was not really as unlikely as it might seem. A New Jersey mob boss named Abner "Lepke" Zwillman was currently leading efforts by organized crime to find the Lindbergh baby. His motives were not entirely civic minded. The police were stopping and searching so many of his beer trucks on New Jersey highways that the bootlegging business was seriously hampered.

There was the chance Wendel might actually be in contact with a gangster who could help Parker recover the baby. And if Wendel actually had some sort of involvement in the crime, his activities might help reveal it. Each man agreed to Wendel's involvement for reasons of his own, and the strange alliance between Parker and Wendel was born.

The next day, Wendel wrote back that he had met with several New York contacts. They were wary because of all the notoriety, he said, but would be willing to help locate the baby and get him returned. He mentioned a New Jersey contact he wished to take Parker to see. A few days later, Wendel took Parker and the ever-present Anna Bading to meet a Mr. Calabrese in Leonia, New York. Wendel said Calabrese was in contact with Al Capone himself. This may have been Giacamo Calabrese, an associate of Capone's who was once accused of impersonating him while Capone was in prison.

Wendel had initially approached his former Al Capone contact, Frank Cristano, and offered to help get Capone released from prison if the baby were returned. Cristano, remembering his former experience with Wendel's claim to be able to convert tar to alcohol, refused to have anything to do with the plan, but referred Wendel to Calabrese.

The meeting was brief. Calabrese suggested he could approach Al Capone and get the baby returned if Parker would use his influence to get Capone released. Parker was noncommittal. After the meeting, Wendel told Parker that Calabrese was willing to get the baby back, but would need $200. It seemed the baby had been taken to Chicago and the money was to cover Calabrese's travel expenses. Parker gave Wendel the $200 and a few nights later found himself waiting on a railroad bridge near Somerville for Calabrese to appear. The plan was for

Calabrese to take Anna Bading to New York to get the baby and then for her to bring it back to Ellis Parker.

Unfortunately, but perhaps not surprisingly, Calabrese didn't show up. Parker never saw him, or his $200, again. Parker concluded that all Wendel's leads would be similar; expensive with no results. These efforts seemed as futile as those of the official investigators he criticized. Still, Parker thought Wendel seemed to know quite a bit about the kidnapping, and in Parker's view, had the sort of personality that might lend itself to such a crime. He decided to keep a close eye on Paul Wendel.

About this time, Parker talked to George Hillman, his former boss when Hillman was Burlington County prosecutor. Hillman was now a Democratic Committeeman for Burlington County and a good friend of Governor Moore. Parker enlisted his help in approaching the governor on his behalf. After all, a direct request from Parker would have been self-serving, but a direct request from a local committeeman would be harder to ignore. Hillman agreed to write the governor and suggest he put Ellis Parker on the Lindbergh case. Since Hillman had suspended Parker to divert criticism from himself during the Rancocas Rumrunning Scandal, he certainly owed Parker a favor.

But while Parker continued to sift clues and impatiently awaited his chance at the limelight of the official investigation, events were moving forward elsewhere.

On the night of March 12, 1932, Dr. John Condon, known as "Jafsie" and acting as go between went to Woodlawn Cemetery in the Bronx to meet with the kidnappers. Only one kidnapper appeared, a man who referred to himself as John. Like the apparent writer of the kidnap notes, Cemetery John, as he came to be known, spoke with a German accent, though he claimed to be Scandinavian sailor from Boston. He met with Jafsie for over an hour, discussing ways to transfer the money and claiming he was only a go between.

The next day, at the New Jersey State House in Trenton, Governor A. Harry Moore was contemplating the letter he received from George Hillman about putting Ellis Parker on the Lindbergh kidnapping. He certainly wanted the case solved and the baby returned as soon as possible, especially since the case would soon be in its third week with no suspects and no baby in sight. Still, he knew there could be problems with inviting Parker into the investigation. Parker and Schwarzkopf didn't get along, and Parker was likely to hog all the publicity that would arise when the baby was returned. Still, Parker was a good detective, one with a better record of detection than anyone else on the case. The baby was still missing and it certainly couldn't hurt to have another bloodhound on the scent. But how could he put Parker on the case without causing problems with the state police? The trick was to take advantage of Parker's skill and doggedness without giving him a stage to grab all the publicity and further alienate the state police. Moore thought for a moment longer, then started to write.

John Reisinger

Chapter 8
A Semi-Official Investigation
1932

When the Governor's letter reached Mt. Holly, Parker read it eagerly, but then frowned. The Governor had finally asked him to work on the "Lindbergh matter", but had not given him any status with the official investigation. Exactly how Parker was to unofficially investigate the biggest case of his life, the Governor didn't say. Well, it wasn't a blank check, but it was a green light. That was all Parker needed. On March 16, 1932, 15 days after the kidnapping, Parker wrote a letter of gratitude to the governor, saying that he had always been interested in children, and, having a large family himself, "could not stand by in a case like this and not work." He also asked the Governor not to mention his name, since there had been too much publicity already.

Parker started out on his unofficial, but governor-approved investigation. One of his first acts was to write another letter to "Dr. Paul H. Wendel, 496 Greenwood Avenue, Trenton, N.J." asking the former pharmacist, disbarred lawyer, con man, and all around questionable character to assist him in the his now somewhat official investigation of the Lindbergh kidnapping.

> *My dear friend Doc:*
>
> *...Now, Doc, I am writing you, asking you if it would be possible for you to assist in any way, among persons whom you might know, under the cloak of secrecy, to see if it is possible to get a contact, to ascertain the whereabouts and to return to me, Charles A. Lindbergh, Jr., who was taken from his parents home several weeks ago.*
>
> *....Also, remember when you communicate with me, that it comes through you, or as you direct, because as you know, I am being watched, telephone lines cut in for every conversation and you know how to reach me and bear in mind, my only interest in this matter is, to return the Lindbergh baby safely to its parents because I have been requested by the Governor, A. Harry Moore, of the State of New Jersey, to make every effort to do so.*
>
> *Please do not fail me and consider every move you make, or your acquaintances, will be kept in strict confidence and advise them to do likewise, as I have a reputation at stake.*
>
> *Your old reliable friend,*
> *Ellis Parker, Chief of Detectives."*

This letter was more open-ended and official than the first letter, and brought Wendel on board for an indefinite period rather than a one shot basis. The part about his phone being tapped and being watched may have been for dramatic effect, or it may have been an early sign of Parker's growing sense of being in competition with Schwarzkopf.

Now that he had the Governor's go-ahead, Parker contacted Schwarzkopf, requesting information discovered so far, and for access to the scene and its clues. Wary of Parker's flair for publicity and his criticism of the state police, Schwarzkopf brushed him off. If Parker wanted to horn in on the investigation and publicly criticize and second-guess the state police, Schwarzkopf thought, he would have to do it on his own.

Without access to the crime scene or to the evidence in state police hands, Parker started sending out feelers to his network of friends, associates, law men, ex-criminals, bootleggers, and anyone else who might be able to provide information. He especially concentrated on the Sourland mountain area around the Lindbergh estate. That area had long been a haven for moonshiners and bootleggers, and Parker had contacts who knew what was going on every minute. He also informally interviewed anyone involved with the case.

In spite of his efforts and his ingenuity, Parker was under a tremendous handicap because he did not have access to either the principals of the investigation or inside information. In spite of the governor's letter, he was still investigating mostly on his own. But within a few days, he suddenly got the official status he wanted and needed, and it came from an unlikely source. The New Jersey Department of Motor Vehicles was conducting its own investigation and Harold Hoffman, head of the Department, asked Ellis Parker to take charge. Hoffman was an old friend of Parker's, and an old rival of Schwarzkopf's. He would become the next governor in 1935, and a key figure in Ellis Parker's impending troubles.

Harold Giles Hoffman was a popular war hero on a political fast track. He had been Mayor of South Amboy, a state assemblyman, a congressman, and had been appointed Motor Vehicle Commissioner in 1930. It was while he was mayor of South Amboy that Hoffman first met Ellis Parker. Hoffman was an energetic and impulsive individual. Although it would not become known until after his death, Harold Hoffman was also an embezzler. He started by borrowing from various state and local funds within his control, perhaps intending to pay it back, perhaps not. By the end of his career, he had taken over $300,000 from the taxpayers, a crime he regretfully admitted in a farewell letter to his daughter years later. This inclination to dip into government funds may or may not have been part of Hoffman's drive for ever-higher office, but it certainly didn't help him make unbiased decisions. Hoffman often made sudden, daring moves, and one of them was his decision to become involved with the Lindbergh kidnapping.

A state motor vehicle department might seem to be the last agency that would investigate a kidnapping, but the New Jersey DMV had a small, motorized investigating force, usually involved in the pursuit of auto theft, license fraud, and the like. On the night of the kidnapping, Hoffman had Andrew Dutch, one of his investigators, set up roadblocks throughout the state. Hoffman hadn't bothered telling Schwarzkopf about his roadblocks, and was met with indifference when he made suggestions to him. As a result, each man felt he had been slighted by the other, and a mutual distrust was born that would last until the end of their careers.

Of course, if Hoffman broke the case, he knew he would have a clear run to the governor's office, and maybe beyond. With his tantalizing prospects in mind, as well as what was probably a genuine desire to see justice done as quickly as possible, Hoffman asked his friend Ellis Parker to officially head up the DMV investigation with his most trusted investigator, Gus Lockwood, as his assistant. Parker eagerly accepted. Now Parker had the approval of the governor to investigate and an official position with a state agency to go with it.

Within a few days, Parker and Lockwood made headlines with the arrest of a car theft ring within two miles of the Lindbergh estate. The ring turned out to have nothing to do with the Lindbergh case, but the discovery of this activity in an area the state police had blanketed for weeks was an embarrassment to Schwarzkopf. Both Parker and Hoffman kept the newspapers abreast of the progress of the DMV investigation.

While Ellis Parker and DMV continued their parallel investigation, the state police were still following Lindbergh's lead in an effort to get the baby back. On April 2, Condon met with Cemetery John at another Bronx cemetery, St. Raymond's, and handed over $50,000 in ransom money. The money was in gold certificates (Paper money backed by gold on deposit in the Treasury), and though it was unmarked, all of the bills' serial numbers had been carefully recorded. Lindbergh opposed recording the numbers at first, but agreed when he was convinced the kidnappers could not tell if the numbers had been recorded or not.

So Condon went to the cemetery and once again made contact with the man who identified himself only as John. Condon insisted on being taken to the baby immediately, but Cemetery John only gave Condon a note saying that the baby was on board a boat named Nelly between Horseneck Beach and Gay Head near Elizabeth Island. A brief description of the boat was included.

The next day, airplanes, led by one flown by Lindbergh himself, searched for the boat named Nelly. All day they searched, then the next, all the way to Virginia, but the boat could not be found. Meanwhile, the state police released the list of ransom bill serial numbers to banks without saying why the numbers were on the list. A teller in a Newark bank suspected the serial numbers were from a Lindbergh ransom and that the baby had not been returned. He told a reporter, who published the story. The story was later picked up by other newspapers and set off the media frenzy once again. At the same time, John Hughes Curtis raised everyone's hopes by reporting he had been in touch with the kidnappers and that the baby was being held on a boat off Cape May, New Jersey. Curtis's story was fantastic, but Curtis was vouched for by a respected businessman and by a retired Admiral Lindbergh knew personally. As a result, Lindbergh spent days on a boat named *Catchalot* looking for the boat Curtis described. Curtis later admitted the entire story was a hoax. But as of the beginning of May, Lindbergh was hopeful.

In response to Parker's letter of March 16 asking his help investigating the Lindbergh kidnapping, Wendel traveled chasing leads. This not only made him feel important, but also kept him ahead of anyone trying to serve warrants on him. Parker told him to make inquiries to find a stoop shouldered man with a German accent. Wendel wrote or stopped by to see Parker at scattered and unpredictable intervals to report on his progress. This was really nothing new, since Wendel had been in contact with Parker off and on ever since his perjury conviction and disbarment 12 years earlier. During the course of several of these earlier visits, Wendel told Parker things that Parker remembered when the Lindbergh kidnapping occurred and Parker's suspicions of Wendel deepened.

Like many unsuccessful people, Wendel blamed others for his self-inflicted bad luck. He expressed his bitterness and frustration that the world was against him, that other people were constantly frustrating his plans and preventing his success. He once said if he could only get a stake of $50,000, he could show the world. When the Lindbergh ransom note demanded exactly $50,000, Parker sat up and took notice. In Parker's mind, pieces started to come together. Could Paul Wendel have somehow been involved with the Lindbergh kidnapping? Could he actually be the kidnapper?

Although it seemed incredible, the more Parker thought about it, the more sense it seemed to make. What better way for the resentful Wendel to show the world; to demonstrate his own superiority? What better way to strike back than to kidnap the child of the most famous man in the world? Over the years, Parker had developed a theory based on his observation of criminals and upright citizens alike. He noticed many middle aged men experienced a personality change. Today we would call it a mid-life crisis, and Parker believed it was responsible for all sorts of erratic and reckless behavior. To Parker's mind, the unstable Wendel, experiencing failure and frustration might react to his mid-life crisis with a reckless and flamboyant gesture to show the world how he had been underestimated. Parker, the master of psychology, believed Wendel had the personality, motivation, and state of mind necessary to pull off something like the Lindbergh kidnapping as a way of showing his power and superiority to the world.

As Wendel provided further information, Parker became more convinced. The press claimed a chisel was used by the kidnapper to pry open the window, but Wendel said it was a screwdriver. He mentioned a local Hopewell resident had a yellow light on the night of the kidnapping. Gradually, Parker thought he was getting to the truth about the kidnapping and Wendel's role in it. He also thought he knew something else about Wendel: if he did do it, he could not fully realize his triumph unless people knew about it. It would be like a golfer shooting a hole in one when playing alone. Sooner or later, Wendel would not be able to stand it anymore; he would have to have the recognition his achievement deserved. He would *have* to tell someone what he had done.

Parker asked Gus Lockwood, the DMV investigator, to shadow Wendel to see if he was in contact with any accomplices and if he would give away the location of the baby. Lockwood was not able to turn up any significant information by shadowing Wendel, but he did help keep track of the Wendel's whereabouts. Wendel continued to report to Parker occasionally, giving him pieces of information that proved to be either trivial or, Parker suspected, fabricated. There was no reappearance of the duplicitous Calabrese, but Wendel supplied several more underworld-related leads that also went nowhere. Parker began to believe Wendel was deeply involved in the kidnapping, perhaps even the kidnapper himself. Wendel continued to drop hints and false leads, Parker reasoned, as a way of bragging about what he had done and taunting the people trying to catch him.

In retrospect, it appears Parker was falling victim to his own desire to score a grand coup over the state police. He was so anxious to pull off one of his legendary deductive surprises that he made the classic mistake of an investigator who accepts evidence that supports his theory and ignores evidence that does not. Parker's most obvious oversight was failing to realize that if he knew "secret" facts about the kidnapping, Wendel could too. Parker or one of his detectives could easily have let such information slip in their dealings with so many people. The newspapers, too, were a constant source of leaks and speculation. Much of what Parker knew about the crime was at least partial public knowledge. Wendel's motive for making the calls, if he had really been the one making the calls is not clear. He might have simply been keeping things stirred up in hopes of becoming Parker's investigator in the most famous case of his life. Parker was right about Wendel's need for recognition. Wendel's later actions prove his desire for recognition for both his cleverness and for his victim status. Wendel's desire to be seen as Ellis Parker's chief investigator while impressing his old friend at the same time would have been more than enough motivation to explain his actions. Unfortunately, Wendel's needs played directly into Parker's.

"Wendel wants to tell me," Parker said to his son Ellis Jr., one day. "He desperately wants me to know about how brilliant he is, but he can't quite bring himself to confess yet. So he gives me clues and keeps himself involved in a way that does not get him in trouble."

Ellis Jr. regarded his father as a great man and had complete confidence in his judgment. If his father said Paul Wendel was the culprit, that settled it.

Besides his faith in his father, Ellis Jr. had his own reasons for suspecting Wendel. Just a few days before, Ellis Jr. had driven by the Lindbergh estate with Wendel and Wendel had seemed strangely familiar with the area and with the night of the kidnapping. He had pointed out areas where a car could be concealed and mentioned a neighbor with a lantern. Investigation confirmed what Wendel said.

"Do you think he'll confess?" Ellis Jr. asked

"You're damned right I do. He'll confess because he won't be able to stand *not* confessing. The longer this goes on without the world knowing about what he did, the more the pressure will build. He's pulled off the greatest crime in America's history. He will have to take a bow. His ego will demand it."

Under gray skies on May 12th, two truckers were taking a load of timber along the road to Hopewell. A little north of the town of Mt. Hope, William Allen pulled the truck over to the side of the muddy road at a place called Mt. Rose Heights. He left his partner in the cab of the truck while he walked into the woods to relieve himself. His partner, Orville Wilson, remained in the truck and idly looked at the countryside through the drizzling rain. A few minutes later, Allen was back, shouting for Wilson and looking shaken.

By late afternoon, the state police had descended on the spot on the Princeton-Hopewell Road to examine what the truck drivers found in the woods. There, lying face down in a shallow depression lay a small and badly decomposed body. Charles Lindbergh, Jr. had finally been found. All the searches, the speculation, the ransom, and the detective work had been for nothing. The baby had been dead all along.

Even in death the Lindbergh baby was not to be spared the glare of publicity. Soon the word spread and crowds of the curious started to gather. The police held the milling crowd of onlookers back while several people picked up dirt and stones as souvenirs and one enterprising entrepreneur set up a hot dog stand. The body was removed to a Trenton funeral home at 915 Greenwood Avenue, just a few blocks down the street from Paul Wendel's house at 496 Greenwood. Both Betty Gow and

Lindbergh himself duly identified the body, and an autopsy revealed that death had been the result of a blow to the head. The autopsy couldn't determine just how the blow on the head had occurred, however.

The discovery of the baby's body changed the case from kidnapping to murder. The public was outraged and called for blood. Schwarzkopf and the state police, almost mad with frustration, were now free to pursue the case as they pleased. Now there was no more need to defer to Lindbergh and to his desire to handle everything with delicacy to avoid spooking the kidnappers so he could get the baby back.

Even though they had more latitude for pursuing the culprits, Schwarzkopf and the state police were now subject to a barrage of criticism for not catching the killer in time and not following leads or procedures people thought might have been successful. One of the loudest critics was the local chiefs of police, who openly called for Schwarzkopf's resignation. Ellis Parker was one of the most vocal.

.

The period immediately after the discovery of the body was not Ellis Parker's finest hour. He gave newspaper interviews mercilessly criticizing and second-guessing the state police. It became almost a form of guerrilla warfare, if not guerrilla theater. Parker's strongest invective was directed not against the killer, but against those trying to find him. He told the New York Times Schwarzkopf's failure to make a thorough search of the surrounding area after the kidnapping was "inexcusable and shameful."

No doubt Parker's genuine outrage and desire for justice were part of the reason for his sniping, but it is hard to escape the conclusion that jealousy, resentment, and a desire to interject himself into the case were equally important. Parker had the skilled craftsman's disdain for those with less talent and ability, especially when they were getting attention and respect he felt they did not deserve. Parker may have started out as a fiddler, but he could never be content to play second fiddle

There were dangers in taking such an adversarial and antagonistic stance. By alienating those who had access to direct information and sources, Parker cut himself off from information and resources he could have used. In addition, his attitude could easily warp his judgment by leading him to automatically take a contrary view of almost any conclusion the official investigation might draw. Being contrary was all well and good when the official investigation was wrong, but what about when it was right?

Whether or not this need to disagree was a factor in what came next is impossible to say, but at this point, Ellis Parker came to a conclusion that was so contrary to the popular wisdom, it would undermine his credibility in the future.

While the baby's body was at the funeral home in Trenton, a reporter was able to take pictures and sell them to the newspapers. Parker got hold of these pictures and studied them. The first thing he noticed was the apparently advanced state of decomposition of the remains. He then checked weather records and found that the weather had been unusually cool since the kidnapping, which would indicate an even slower rate of decomposition.

Parker also noted the wanted poster asking for the return of the baby had given his height as 29 inches, but the body's length was given as 33 inches. Parker theorized the body was too decomposed to have only been dead since March 1st and that the discrepancy in height meant that the body was not that of the Lindbergh baby. He believed either the body had been placed there by bootleggers to get the police to stop searching vehicles and disrupting their operations, or it had been placed there by the police themselves to draw the real kidnappers out into the open.

In fact, Lindbergh himself had positively identified the body, as had Betty Gow, the baby's nurse. In spite of its state of decomposition, the baby's face was reasonably well preserved, since it had been face down in mud. The features were clearly distinguishable. In addition, the hair on the head of the body matched the samples of curly blond hair the Lindberghs still had in their possession, and the body was clad in a homemade shirt that had been hand stitched in blue thread. The toes and teeth matched those of the baby as well.

The controversy about the baby's length was due to a misprint. The corpse was about 33 inches in length, but a widely circulated wanted poster published by the state police on March 11 stated the length was 29 inches. The 29 inch figure, however, was actually supposed to read 2 ft 9 inches, or 33 inches. Ellis Parker, of course, was not aware of this. He was also influenced by Paul Wendel, who assured him that the body was not that of the Lindbergh baby. Parker believed Wendel's insistence that the corpse was not the Lindbergh baby made his guilt even more certain. If he had not done the kidnapping, Parker reasoned, here was a perfect opportunity for Wendel to distance himself from the crime. He had only to say that he must have been mistaken when he thought he knew who did it and that the baby was still alive. But Wendel assured Parker the corpse was someone else, thereby confirming Parker's suspicions even more.

The March 11 wanted poster. Note the height listing of 29 inches rather than two foot, nine inches.

(Photo courtesy of the New Jersey State Police Museum)

Now Ellis Parker had to find a way to convince everyone he was right and everyone else was wrong. He had to not only beat the kidnapper, but the state police, state's attorney, and public opinion as well.

Bagging Wendel, or securing his confession would not be easy. Wendel was still wanted on the embezzlement and bad check cashing charges and had gone into hiding in New York where Parker had no jurisdiction. There the matter rested. Parker's investigation seemed as stymied as that of the state police.

A little over a month after the baby's body was discovered, Congress passed a law making kidnapping a federal offense when the victim was transported across state lines or when the victim was missing for more than three days. The new law was soon dubbed the "Lindbergh Law". Such a law had been contemplated for years, but became inevitable in the frenzy of public indignation once the Lindbergh baby was kidnapped. Curiously, future Supreme Court Justice Felix Frankfurter, then a Harvard law professor, was one of the few opposing such a law, saying there were already too many statutes in the federal code.

Meanwhile, some of the ransom money began to appear in New York and the surrounding boroughs, but mostly in the Bronx. At the insistence of Elmer Irey of the Treasury Department, the serial numbers of the ransom bills had been recorded and the list had been circulated to banks across the nation. Now banks started reporting that some of these numbers were showing up. The kidnapper was being cautious, it seemed, spending only about $40 a week and leaving no real trail, but the bills were appearing. The more bills that appeared, the more likely someone would be able to identify the person who was passing them.

Throughout the rest of the year, the official investigation gathered and sifted information and ran down numerous false leads, all the while bombarded by scathing criticism.

"If you weren't such a bunch of saps and yaps, you'd have already captured the Lindbergh kidnappers," wrote columnist Walter Winchell. Al Dunlop of Detective Magazine said the investigation "was miserably bungled from every angle" and even New Jersey State Senator Emerson Richards took a shot, saying that the state police "were fine for catching speeders, but not equipped for detective work." The police tried to avoid being distracted by all the public criticism, but it was like a man trying to figure out his income tax return in the midst of a cloud of hungry mosquitoes. According to one report, the state police were so frustrated by the end of 1932 that they recruited a World Telegram reporter named Dawes to interview Ellis Parker and quietly report back what he had learned of Parker's progress on the case. The year ended with little hope for a solution and the outlook didn't improve until the next spring.

On April 15, 1933, President Franklin D. Roosevelt, in another effort to break the stubborn grip of the Great Depression, issued an executive order to stop people hoarding gold. Gold bullion, gold coins, and gold certificates of $100 or more were to be deposited in a Federal Reserve Bank by May 1,

1933. For the police, this order did two things that would make catching the kidnappers easier. First, the order would make any kidnap money in denominations of $100 or more worthless after May 1, so the kidnappers would be forced to dispose of it quickly. In addition, it would make the supply of gold certificates dry up, so that anyone who passed even a small denomination gold bill would likely be noticed.

As the May 1 deadline approached, more and more ransom bills began to appear, including an exchange of $2,980 by a man using the alias of J.J. Faulkner. No one could give a description of this man. There are several theories, even to this day, but J.J. Faulkner was never found or identified. In spite of the hope offered by recalling the gold certificates, the elusive kidnapper, or kidnappers, remained unknown to the police for another long year.

Chapter 9-
Bradway Brown and
an International Fugitive
1933-1934

Without new developments, even a public frenzy such as the Lindbergh kidnapping dies down eventually. More urgent news was pushed the case off the front pages. Adolf Hitler became Chancellor of Germany, and a month later, the Reichstag burned under mysterious circumstances, giving him the excuse to purge Communists and consolidate his power. The Japanese had overrun most of China, and Gandhi continued his campaign of civil disobedience in India. In America, President Roosevelt signed the National Recovery Act, designed to help the country break out of the lingering Depression. Prohibition finally ended in December of 1933, an event that was widely saluted by celebrations and toasts. If the Lindbergh case was no longer front-page news, there was still a high level of interest, and it would only take some new development to start the bandwagon rolling once again.

Ellis Parker worked behind the scenes, his eye still fixed on Paul Wendel, thinking of ways to encourage him to confess, but other cases vied for his attention.

On the night of January 16, 1933, Ellis Parker was just finishing a hand of cards in the upstairs bar of the Elks Club on High Street when someone handed him the phone. On the line was Morris Beck, the local police chief at Palmyra.

"It's Bradway Brown," Beck began, "You know; the fellow that was involved in that Wilson-Roberts case a while back. He's dead. I'm at his place on Highland Road now. He's lying on the floor and the room was locked. I had to break in. It looks like he shot himself, but what with all the possible publicity, I have to be sure. Ellis, I'd be grateful if you could help me out."

Soon, Parker was on his way to Palmyra, along with Deputy Clint Zeller.

"Wasn't Brown involved in that case of the society couple shot to death in Moorestown?" Zeller asked. "You proved it was a murder-suicide."

"Right," said Parker. "Brown was a classmate of Roberts and a friend of Wilson. He's been hanging around speakeasies saying he knew the real story. People tend to get suspicious when they hear things like that, but I knew there was nothing to it. Still, it's strange. Morris Beck says he died the same way as Wilson and Roberts; in a locked room."

Sure enough, the body of Bradway Brown was lying face down in the living room of the Brown home. Nearby was a Holtz .32 revolver with Brown's hand still touching it.

Chief Beck reported the lights were on and the doors locked when he got there. A lady who lived next door heard the shooting and reported the crime. Brown's wife and two-year-old child were in Florida. At first, Beck believed Brown must have shot himself, then Beck decided it was murder after all. Articles in both the Washington Post and the New York Times claimed Beck was convinced it was murder while Parker thought it was suicide. Parker later claimed he knew it was murder all along and implied he was merely trying to trap the killer. When asked about his earlier insistence that the case was a suicide, Parker answered cryptically that "I will admit that I can lie, and have lied, and I will do it every time when it comes to defeating the ends of justice." Exactly what this meant was anyone's guess.

According to Parker's later account, Brown was still wearing his overcoat and two chest high bullet holes were apparent, along with two corresponding chest wounds. Parker looked at the coat, then started looking around the room. Beck asked what he was looking for.

"The third bullet," Parker replied. "Just look here at his overcoat. There are two holes chest high. Those are the ones you saw, but there is another one much lower, near the seam. There is no wound from the third bullet. We have three shots and only two wounds,. The third shot missed. The question is, where is the third bullet?"

"Well....."

"There can be only one answer," Parker continued, "The bullet is outside and that means the third shot was fired outside. So if Brown shot himself, he must have started outside, then come in here, turned on the lights, locked the door, then finished the job. Does that seem likely to you?"

"Well, no," Beck admitted, "but then how did the doors get locked?"

"We'll get to that," said Parker, "but look at the gun. It has dirt in the barrel, like it was dropped outside. Brown was shot outside and brought in here. The gun was dropped and then brought in here too."

Parker went to the garage and found Brown's car. Morris Beck said the engine was still running when the body was discovered. One of the other policemen noticed a fresh gouge in an old wooden boat stored there. The third bullet had been found. Parker surmised the killer had fired at Brown in the garage, hitting the boat. Brown ran out the door and the killer shot him twice. He then dropped his gun to pick up the body and move it inside. The dirt in the barrel matched the dirt and cinders in the path to the house.

Parker also found two hats under the boat. One was Brown's, but the other was a different size, so Parker had it analyzed. The hat belonged to a man with blond hair and dandruff. The hat itself was an Adam hat, the Clark Gable model.

To Parker, the gun seemed like a better clue, but the serial numbers had been filed off. Parker soon noticed, however, that the metal was too hard and the numbers stamped in too deep for filing. The numbers had been filled with lead and some file marks added to make it appear that the numbers had been filed off. The gun was sent to a chemist in Trenton who removed the lead and reported the gun's serial number was 59237. The gun was traced to a garage mechanic in Peoria, Illinois, who reported the gun stolen several months before. The mechanic had black hair.

There the case stalled, but it brought another case back to life. The press and the public breathlessly speculated that the Bradway Brown murder was connected to the Wilson-Roberts murder-suicide of 1929, but Parker found no link at all. Horace Roberts, the dead boy's father, was having Depression-related financial problems and had his eye on a $30,000 insurance policy his son had taken out. The insurance company was not obligated to pay if the death was a suicide, but it would pay if the death was murder. Roberts contacted the governor and found a number of witnesses who had not been satisfied with the original finding of murder-suicide. The coroner in the case revealed that an attempt had been made on his life and that he had been pressured by an important political figure to drop the original inquest.

Rumors flew about a ladder, a mystery woman witness, a duplicate key, suppressed testimony, doctored reports, and two mysterious figures reportedly seen on the front lawn of the Wilsons' house the night of the killings. Much was made of Bradway Brown's relationship with the deceased since he was a neighbor of the Wilsons and a college classmate of Horace Roberts. Several people also reported that Brown had recently bragged he was about to reveal the name of the "real" killer. Ellis Parker, no doubt smarting because his conclusions were being questioned, was dismissive of all the speculation, declaring in the press that if the insurance money were paid, the questions would go away. He further stated that anyone who changed or added to his previous testimony should be arrested for obstruction of justice. This statement led Arthur Carabine, formerly one of Parker's detectives and now in private practice, to complain that Parker was hindering the case by intimidating possible witnesses. Parker stated that the case was settled and he would say no more about it, adding that if he had his way he'd "appoint a lunacy commission and have all these people committed to the same asylum."

Howard Eastwood was now Burlington County Prosecutor, however, and so great was the level of speculation and rumor, and the claims of new evidence (along with political pressure from the governor a New Jersey Supreme Court Justice) that he sent the matter to the Grand Jury in February. Fifty witnesses were called, the last of which was Ellis Parker, who was questioned for over two hours. Though they noted some deficiencies in the original case, the Grand Jury agreed with Parker's original finding of murder-suicide. The Wilson-Roberts case was finally over.

In the Bradway Brown case, however, Parker was at a dead end, so he kept the case in the active file and went on to other matters.

About this time, Ellis Parker attended a conference of local police from the counties and towns on the New Jersey side of the Delaware River. They were trying to get to the bottom of a series of very similar burglaries plaguing the area. The burglaries all occurred while the victimized family was out to dinner. The burglars were well informed about each family's movement and arrived in a car. In addition, the burglaries were always about 25 miles and a week apart. Criminals, the police knew, could be very systematic sometimes. Parker followed the line of burglaries on a map and found the "schedule" called for a burglary on the night of January 16, at Palmyra; the exact date and place of the Bradway Brown murder! Had Bradway Brown surprised the after dinner burglars?

Theorizing the murder could have been the result of a burglary gone bad, Parker followed the line of subsequent events to project the time and place of the next burglary, and found it was due that same night in Florence, New Jersey. Parker called the police chief in Florence.

"Have you had any burglaries in your town recently?" he asked.

"No, " was the reply. "No a one."

"Well, you're going to have one tonight."

On that foggy night in Florence, police staked out the town looking for the after dinner burglars. Parker's deductions paid off. A policeman saw three men running out of a house toward a parked car and ordered them to halt. One man pulled a gun and fired at the policeman. He returned fire and the man fell dead while the others scrambled in the car and roared off, leaving the police with a corpse and a partial license number.

The dead man was a notorious burglar named Joe Ferguson, so Parker began to check out Ferguson's known criminal contacts. He questioned them about their whereabouts on the dates of the burglaries. One of the men, named Edward Adamski, had just been picked up by the Newark police for trying to pawn a ring later identified as stolen in one of the earlier after dinner burglaries. When Parker checked Ferguson's and Adamski's record, he found another tie-in. Adamski had been arrested for burglary in Pekin, Illinois, and released for lack of evidence. Pekin was next to Peoria, where the Bradway Brown murder weapon had been reported stolen around the same time. A few weeks later, in Philadelphia, Ferguson had been arrested on a concealed weapons charge, but released for lack of evidence. This seemed strange. How could it have been lack of evidence? The evidence would be the weapon itself. If the weapon wasn't there, the police wouldn't have had any reason to arrest the man in the first place. If the police *had* found a weapon on the suspect, what happened to it?

Parker went to Philadelphia and called on the prosecutor in the case to ask how a concealed weapons charge could have been dismissed for lack of evidence. He was told that the gun in question had been marked as an exhibit, but disappeared in the courtroom under everyone's noses, so the case had to be dismissed. Parker asked if the record showed the make and serial number of the gun.

"Yes," was the reply. "It was a Holtz .32, serial number 59237."

Parker was elated. The case was solved, and he had enough evidence to convict Adamski and to find the third member of the after-dinner burglars. But when he got back to Philadelphia Police Headquarters, he was told that Adamski had escaped from the Mt. Holly jail. Parker's bubble was burst. One

burglar was dead and one had escaped, but he had no idea who
the third might be.

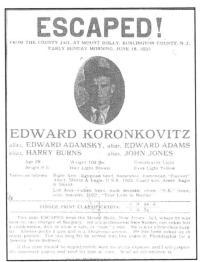

Wanted poster for Edward Adamski aka Koronkovitz
(Author photo)

Thinking it out, Parker remembered that the after dinner
burglaries had started just a few days after Ferguson and
Adamski had been released from that Philadelphia court. There
was a good chance that the after dinner gang had been formed on
the spot. Parker went through court records to see who else had
been on trial that day. He even checked the witness lists. Slowly,
he eliminated names.

The most likely suspect seemed to be a burglar named
Adam Szewczak, who had also been released that day. Parker
asked the Philadelphia Police for a photo of Szewczak and saw at
once that the man had blond hair and was wearing an Adam hat,

the Clark Gable model. Szewczak was the third man, but where was he, and where was Edward Adamski?

Once again the case stalled momentarily.

Sometime later, two Philadelphia narcotics detectives found a negotiable bond on a suspect and discovered it was part of the loot from one of the after dinner burglaries. The man with the bond said he got it from a man named Zeleski. Based on this information, the police located Zeleski and followed him, thinking he was involved in drugs. They saw Zeleski meet another man in a drug store, and hand him a set of car keys. The police raided Zeleski's room, found more loot from the after dinner burglaries, and contacted Parker. Parker went back to Philadelphia and his suspicions were confirmed when he saw the prisoner. The man calling himself Zeleski was actually Adam Szewczak.

The police followed the man in the drug store who had apparently loaned Szewczak a car. The suspect, a man named Lutz, a barber with no criminal record, was apparently friendly with Szewczak. The police followed Lutz for two weeks without turning up anything suspicious and were on the verge of giving up when Lutz walked into the same drug store in which he had met Szewczak.

There, in that same drugstore, was Edward Adamski.

When Ellis Parker brought Lutz and Adamski back to Mt. Holly, reporters and photographers were waiting. Ellis Parker's cleverness and his success in finding the killers after 15 months of dogged determination were splashed all over the newspapers, providing a stark contrast to Schwarzkopf's unsuccessful efforts in the still-unsolved Lindbergh kidnapping. The April 14, 1934 edition of the Camden Courier told of the Bradway Brown case in a banner headline and a smaller line that said "ELLIS PARKER IS CERTAIN ROBBERS SHOT CLUBMAN". (Bradway Brown was often referred to as a "clubman" in the newspapers, a reference to his frequent appearance at the local speakeasies.) The article, full of praise for Parker, went on for two pages and included pictures of all the principals in the case, Bradway Brown's house, and the Holtz revolver. The only article related to the Lindbergh case in the same paper was a small item claiming that two federal Justice Department officials had improperly questioned Charles Lindbergh while the famous flyer was on a recent visit to Washington. Parker must have gotten no little satisfaction out of the situation.

In court, Lutz gave evidence against his former friends, testifying he rented them the car for five dollars and Szewczak told him there had been a shooting. As Parker deduced, Bradway Brown had come home and surprised the after dinner burglars in his garage. They had read a newspaper announcement that Mrs. Brown had recently left for Florida and assumed the house would be empty. There was a brief struggle and Brown was slain. The door to the house had a lock that could be engaged by pulling the door shut from the outside. The burglars tried to make the killing look like suicide by locking the body in the room along with the pistol. Adamski and Szewczak were found guilty and hanged.

A few weeks later, on May 1, 1934, Ellis Parker was guest at a testimonial dinner at the Log Cabin Lodge at Lake Medford to honor his 41 years of service. The speakers said some very complementary things about the Old Chief. Judge Harold B. Wells from the Court of Errors and Appeals said "Parker possesses a common touch. One time on the bench, I had a case of a boy who had stolen a bicycle. Ellis said it would be wrong to send the boy to an institution for something like that when all he really needed was a bike. So we took up a collection and bought the boy a bike, and that boy was never back in juvenile court."

Robert Peacock, Parker's secretary before Anna Bading, told the story of Rufus Johnson, the condemned man who told Parker that he had treated him fairly, even though the man was on his way to be hanged.

George de Benneville Keim, secretary of the Republican National Committee summed up the feelings of the group best. He said, "There is only one Ellis Parker. His success is grounded in his devotion to fair play."

When it was Parker's turn to speak, he was suitably modest, saying his success was due to a "good wife and a contented mind."

Just how contented his mind was with the Lindbergh case still unsolved and Paul Wendel still at large is questionable, but there is no doubt Parker accomplished a lot in his long career, and that most people knew it and respected him for it. If only his mind could have been contented enough to stay away from the Lindbergh case.

Program from Parker's 1934 testimonial dinner
(Author photo-Program courtesy of Andy Sahol)

In the summer, Cora and the remaining children and grandchildren went off to the Brant Beach house to enjoy the New Jersey shore. Ellis came down to see everyone as often as he could. If he had made a balance sheet of his life at this point, he would have had to admit he had every reason to be satisfied. He had a worldwide reputation, was respected by his peers, and almost worshipped by the local people. He had a good wife, children, and grandchildren, all of whom called him Ellis. He had a fine house in Mt. Holly and a beach house at the ocean. Any man should have been content with all these accomplishments, but there was still one nagging piece of unfinished business that gave him no rest; one case that stubbornly resisted every attempt to unravel its secrets. The Lindbergh kidnapping was still unsolved, and he was still not recognized as an official part of it.

He knew all that would change as soon as he got a confession from Paul Wendel.

During this time, Parker continued to investigate the Lindbergh case, sometimes going to surprising lengths, including turning to J. Edgar Hoover for help. Hoover and his Division of Investigation had something in common with Parker. He too was officially snubbed by the New Jersey authorities and was conducting a parallel investigation without benefit of all the evidence. Unlike Parker, however, the wily and aggressive Hoover successfully maneuvered his way to the head of the line. On October 19, President Roosevelt officially placed the Division of Investigation in overall charge of the Lindbergh case at the federal level, elbowing aside a very unhappy Elmer Irey and the Treasury Department. Schwarzkopf reluctantly agreed to share information with the newly empowered Division, hoping no doubt Hoover would share some of the criticism as well. Ellis Parker had contacted Hoover earlier, and on October 27 of 1933, went to Washington to meet with him. Parker made a plea to work together and asked for Hoover's help obtaining a list of the denominations and locations of ransom money that had turned up. Hoover questioned Parker about his notorious March 5, 1932 statement to the press, and Parker explained it was to encourage the kidnapper to contact him. Or, as Parker put it in a follow up letter, "for the purpose of baiting the sucker on."

In this meeting, and in his follow up letter the next day, Parker made an extraordinary proposal that showed his increasing willingness to combine deception, bending the truth, and play acting in pursuit of the kidnapper. Knowing the

Division had contact with "Jafsie" Condon, the man who had acted as intermediary to the kidnappers, Parker proposed a scheme to enable himself to question Condon secretly. As he put it in his letter to Hoover the next day,

"It would seem to me, in your communication with Condon, you could state the fact you were going to send a man from your office, who is sent throughout the United States on various matters, to get the facts and study them, in order to come to a proper conclusion. If you have a man who is built and looks something like me, the name might be substituted, as I realize that Condon might go back to the New York office and attempt to contact again, but if he is lead (sp) to believe the man is sent there especially, he won't bother.

In the mean time, I will gather up all the data I can to question him at length, in order to get all the details of the whole transaction, as I told you yesterday, Mr. Condon, in my judgment, was only one of hundreds who like to have done something in the matter and through his...eagerness and overzealousness (sp), he was taken over by a person whose mind was supreme."

Aside from Parker's attempt to deceive both Condon and the official investigation, this letter reveals that a year and a half after the kidnapping, Parker was still investigating, and was doing so without the most basic evidence that was freely available to the state police. He could not review the actual ransom notes and could not question the one man who had had direct contact with the kidnapper. In all the other cases in which Parker had dazzled everyone, he always had access to all the information available. In no other recorded case was Parker compelled to work in the dark as he was now. The fact that he felt he had to resort to this rather transparent subterfuge to question a man who had been questioned extensively by everyone else shows just how far out of the loop he was. Nevertheless, Parker plowed on, determined to crack the case even with one hand tied behind his back.

Parker was naive if he assumed J. Edgar Hoover was willing to help an outsider in the interests of solving the case. The territorial infighting of the various agencies on the Lindbergh case reached the federal level as well. All of Hoover's efforts had been directed towards enhancing his and the agency's power and reputation. He was no more willing to help Ellis Parker than Schwarzkopf was, and for much the same reason. It appears Hoover, knowing Parker's reputation, feigned cooperation to find what the Sherlock Holmes of America had turned up. Hoover hoped to put Parker's resources at the service of the Division of Investigation, not the other way round. To a man such as Hoover, accustomed to gathering dirt on potential enemies and rivals, Parker's complaints about state police shortcomings must have been eagerly welcomed. In the end, though, Parker got no help from Hoover.

Even though Ellis Parker had plenty to do in his own bailiwick during this period, he still got requests to lend his talents to police in other places. Like a skilled juggler, he pursued cases in Burlington County while serving as consultant and directing investigations elsewhere. In one such case, he tracked a fugitive all over the world without leaving Mt. Holly.

About the time of the Bradway Brown murder, Parker got a call from an old acquaintance named Guard Darrow, who was the district attorney in San Francisco. Darrow wrote to Parker about an unusual case that had them stumped. Six months before, a man named Tom Coumas burst into a schoolroom and shot the teacher dead while all the children looked on in horror. A janitor was nearby and tried to intervene, but was shot in the shoulder for his trouble. Coumas dropped the gun and ran out. No one had seen him since. Coumas had two children in the school, but no one was sure just what his motive was. Coumas, a Greek immigrant, was married and had four children ranging from 9 to 15. His wife had died the year before. Now he had disappeared and the local police were at a loss how to proceed. There just weren't any clues.

Parker knew better. As far as he was concerned, there were always clues. You just had to know where to look. This case promised to be different. Usually, he had to determine *who* the killer was, but that wasn't in question. In this case, he would have to determine *where* the killer was.

Parker wrote back and said that in his experience, a fugitive always returned home sooner or later. There, on familiar and friendly ground, he could blend in and lose any pursuers. He asked for any more information Darrow could send.

Darrow wrote back kidding Parker about getting old so that he wasn't thinking as clearly. The police in California had already investigated the possibility Coumas might return to Greece, but Coumas had lived in Stockton for ten years, and there was no trace of where he came from before that. They had even checked with various Greek charities and social clubs, but got no results. With his usual talent for deduction, Parker started thinking about how best to track Coumas, and thought about the children. Based on the number and spacing of the children, it was apparent that there "wasn't a whole lot of birth control in the Coumas family." That would imply that the oldest was born within a year of their marriage, and that would mean they were married about 16 years before, since the oldest was 15. So Parker sent letters to marriage bureaus in all 48 states asking for any record of a Thomas Coumas getting married around 1914-1916.

Several months passed while this correspondence was in progress, and Darrow wrote Parker several letters needling him about his lack of progress. Finally, Parker got the answer he was looking for from the state of Washington and sent Darrow a telegram.

HAVE ESTABLISHED COUMAS MARRIED IN VANCOUVER, WASHINGTON NINETEEN FIFTEEN. COME EAST AND LEARN.

ELLIS PARKER

Humbled, Darrow wrote back asking what they should do next, much to Parker's satisfaction. Parker examined the marriage records sent from Washington and noted that Coumas was a naturalized citizen and his occupation was listed as a cook.

Parker knew that a cook could easily move from job to job without leaving much of a trace, but he also knew that most states required a medical examination before a cook could start work, so he told Darrow to contact health departments in nearby states and towns.

Meanwhile, Parker contacted the immigration authorities in Washington, D.C. to find out about Coumas's immigration papers. He was told Coumas was from Raemo, Greece, and had been naturalized in 1914 in Portland, Oregon, just across the river from Vancouver, Washington. Parker told Darrow to have a few of his people go up to Portland and search through records to see if anything about Coumas's past might turn up, and also to have restaurant owners between San Diego and Portland questioned about any recent hires. A few weeks later, a report came back that a restaurant owner in Merced, California had recognized the photograph of Tom Coumas as the cook he had hired, but who had since disappeared. The location indicated Coumas had gone south, possibly heading for Mexico.

Parker deduced that Coumas was going to Mexico to have a jumping off place to return to Greece. Parker contacted a professor at Princeton who was fluent in Greek and asked him to write to the Greek authorities in Raemo. At the same time, he contacted authorities in Mexico to check cooks on ships in Mexican ports. The Mexican inquiry came up empty, but when the answer arrived from Greece a few weeks later, it was even more surprising. Not only did they have no record of Tom Coumas, they had no record of a Coumas family anywhere in the province!

This surprised even Ellis Parker. Why would a man with a previously clean record change his name? What's more, he changed it before he became a naturalized citizen, since his papers showed him as Tom Coumas. Of course, many foreigners with long or awkward names changed them upon arriving in America. Maybe that was what happened. But what was his original name? Parker had the Princeton professor write again, this time asking the Greek authorities for any record of a man leaving for America from Raemo around 1905-1914.

Before he received a reply, however, Parker received a telegram saying the police who were looking through records in Portland had turned up the court case in which Coumas had changed his name just before being naturalized. His original name had been Smyrno Smyrnogranis. This changed everything. Parker contacted the Mexican authorities who promptly turned up a cook named Smyrno Smyrnogranis who had recently boarded a steamer at Tampico bound for Brazil. Parker tracked the ship through a few more stops, then sent another letter to Greece.

When Parker's final letter arrived in Raemo, Greece, the local police had already arrested the ex-cook, Smyrno Smyrnogranis, a.k.a. Tom Coumas and charged him with murder. Because there was no extradition treaty, they didn't send him back, but imprisoned him in his native country. Parker was out fishing when the telegram from his friend Darrow arrived at Mt. Holly.

COUMAS ARRESTED KEEPING SHOP IN GREECE. HEARTIEST CONGRATULATIONS.

Anna Bading read the telegram, and then sent a reply.

DETECTIVE PARKER HAS GONE FISHING. WE REJOICE WITH YOU.

Ellis Parker had tracked down an international fugitive without leaving Burlington County.

While Parker was still tracking Tom Coumas, and closing in on the Bradway Brown killers, he was drawn into still another unusual and confusing case.

In Florence, New Jersey, in January 1934, farmer Adam Gibner opened the door to find a distraught young woman who claimed her husband had just shot himself. This was the start of what the newspapers would call he "Honeymoon killing".

A few hours later, Ellis Parker was inspecting the scene along with the county medical examiner, Dr Remer. In the woman's car, a Nash with a California license plate, they found the woman's husband, Milard Edouard, slumped sideways over the wheel. He was a big man with a bald head, a head that appeared to have been struck by a bullet traveling from one temple to the other. His left hand was still on the wheel and his right was under him. His hat was on the floor between the steering column and the driver's side door. There was no bullet in the car; it might have exited through a partially opened window on the driver's side. A .25

caliber revolver was lying on the floor on the driver's side. The ground around the car was frozen, so there were no footprints.

Burlington County prosecutor Howard Eastwood joined Parker and the medical examiner, and the three of them removed the body and searched the pockets. They soon had a collection of seemingly unrelated items; an insurance policy on the car, made out to O.M. McLeod, and a wallet. In the wallet were two calling cards, one with the name of W.G.Foster of Vancouver, and one that had the words "Tony Mouroboli, Midnight Follies, Tijuana" written in pencil. Also in the wallet were two photos showing several people leaning against a sign that said Mundelein Park. One of the men was clearly the late Mr. Edouard and he had his arm around a woman who was not his wife. On the back of the photo was written "Milard Stephen". There was also a key case with the initials O.I.M.M. and a numbered tag saying the case was registered with a company that would return it to its owner if it was to be mailed to them. Finally, there was an envelope with a woman's name and an address in Tucson, Arizona.

Parker took this odd assortment of artifacts back to his office, gathered the county prosecutor, several state police, and Anna Bading. He then had the woman brought in. Her name was Anna May Edouard, formerly Anna May McLeod. Her now-deceased husband was a Frenchman who was also divorced. He was very well off, she said, and had over $110,000 in two safe deposit boxes in New York City.

"But there were complications," she said. "Eduoard's former wife was able to place some kind of attachment on the money, and as he was not an American citizen, Edouard was effectively cut off. All that money and he couldn't touch it. Why, I even had to borrow $200 from my sister for the wedding and the trip east."

"You're a long way from California," Parker remarked. "Where were you going?"

"To New York. Edouard said that as an American citizen and his wife, I would be able to withdraw the money. He had given me Power of Attorney. I have the paper with me. We have been traveling for several days. But it was so strange. Each day he became more withdrawn and worried. He never told me what was wrong. Finally, last night, he suddenly picked up the gun we kept under the seat and shot himself."

"Whose gun was it?"

"It was mine. I bought it for protection two years ago."

Further questioning revealed that Edouard had his hat on when he shot himself. He was also smoking and that is why the window was partially opened. Parker informed Mrs. Edouard that she would have to be held as a material witness and Anna Bading escorted her out.

"Well, it's plain what happened," said one of the state police. The others nodded agreement. "She marries him for his money, gets him to fill out the Power of Attorney, then bumps him off. The whole story about the money locked up in New York is just to explain the Power of Attorney. If there were really a court order of some kind on that safe deposit box, she wouldn't be able to get to it any easier than he could."

"That's the way it looks, Ellis," said the County Prosecutor. "Murder for money. It's not the first and it won't be the last."

Parker didn't reply. He turned to the medical examiner.

"Doc, what does your examination show?"

"He was shot in the right temple at close range. There were distinct powder burns. From that and from the angle of the shot, I'd say it was possible that he could have shot himself, or that she could have shot him."

"And another thing, Chief," said one of the Burlington County detectives. "Why would he use her gun? How would he even know where it was? She shot the guy and that's for sure."

"I think she's telling the truth," said Parker finally.

"He shot himself? But the story doesn't add up."

"Oh, I know the part about the safe deposit boxes and the court order doesn't add up," agreed Parker, "but most of the story does. She said he opened the window and that's what we found. We know the window was open before the shot because the bullet wasn't found. She said he had his hat on and there it was, but most important was the position of the body. If she had shot him while he was driving, he would have been sitting back in the seat and his hat would be blown in the back or between him and the seat. But the hat was found on the floor, indicating that he must have been leaning forward and not driving when it happened. That would also account for where the gun was found. And even the gun checks out. She said she bought it two years ago and hadn't fired it since. Well, the gun is dirty and has rust spots on it, which backs up her story once again."

By now the others in the room were exchanging glances. Parker was making sense. Maybe it wasn't a murder after all.

"All right," one of them said. "Let's say he shot himself. Why?"

"I think we can get some clues from his possessions," Parker replied, picking up the box of evidence from the desk. "The initials on the key tag match the initials of Edouards ex-wife. Now, he had a snapshot showing himself with another woman in front of Mundelein Park, which is a real estate development outside of Chicago. It looks as if he and the lady were at least contemplating buying a house or lot in the development. And even though the man in the photo is Edouard, the name on the back is Millard Stephan, which tells us that Edouard used another name with another woman."

"Next we have a card from a real estate company in Vancouver with the name of Foster on it. Because the card is clean and new, it appears Edouard met this Foster fairly recently. There are also these pamphlets from several gold mining companies headquartered in Vancouver. But Foster is not connected with these companies. Then there is this envelope with the name of still another woman and a Tucson address. The date indicates it was between the woman in Mundelein Park and his marriage to the present Mrs. Edouard."

Eastwood shook his head. "The man certainly got around."

"Finally," said Parker, "there is this card with the name and address of some place called the 'Midnight Follies' in Tijuana. You don't have to be a detective to figure out what kind of a joint that is. Based on this evidence, what sort of man was Mr. Edouard?"

"He was a nut about women. He gained their confidence and sponged off them. He even used his wife's money to come east. But it still doesn't explain why he would shoot himself."

"Don't forget he changed his name at least once," added Parker. "We have a man who changes his identity, moves from place to place, speculates on gold mines, and lives off women one after another. In short, a man with something to hide. My secretary, Miss Yoos, will contact the New York police in the morning and ask them to find out who holds the deposit box numbers Mrs. Edouard gave us. I am willing to bet it won't be anyone named Millard Edouard."

"But why did he shoot himself?" someone asked with exasperation in his voice.

"We will have to wait until all the information is in to be sure," said Parker, "but I believe this Edouard told his newest wife that story about money in the safe deposit boxes just to string her along so he could milk her for whatever money she had. That seems to have been his practice. But this time, he was dealing with a strong-willed woman. She insisted on the Power of Attorney and on making a trip east to recover the money. I don't doubt he tried to talk her out of it along the way, but finally realized he couldn't, and she would soon find out that there never was any money. His wife would no doubt raise a stink and he would come to the attention of whatever authorities were looking for him. Judging by the way he was moving around, I'd say the police must have wanted him pretty bad. That is why he shot himself. He was trapped and that was his only way out."

In a few days, and after some more checking, the rest of the puzzle was put together. Edouard had married seven different women, and had told most of them the same story about the New York money. Anna May was the first to actually insist on recovering the fictional $110,000. Further checking revealed Edouard, whose real name turned out to be Milan Felippe, was wanted by the French police for espionage and murder. Once again, Parker had seen beyond the surface to the truth beneath.

Ellis Parker
(Photo courtesy of William Fullerton)

The crimes Parker investigated during these years, especially the Bradway Brown case, showed he had lost little of the famous abilities that had served him so well in the past, even though some of those closest to him later claimed his memory was starting to slip somewhat. But he could still cut through the confusion of a case and zero in on what was important. He could still use his powers of observation and his uncanny ability to reconstruct the actions and motivations of a crime's participants. His memory might have been slipping and he might have been losing some of his edge, but his instincts were still good, and his senses were still sharp for the most part. Soon these abilities would be put to the test, for the Lindbergh kidnapping case was about to hit the headlines once again.

Chapter 10
The Most Hated Man in America
1934

By September 1934, the Lindbergh kidnapping was well over two years old and still no suspect had been arrested. Numerous rumors, tips, and reports from various sources continued, but nothing of substance. The state police, the governor, and the federal Bureau of Investigation still received letters from citizens convinced their neighbor or their brother-in-law was the Lindbergh kidnapper, but no credible leads were in sight. After the thousands of man-hours expended, the trail seemed to lead nowhere. The case had gone cold. To the public, it seemed someone had committed the worst outrage in the nation's history and gotten away with it despite the great concentration of police resources. To a nation struggling through the Depression and uneasy about ominous developments in Germany and Japan, the Lindbergh kidnapping case was deeply unsettling, another sign that the familiar and comfortable world of the 1920s was gone forever.

Ellis Parker's triumph (and publicity) solving the Bradway Brown murder a few months earlier had been an unwelcome reminder to the state police of just what a smart and determined investigator could accomplish. The public was reminded as well. On the surface the Bradway Brown case seemed more complex and puzzling than a simple kidnapping, yet Ellis Parker had cracked the case without the state police or a nationwide manhunt. More than a few people were of the opinion Ellis Parker should be put on the Lindbergh case to straighten things out once and for all. Parker himself made no effort to discourage this view. Schwarzkopf's reaction was to put his head down and push on. There were still dozens of police departments involved, and some freelance private detectives. Sooner or later, Schwarzkopf thought, the kidnappers would make a mistake and land their heads in a noose.

What information the police did have seemed to indicate the kidnappers were based in or near the Bronx. The kidnappers initially contacted Condon (Jafsie) based on his notice in a small Bronx newspaper; the two cemeteries involved in the ransom payoff were in the Bronx; and, the Bronx was within a few hours driving range of Hopewell. Some of the ransom money turned up in and around the Bronx, too. In spite of the size of the Bronx and the large number of people who lived there, the manhunt was now narrowed down quite a bit, but the police needed to narrow it down further.

A New York psychiatrist Dudley Schoenfeld contacted the New York police with a completed "profile" of the kidnapper, one of the earliest on record. Schoenfeld had studied all the evidence and worked backwards to see what kind of a person would be the most likely suspect from a psychological point of view.

According to Schoenfeld, the kidnapper was a man of relatively low status in life but who nevertheless felt superior and omnipotent. He blamed others for his lack of success and, subconsciously at least, kidnapped the Lindbergh baby to humble Charles Lindbergh because Lindbergh represented the fame and success the kidnapper felt was rightfully his. The kidnapper believed kidnapping the child of such a man would demonstrate he was superior to someone the world held in high regard. The kidnapper was a man who would work alone and take great personal risks. He would be about 40 years old, German, and have served time in prison. He would be secretive, mechanically inclined, and not likely to confess. Schoenfeld further predicted the man would carry a ransom bill on him at all times as a memento of his triumph. This turned out to be a remarkably accurate profile of the man who was eventually caught and tried for the crime. Unfortunately, it also is a reasonably accurate profile of Paul Wendel, a fact not lost on Ellis Parker, who was a pretty good analyst himself.

With the failure of the New Jersey State Police, the Lindberghs turned to James Finn of the New York City police. Finn was assigned to Lindbergh's bodyguard detail when Lindbergh visited New York in 1927 after his historic flight. Lindbergh remembered him and sought him out when Schwarzkopf seemed to falter. Even before this time, Finn had not been idle. He sent his men to interview subscribers to the

Bronx Home News, telling them to look for anyone resembling Condon's description of Cemetery John. Like Ellis Parker, Finn soon ran up against Schwarzkopf's reluctance to share information and decided to try another approach; carefully and systematically tracking the appearance of the ransom money. Frank Wilson of the Treasury Department was involved in this task too, along with special agent Thomas Sisk from the Department of Justice. They were aided in this plan by some fortunate circumstances.

When Roosevelt outlawed gold certificates in April 1933, and gave a limited time for these bills to be turned in, the police thought they had a chance to trace the kidnappers by tracking the ransom money. The kidnapper had to convert the bills before they became worthless. There was a good chance the kidnapper would turn in all or part of his loot and be identified. Sure enough, portions of the ransom money were turned in to banks here and there, but none of the descriptions led back to a potential suspect.

Finn decided to track the ransom bills as they appeared in circulation, a tedious and frustrating task. Several of the smaller denomination bills soon appeared, mostly scattered around New York and the Bronx. The police kept careful track of where each bill turned up, using pins in a large wall map, but the notes being passed did not lead to a description of a suspect. People seldom noticed or remembered who gave them a particular bill. The few descriptions that were offered were so vague as to apply to almost anyone. Since the ransom notes were in the rapidly disappearing gold certificates, however, the police continued to hope a bill would stand out enough to cause someone to notice and remember who passed it. As time went on, Finn noticed the bills were turning up in larger denominations, indicating the kidnapper was running out of the smaller bills. This was good news, because people would be more likely to notice and remember a large bill, and might eventually lead the police to whoever had passed it. When that happened, the police believed the man identified would be a German speaker experienced in woodwork or carpentry, and lived in the Bronx.

The police finally got the break they'd been looking for. The head teller at the Corn Exchange Bank in the Bronx noticed two gold certificates, each for $10. The teller checked the serial numbers against the ransom serial numbers and called the Bureau of Investigation when they both matched.

The BI called in officers from Finn's task force who had been trying to track ransom bills. They found "4U-13-41 NY" written on one of the bills and assumed it was a license number, especially when they tracked the bill to a gas station. The attendant remembered receiving the certificate, and remembered the man who had given it to him. As police hoped, the attendant noticed the gold certificate and wrote the car's license number on it in case the bill was counterfeit. He described the driver as a man with a German accent. Incredibly, the attendant said the man had told him he had more of the certificates at home. The police called the Motor Vehicle Bureau and found the car was registered to Bruno Richard Hauptmann of the Bronx. Now after all the time and all the frustrations and all the false leads, the police had a suspect. And he was a German living in the Bronx.

The New York police immediately told Schwarzkopf and J. Edgar Hoover of their suspect, setting off yet another jurisdictional squabble over who was going to make the arrest and how many agents each department would have on the scene. Several days later, when all the details had been negotiated, the police finally moved in. Separate unmarked cars carrying men from the New York Police, the New Jersey State Police, and the Bureau of Investigation converged on Hauptmann's Bronx neighborhood, each group fearful of the others jumping the gun and getting the credit. Thinking Hauptmann might lead them to accomplices, the police followed him for blocks, but Hauptmann soon noticed the cars behind him. At this point, the lawmen, jealous of who would make the arrest, were watching each other as much as their suspect. Finally, Hauptmann's car was forced to a stop and he was arrested. Just as the psychiatrist had predicted, Hauptmann had a thick German accent and was carrying a ransom bill.

Although he denied having more of the money, a subsequent search turned up over $14,000 in ransom money hidden in his garage. When the police learned Hauptmann was a carpenter, they were sure they finally had their man. He was the right nationality to have written the ransom notes; he lived in the Bronx where so much of the trail seemed to lead; he could have built the ladder since he was a carpenter; his handwriting was very similar to that on the ransom notes; and, he lied about having the ransom money. He seemed like the perfect suspect.

The only thing that was needed to wrap up the case was a confession.

Arrest photo of Bruno Richard Hauptmann
(Photo courtesy of the New Jersey State Police Museum)

But Bruno Richard Hauptmann had no intention of confessing to anything. He vehemently denied any involvement in the crime, and insisted he didn't know the money found in his garage was part of the ransom. He claimed the money had been in a box left with him for safekeeping by his business partner, another German named Isidore Fisch. Fisch had gone on a visit back to Germany and died there. Hauptmann claimed he had discovered Fisch had cheated him out of his investments. When Hauptmann discovered the money in the box Fisch had left him, he decided to keep it as compensation for his losses. Of course with Fisch dead, there was no way of corroborating this tale, which soon became known as Hauptmann's "Fisch story".

There was more evidence against Hauptmann. Arthur Koehler, an expert on wood, had been studying the kidnap ladder even before Hauptmann was found and had traced the wood to specific mills. He had further traced the wood to a lumberyard in the Bronx, a yard Hauptmann was later found to have patronized. After Hauptmann was arrested and his house thoroughly searched several times, Koehler matched a board in the ladder to a board from the flooring of Hauptmann's attic. This board became known as Rail 16 from its position in the ladder.

Despite Hauptmann's steadfast denials of involvement, his actions seemed suspicious as well. He claimed he had no more than a few dollars in gold certificates when he was arrested, but police had found another $14,000 hidden in his garage. Hauptmann had ceased working as a carpenter from the time the ransom was paid and lived on his investments. Among his papers was a document indicating he had attempted to rent an apartment in Manhattan in a phony name starting on the day of the kidnapping. This was thought to be where he intended to hold the baby.

Hauptmann stowed away on a ship and come ashore in America illegally several years before. He had a criminal record in Germany of several burglaries and armed robberies. One of his burglaries was accomplished using a ladder to gain access to a second floor window of a prominent local mayor. In addition, Hauptmann was a fugitive, having escaped from the German jail where he was serving time for his crimes. It was circumstantial evidence, but there was a lot of it and it fit together perfectly.

Even though Hauptmann seemed a likely suspect, there was no direct evidence placing him at the scene of the kidnapping except some vague eyewitness testimony that seemed to shift over time. In addition, Hauptmann was so consistent and so vehement in his denials he made some people less certain he was the right man.

In the years since this case, much has been written about Hauptmann and the evidence for and against him. Some accounts have put forward an image of Hauptmann as a wronged innocent, even a saint-like figure, proclaiming the truth to a corrupt and uncaring world that refused to listen. One of the reasons for this view is Hauptmann's stubborn refusal to confess or to make any kind of deal with the prosecution. He was telling the truth, he insisted, and he was innocent. Hauptmann was very convincing when he spoke of his innocence and persuaded more than a few people of his sincerity. How could a guilty person be so insistent? One clue might have been an incident that occurred in September, while Hauptmann was being held in jail in Brooklyn before he was extradited to New Jersey for trial.

Hauptmann had finished his breakfast and returned the tray. Some time later, the guards noticed the large pewter spoon was missing. Knowing of their prisoner's previous escape from a jail in Germany, the guards demanded the spoon back. Hauptmann looked them in the eye and insisted he had returned the spoon and didn't know what they were talking about. After some more such give-and-take, the guards searched the cell, finally finding the spoon broken in four pieces and concealed among the plumbing. One part of the spoon had already been fashioned into a crude knife. Of course this incident doesn't prove Hauptmann was guilty of the kidnapping, but it does show a tendency to stubbornly insist on his innocence even when he was guilty.

Hauptmann was extradited to New Jersey for trial and the state Attorney General; David Wilentz headed the prosecution. His first problem, strangely enough, was what crime to charge Hauptmann with. Kidnapping was the most obvious, but kidnapping in itself was a relatively minor crime, punishable by up to 30 years imprisonment. Of course, he could add extortion, which carried a penalty of up to twenty years, and if he added illegal immigration and illegal possession of the gold certificates, Wilentz thought he could get Hauptmann put away for life. But he also knew it wasn't enough. For a crime as heinous as this one, only the death penalty would satisfy the public. First degree murder carried the death penalty, but Wilentz wasn't confident he could meet the burden of proof since it was possible the baby died accidentally.

Finally, Wilentz settled on felony murder as the charge. Murder committed in the course of a felony carried the death penalty even if the death is accidental. This charge often was applied to bank robberies when a guard or bystander was shot and it was impossible to prove just which bandit did the shooting or why. Wilentz took the position that a felony murder had been committed because the baby had died in the course of a burglary. The burglary was the stealing of the baby itself, or more specifically, its sleeping suit. It was a clever and somewhat devious tactic, but it offered the best chance of obtaining a sentence the public would consider sufficient.

Once he had decided on the charges, Wilentz felt he needed to deal with Ellis Parker. To Wilentz, Parker was potentially dangerous. From the beginning Parker second-guessed the official investigation and its conclusions, and although maddeningly cryptic and vague about his findings, strongly implied he had evidence someone else was the real kidnapper. Wilentz knew that Parker's flair for publicity, coupled with his reputation and his legendary investigative prowess could prove a deadly combination capable of derailing the state's case against Hauptmann. If Parker really did have something pointing to a different kidnapper, or was about to find some such crucial missing evidence, he was likely to spring it on the public during the Hauptmann trial. The result could be embarrassing to the state, maybe even disastrous. It could make the state a laughingstock and arouse an angry citizenry to demand the heads of those who wasted so much public time and money in a flawed investigation.

Determined to neutralize this threat, Wilentz called a conference in his office in early December. He had Assistant Attorney General Robert Peacock invite Parker, along with several representatives of the state police. The idea of the meeting was to smoke out anything Parker might have found that could be used against the prosecution, and possibly enlist Parker as an ally. After all, Parker might have found something that would help the prosecution.

At the meeting, the state police assured Parker they were only interested in the truth, and that he could have access to all its facilities to conduct whatever investigations he cared to make. With the trial less than a month away, this offer was essentially meaningless, but it was at least a gesture of cooperation. Wilentz asked Parker to attend the upcoming trial and to testify for either the defense or the prosecution as he saw fit. Parker was non-committal. Finally Wilentz asked Parker directly if he had any information of value they should consider.

"Frankly, I haven't got a single lead," Parker replied, "and furthermore I am convinced Hauptmann is the man."

Just why Parker claimed he had nothing is not clear. He may have been suspicious of Wilentz's sincerity, and elected to keep his true feelings to himself, or he honestly may have felt the game was lost. He read the papers and knew the almost overwhelming evidence against Hauptmann. Maybe in the face of this evidence, his rational detective instincts won out over his ego and self-confidence. Whatever the reasons, Parker indicated he had no information and little interest in the case at this point.

Wilentz was relieved. Now they could proceed with confidence. The state could throw everything they had at Hauptmann and secure the conviction unhampered. They had nothing to fear from Ellis Parker.

The trial was held in Flemington, (the Hunterdon County seat) New Jersey in the dead of winter. The old courthouse had never seen anything like the Hauptmann trial. The usually sleepy town was packed with excited crowds wanting a glimpse of the famous people and the notorious kidnapper. An estimated 700 reporters from all over the world, joined thousands of others in the carnival. Traffic jammed the roads leading in and out of Flemingtion for miles around. The Union Hotel across from the courthouse was full and local people rented out rooms in their homes to accommodate the crowds. The owner of the hotel, however, had anticipated the demand and had rented almost every local room available in private homes for one dollar a night. He then rented the rooms out to reporters for five dollars a night. Even so, many of the visitors had to stay in Trenton or even New York.

The Flemington County Courthouse
(Author photo)

The Union Hotel was host to both the jury members on the third floor, and a number of reporters elsewhere. Although the jury was supposed to be sequestered, they ate in the same dining room as the reporters, separated only by a screen. Outside, the excited crowds debated every development in the trial, and shouted advice to jurors when they saw them. Most of the advice consisted of exhortations to convict Hauptmann. Scalpers did a brisk business selling tickets to the trial, and the Hunterdon County Sheriff created a minor scandal by collecting a surcharge on seats. Onlookers crammed themselves into every possible nook and cranny of the second floor courtroom, including the windowsills. The floor was soon littered with trash and food scraps. Souvenir hunters in the crowd promptly stole everything in the courthouse that wasn't too big to carry. One even tried to carry off the witness chair. Finally, local members of the American Legion, Kiwanis, and Rotary Club were called in to act as combination tour guides and guards. Local entrepreneurs sold models of the kidnap ladder and "autographed" pictures of the Lindberghs. One enterprising youngster, in concert with a blond-haired friend, sold locks of the "Lindbergh baby's hair" to gullible souvenir hunters. A local restaurant featured Lindbergh Steak, Hauptmann Beans, Jafsie Chops, and Jury Pie.

As in later sensational events, the same news was filed by the hundreds of reporters who almost tripped over each other in their efforts to get the same story. H.L. Mencken, only one of a number of famous writers on the scene called the event "the biggest story since the Resurrection."

Ellis Parker appears to have been somewhat ambivalent about the trial at first. Although invited to attend by Wilentz, he stayed in Mt. Holly as if resigned to Hauptmann's guilt and washing his hands of the whole business. For once, Parker seemed content to quietly back away and leave the spotlight to others. But as so often with Ellis Parker, looks were deceiving. His real attitude was to wait and see. A lot could happen in a trial like this. Maybe they had more conclusive evidence than he thought, or maybe they would inadvertently back up his conclusions. Parker's theory at this point appeared to be that Wendel had done the kidnapping but had been cheated out of the ransom money when he asked Isidore Fisch, an old client, to launder it. Maybe Hauptmann would implicate Wendel and vindicate Ellis Parker after all.

Parker was well aware of the frenzied trial atmosphere, and the public's insatiable appetite for anything to do with the Lindbergh kidnapping. His resentment at being passed over must have been acute as the sensational case sped towards its climax without him.

David Wilentz and the prosecution had several strong pieces of evidence. Hauptmann had $14,000 of the ransom money hidden in his garage and lied about it. On top of this damning evidence, experts testified that the ransom notes were similar to Hauptmann's handwriting and contained misspellings and grammatical quirks that also appeared in Hauptmann's notebook. Wood expert Arthur Koehler told the court how he had traced the wood in the ladder to a piece from Hauptmann's attic. This board, known as Rail 16, would become controversial after the trial, (and ever since for that matter) but was devastating to Hauptmann's defense at the time. A 3/4" chisel had been found at the Hopewell estate and a 3/4" chisel was missing from

Hauptmann's toolbox. Finally, the prosecution had several witnesses who testified they sawHauptmann, or identified his voice. Among these witnesses were Condon (Jafsie) and Lindbergh himself. The fact that their identifications had somehow become more positive with time didn't seem to concern the jury.

But there were weaknesses in the prosecution's case as well. The evidence actually placing Hauptmann at the Lindbergh house was thin. There were no fingerprints, no identifiable footprints, no items in Hauptmann's house or car from the crime, and no forensic evidence. Even the testimony of Lindbergh and Jafsie only placed Hauptmann at the cemetery to collect the ransom, not in Hopewell and certainly not in the baby's room. Several eyewitnesses from Hopewell gave vague accounts of seeing someone who seemed to resemble Hauptmann in the area.

There were some more basic problems as well. Up until the capture of Hauptmann, the police were convinced the kidnapping was the work of several people. Now they were prosecuting one man and proposing he acted alone. They could not explain how Hauptmann could have known the Lindberghs would be at home the night of the kidnapping, nor how he could have broken into an unfamiliar occupied house and take a baby away undetected, nor how or when the baby had died. Still, they had a mountain of circumstantial evidence, a heinous crime, a famous victim, an unsympathetic accused, and a public clamoring for blood.

The head of Bruno Hauptmann's defense team was Edward Reilly, a well-known and flamboyant New York defense attorney somewhat past his prime due to excessive drinking and personal problems. His fee was paid by the New York Herald in exchange for exclusive stories. Most accounts of the trial give low marks to Reilly, citing his efforts as lackluster and detached. He spent less than an hour with his client preparing for the trial and privately confessed to thinking him guilty. Most analysts agree Reilly did not give Hauptmann the defense he deserved.

Reilly's general strategy, however, was basically sound. He intended to cast doubt on certain shaky areas of the state's evidence and to hammer on the inconsistencies in the state's case. In its place he attempted to plant his own theory he claimed was more consistent with the facts. While the state contended Hauptmann was the lone kidnapper who drove from the Bronx on the night of March 1, 1932 and climbed the ladder to steal the baby, Reilly argued this was highly unlikely. How could Hauptmann have known the Lindberghs would be at the Hopewell estate that Tuesday when previously they had always departed on Monday? To Reilly, there was only one logical answer: the kidnapping was an inside job by someone in the Lindbergh household.

To pursue this inside job theory, however, Reilly had to attack and discredit the members of the household staff, and even ask pointed questions of Lindbergh himself. This was not a strategy likely to endear him to the jury. Most good attorneys could pursue this theory in a sensitive way if careful. Reilly, however, wasn't. He grilled Lindbergh on how much research he had done before hiring the members of his staff, suggesting Lindbergh had been negligent. He almost implied Lindbergh himself was partly to blame for the kidnapping. Predictably, the jury was less impressed with Reilly's theory than with how callously and offensively he was pursuing it. Reilly was further handicapped by his defense witnesses, many of whom were unimpressive and were promptly discredited by Wilentz.

Reilly decided to put Hauptmann on as a witness, thus exposing him to a withering cross-examination by Wilentz. Hauptmann had trouble with his limited command of English, and with explaining much of the state's incriminating evidence. He also sometimes came off as arrogant. Wilentz was able to undermine his credibility and force him to admit lying to the police. Hauptmann's testimony probably hurt his chances considerably, but Reilly had little choice. No jury was likely to acquit anyone who wouldn't speak for himself on a case of such importance. Besides, Reilly hoped Hauptmann's steadfast insistence on his innocence might impress the jurors.

The trial and the accompanying carnival went on. The testimony was sometimes dramatic, sometimes mundane, and sometimes even boring. The defense and the prosecution battled and Hauptmann shouted at several witnesses accusing them of lying. Experts testified and parried with their cross-examiners, and newspapers printed daily summaries under breathless headlines. The evidence against Hauptmann piled up higher and higher, until the inconsistencies and doubts were buried by the sheer weight of it.

Jail behind Flemington Courthouse.
The rounded doorway is where spectators lined up to
be admitted to the courtroom for the trial.
(Author photo)

Finally, after 29 court sessions, 162 witnesses, 182 exhibits, and over a million words of testimony, the case was given to the jury. A few hours later, they returned their verdict: Bruno Richard Hauptmann was guilty of felony murder. There was no recommendation for mercy, and Hauptmann was sentenced to die in the electric chair.

John Reisinger

Chapter 11
Second Opinions and Second Guesses
1935- 1936

Ellis Parker cursed softly to himself when he learned of Bruno Hauptmann's conviction. Of course, he had been expecting it, but now that it had actually happened, he felt the pressure on him rising. The state police, along with the Treasury Department and the New York Police had found the kidnapper, tried him and convicted him, all without his help, but did they get the right man? Parker had followed the trial closely. He knew there was a lot of evidence against Hauptmann, but that the evidence was mostly circumstantial. He also believed Hauptmann's explanations might just be true. No, Parker wasn't satisfied. Nothing he had seen or heard had changed his opinion that the real kidnapper was his old friend Paul Wendel. Parker made his opinion known to anyone who would listen, especially the new governor, Harold Hoffman.

Hoffman also watched the trial and ultimate conviction of Bruno Richard Hauptmann with interest. His old friend and political rival David Wilentz had been devastating as prosecutor, but then he had a lot to work with. If Hauptmann wasn't guilty, he had to be the unluckiest man on earth. But what about the others? Everyone had been in agreement that the kidnapping was the work of at least two people. Where was the accomplice and why was everyone suddenly satisfied Hauptmann acted alone? Even before the trial was over Hoffman directed Schwarzkopf to continue investigating to find out if Hauptmann had accomplices, but he really didn't expect the reluctant Schwarzkopf to come up with anything new, and so far, he hadn't.

Hoffman stared moodily out the window of his suite in Trenton's Hotel Hildebrecht. The whole situation left a very bad taste in his mouth. It was the worst of all possible political and moral outcomes. His political rivals were making themselves national heroes prosecuting the most hated man in America and bringing him to justice while the governor was pummeled in the press about his proposed two percent sales tax. And the worst part was, in spite of Hauptmann's conviction, the real story still hadn't come out. So many things just didn't add up.

At least, that's what his friend Ellis Parker insisted. Ellis kept claiming the investigation had been botched. He said the evidence was suspect at best and rigged at worst. He wasn't even convinced the body was that of the Lindbergh baby. Harold Hoffman knew Parker was the best detective in America, and if he said the case was botched, you could be pretty sure he knew what he was talking about. But even if there had been a miscarriage of justice, what could he do about it at this point? Hauptmann had been tried and convicted in accordance with

New Jersey law. There was still a series of appeals available to him that his attorneys would no doubt use to his best advantage. Hauptmann had just gotten his first delay when Judge Trenchard announced the execution would be postponed until June to give Hauptmann's attorneys time to file appeals.

Harold Hoffman had his doubts about the Lindbergh matter but his dilemma was how to choose between two undesirable alternatives. If he did nothing further, he would watch a possibly innocent man die while his political rivals became heroes for bringing it about. If he attempted to intervene, however, he risked being seen as sympathetic to a baby-killer. Of course, if he intervened and Ellis Parker proved him correct, Hoffman would be a courageous hero who risked his career for justice. His future would be assured. The great unknown, of course, was whether Parker was right, and more importantly, whether he would be able to prove it.

Hoffman needed more facts before he committed himself, and he knew just who could get them for him. Whether what happened next was Hoffman's idea or Parker's will probably never be known. The action had the earmarks of both men, showing Hoffman's boldness and Parker's willingness to bend the law in a good cause. What is certain is that Parker acted with the full knowledge and approval of his old friend the governor.

On the night of April 11, 1935, Ellis Parker secretly visited Bruno Richard Hauptmann in the condemned man's prison cell for a two hour interview. New Jersey prison regulations prohibit anyone except family, attorneys, and clergy from visiting a prisoner on Death Row without a court order. Warden Mark Kimberling, however, was an old political ally of Governor Hoffman's, and allowed Parker full access. In prison cell number 9, just a few feet from the electric chair, the world's greatest detective and the world's most hated man met face to face. In a confidential letter written to Hoffman the next day Parker tells what happened.

"The fellow placed all confidence in me, was free to talk with me and did most of the talking and wants his wife to come and see me because she can talk and explain things better and I am going to let her come.

I can see a great possibility where this fellow can be a victim, even in the extortion. I don't think he had a damn thing to do with the kidnapping, or had any knowledge of it; however, I am going to suspend judgment until I get further into it".

Nothing in the letter indicates Parker learned anything new as a result of his visit, but it didn't matter. Parker clearly was hooked. Hauptmann's plausible story coupled with his unwavering insistence on his innocence played directly into Parker's predisposition to prove the state police wrong and himself right. Even though Parker says he is suspending judgment, it is obvious his mind is made up. Parker then draws Governor Hoffman directly into the fray on the side of Hauptmann.

"I told him of the fact that you were one of my best friends and that you wanted to do the right thing by him and that you wanted him to tell me everything."

For the desperate Hauptmann, word that the governor was taking a personal and sympathetic interest in his case must have been like a life raft thrown to a drowning man. Any thoughts he might have had of confessing must have evaporated in light of this encouraging development.

Hauptmann told Parker what he wanted to hear and Parker told the governor what he wanted to hear. Instead of a fact-finding expedition, Parker's visit to Hauptmann merely reinforced what he and the governor already believed. Now both Parker and Governor Hoffman were set on a course that would lead to disaster.

Bruno Hauptmann's first appeal was filed with the New Jersey Court of Errors and Appeals on May 20, and arguments were heard on June 20. Hauptmann's attorneys Lloyd Fisher, Frederick Pope, and Egbert Rosecrans (Anna Hauptmann had just fired Edward Reilly) had several different arguments in the 178 points they filed. Most basic was the claim that the state's charge of felony murder, that is, murder during the commission of a felony was inappropriate. The felony the state had claimed was grand larceny for the theft of the child's sleeping suit. Rosecrans argued there had been no intent to steal the sleeping suit because it had been returned. Besides, at most the sleeping suit could justify no more than petty theft. Rosecrans then claimed Judge Trenchard's charge to the jury had unfairly directed a finding of guilty. Finally, Hauptmann's attorneys claimed the atmosphere in the courtroom, the media attention, and the angry crowds made a fair trial impossible. After a rebuttal by David Wilentz, the 14 judges adjourned to deliberate. A decision was not expected until some time in the fall.

While many people anxiously waited to see what the Court of Errors and Appeals would do, Ellis Parker continued with his investigation of the case that was considered closed by almost everyone else. All through that summer and into the fall, Parker questioned many of the principal witnesses in the Hauptmann trial and found holes in their testimony. He went to New York and talked to friends and associates of Hauptmann. He interviewed the agent who had sold Isidore Fisch his ticket back to Germany and found Fisch paid in cash. In addition to this tireless search for answers, Parker found time to study the Hauptmann trial records as well.

On October 2, 1935, Parker sent a 13 page written report of his findings to Harold Hoffman.

For the product of such an organized mind, the report is strangely uncoordinated, almost rambling. Points are made, remade, set aside for a while, then made again. Stranger still, many of the points are based on hearsay, third hand testimony, or even rumors. In addition, it is probably the only official report a governor ever received sprinkled with grammatical errors and curse words. Ellis Parker often mangled his wording, but this report almost seemed to have been written by someone with a confused mind.

The report starts out criticizing Hauptmann's attorney, Edward Reilly, saying Hauptmann had poor representation. As Parker puts it,

> *"..whether Hauptmann is guilty or innocent, he never had a chinaman's chance."*

Parker predicts, correctly, that the Court of Errors and Appeals would sustain the conviction. In this opinion, Parker was more realistic than Hauptmann's attorneys, who thought they would prevail.

Parker then attacked the testimony of Arthur Koehler, the prosecution's wood expert who matched the wood in the kidnap ladder with wood from a Bronx lumber yard Hauptmann patronized by carefully matching saw and plane marks with marks left by equipment in different mills and lumber yards. Parker is not impressed.

> *"He is a damn liar, as there couldn't be over 2,000 feet of lumber sawed by any saw mill, or planer, without having the saw reset, or resharpened or plane resharpened. This I have gotten from sawyers who know, and besides, the house where Bruno Richard Hauptmann lived, was built eight years ago."*

This is an interesting and important point. How could wood cut and planed at least eight years earlier have plane or saw marks identical to those left by present day blades certainly reset and sharpened many times since? This point should have been brought up as rebuttal in cross examination of Koehler, but it wasn't. Defense attorney Frederick Pope made an objection based on this idea during the trial, but he was overruled. Parker's point about saws being sharpened in the years since the crime is interesting, but Koehler had actually begun checking sawmills and the kidnap ladder in 1932, long before the police had a suspect. Furthermore, saw marks were only part of his evidence. He determined the cutting speed of the various sawmills as well as the number of blades used and classified the mills accordingly so he was able to narrow down the source of various lumber shipments and look for matches. Accordingly, he was able to match a mill with a lumber yard with the ladder. He was also able to match an attic board in Hauptmann's attic with one of the side rails of the ladder. His evidence was so devastating because it was so thorough.

Parker talks about the jurisdictional inconsistencies of trying to decide the county in which the death occurred and points out how the prosecution talked of the baby dying three different ways. He then returns to the attack on Reilly in a passage of pure hearsay that is unintentionally funny.

"Some newspaper men told me that during the trial at Flemington, that Riley was drunk all the time, was doing a tap dance in the street, raising a flag up and down, and making speeches in front of the hotel where the jury could look out and see him, and then in his summation to the jury he quoted scripture from a Bible. You can imagine what effect this would have on a jury."

Parker then goes on about questioning several witnesses, including Benjamin Lupica, a Princeton student who said he'd seen a car with a ladder in the back. As usual, Parker pulls no punches, as when he is describing Amandus Hochmuth, the man who claimed he saw Hauptmann in the vicinity of the Lindbergh estate.

"The nearest was a man, who in my judgment, is crazy, by the name of Hocsmuth and I think, if you will read his testimony, you will agree with me, as he couldn't answer any question intelligently. His neighbors say he doesn't know who they are until they tell him."

The remainder of the report is mostly a series of things that don't quite fit, something Parker looked for in all his cases. He mentioned his suspicions about others writing the ransom notes, inconsistencies in where the bills turned up, Condon's on-again off-again identification of Hauptmann, and the fact that at least two identical sleeping suits were purchased from Macy's immediately after it was described in the press. Any opportunist extortionist, therefore, could have sent the Lindberghs an identical sleeping suit as "proof" they were the genuine kidnappers.

On page eight, Parker shows he still had Paul Wendel very much on his mind. This statement all but names Wendel as the kidnapper.

"*The kidnapping was long planned, as the facts around the case will positively show. In my judgment, no one around the Lindbergh home, or connected with it in any way had anything whatsoever to do with this affair. Gangs don't kidnap babies. The only persons who kidnap children are persons with distorted minds. A person who has undergone an after-change in life, who imagine they are the smartest people on earth and they are pretty near right, because if you think you can outguess a crazy person, you are crazy for thinking it.*"

But for all the ramblings and thinly veiled allusions to his theory of Paul Wendel, Parker's sense of fair play and justice still burns brightly in an eloquent and memorable passage on page 10.

"*I think, when it comes to taking a person's life, you should be morally convinced of their guilt. In this case I could not see it and don't see it as yet.*

Governor, I don't want you to think that Bruno Richard Hauptmann should be turned loose, because I have no sympathy with any person who would be a party, in any way, in extorting money from a parent who has had a child stolen, whether they had anything to do with the kidnapping or not, but to take a person's life when there is an uncertainty, I don't think it is right. Should Bruno Richard Hauptmann be electrocuted and later it revealed that some one else committed the crime, it would do more to break down justice than anything that could ever happen."

After making a few more minor points, Parker concludes the report with yet another attack on Reilly.

"I am enclosing with this report, a letterhead issued by Mr. Riley (sp), the lawyer who represented Hauptmann, which I think is the most damnable thing I have ever seen."

The stationary he enclosed was made up especially for the trial and featured a sketch of the kidnap ladder on one side. Parker was not the only one who was appalled by it.

In spite of its shortcomings, Parker's report confirmed what Hoffman had suspected; Bruno Hauptmann was most likely innocent of the kidnapping, or at least had accomplices. If Ellis Parker said so, Hoffman knew, you could bet on it. But what should he do about it? The governor, knowing Hauptmann's appeal was still pending, decided to wait and see if the court would make his intervention unnecessary.

One week later, on October 9, the Court of Errors and Appeals announced their decision. As Parker predicted, the 14 judges unanimously upheld the conviction. Hauptmann was one step closer to the electric chair.

After digesting the report from Parker, and seeing the appeal turned down, Governor Hoffman decided he had to intervene in the case before it was too late. He still hesitated. He needed something more; something dramatic to jolt him into action. On October 16, he got it. Hoffman found he had an opening in his evening schedule, and decided to visit Hauptmann himself. His political ally, Warden Mark Kimberling had earlier brought him a message that Hauptmann had asked to see him and here was his chance. Knowing Hauptmann's English was not fluent, Hoffman decided to bring a stenographer who spoke German and was dependably confidential. There was only one person he knew who fit the bill: Ellis Parker's secretary.

Anna Bading was attending a formal dinner in Mt. Holly for the Order of the Eastern Star, an organization she had been active in for years. When the governor asked her to meet him at Warden Kimberling's house in an hour, she duly turned up, along with her steno pad. Coming directly from the dinner, Anna Bading was still dressed in a formal gown. When the governor told her of their mission, she objected she couldn't go dressed as she was. It wouldn't be proper. Mark Kimberling gave her one of his overcoats to wear to be less conspicuous, giving rise to later stories that she had gone disguised as a man.

The governor left Anna Bading in the room with the electric chair while he was taken to nearby cell 9. As it turned out, he did not need her services; Hauptmann had no trouble making himself understood. The condemned man treated the governor to the same indignant protestations of innocence Ellis Parker heard six months earlier. The governor tried to be noncommittal to Hauptmann, but emerged determined to follow his reinvestigation through to the end. A few days later, his determination was reinforced by a call from Charles Curtis, Vice President of the United States under Herbert Hoover. Curtis asked about the Lindbergh case and gave his opinion that Hauptmann did not get a fair trial. He suggested the governor talk to Mrs. Evalyn Walsh McLean, a Washington socialite who had taken an interest in the case. This amounted to a green light from the Republican Party for Hoffman to intervene in the Hauptmann matter.

The New Jersey Court of Pardons met on October 29. As governor, Harold Hoffman was a member of this court and told his fellow judges the case of Bruno Hauptmann would soon be "in our laps." and there were several puzzling aspects to the case. Hoffman then casually mentioned he visited Hauptmann only two weeks earlier. If the other members were shocked, they didn't say so, and no one told the press. Hoffman's secret visit was still secret ... for the moment.

On November 12, Egbert Rosecrans petitioned the Supreme Court of the United States, asking it to review the decision of the New Jersey Court of Errors and Appeals.

Although Parker's public posture at this time was low profile, the press believed he was still involved in the Lindbergh case. A remarkable example of this attitude came when Jacob Ciemiengo wrote to Parker from the Trenton State Prison in November, requesting a meeting. At 16, Ciemiengo was the youngest person ever to receive the death sentence in New Jersey. He and an older man, George Hildebrand were convicted of the murder of Thomas Eilers, a Florence poultry farmer. In correspondence Parker made available to the press, he declined to visit because "my visit there at this time I know would be misconstrued. I have just learned that your lawyers have filed an appeal, and as soon as things die down a little, I will come up and have a talk with you and George." Clearly, Parker does not wish to get involved with Ciemiengo's appeal, but the newspapers reported Parker would visit Ciemiengo "as soon as interest in the case of Bruno Richard Hauptmann blows over", something Parker never said. Though Ciemiengo was on death row along with Bruno Hauptmann, Ceimeingo's sentence was later commuted to life imprisonment.

On December 5, Parker sent another report to Governor Hoffman, about a letter received by the Trenton Chief of Police. Postmarked March 10, 1932, the letter was apparently from a semi-literate member of the kidnappers who had gotten cold feet and was fleeing to Canada.

"I promised not to squeal and they gave me money and I am going home...
We all thought we could make some easy money. We got a place near Elizabeth, N.J., and one of the fellows who was pretty smart runs a wire to this place and listened to everything the Linberg people say....The fellows don't want no more ransom. They are all sorry and afraid. There is three more left now.......Follow the Linbergh Telephone wires and you will find the baby and the three fellows. The fellows were pretty nervous. If I did not like the baby I would not write this. But if you want the baby and the fellows, you must keep this a secret.
(Signed)...Thank you"

When read carefully, the letter is unconvincing. It gives few details and implausibly claims the kidnappers somehow ran a wire to the Lindbergh home. Needless to say, none of the constant searches ever discovered such a wire. There is little to distinguish this letter from the hundreds of similar crank letters circulating at the time, but Parker accepted the letter as genuine because the baby was found about 60 feet from where temporary telephone lines had been run to the Lindbergh estate. Since the wires were run on March 3rd and the letter was postmarked March 10th, Parker figured the writer knew where the body was two months before it was found because he placed it there between those dates.

An equally likely explanation, however, is that the body was left within a short distance of the road leading from the estate because that was presumably the route taken by the kidnapper as he escaped. Temporary telephone lines were also run along the same road because it was the most direct public right of way available, so it is not surprising that the telephone lines passed fairly close by the body. It would have been more surprising if the body and the telephone had been miles apart.

Even though the writer, the references to fleeing to Canada, and the claims of a kidnap gang seem to bear no resemblance to Parker's theory of Paul Wendel as the lone kidnapper, Parker says the letter "convinces me of the party that I have in mind."

In spite of Parker's earlier statements to the contrary, he now seemed to believe the body on Mt. Rose heights *was* that of Charles Lindbergh, Jr., and that the extortion of the ransom was by someone other than the kidnapper (but seemingly in collusion). He even claims he said so from the start.

" *This positively bears out what I have always contended, that the baby died somewhere else and was taken there. The baby could have been placed there any time between the 3rd and the 10th and must have been placed between those dates. To me, I believe they got cold feet and didn't intend to go on with the ransom, but when it was not discovered the kidnapper hooked up with these other birds (I don't mean Hauptmann), to get the money.*"

Of one thing Parker was still certain, however; Bruno Richard Hauptmann was not the kidnapper. The letter also reveals another part of Parker's investigation.

"*As you will recall, Gus Lockwood learned from Al Reich that Dr. Condon said a man sat on the bench with him in this cemetery, for an hour and he had his hand on a big gun, in a holster. The particular individual took a big gun and holster to a place, to keep for him, one time when he was frightened. I traced this gun from the factory to the dealer and from the dealer to a man who had been dead five years. I finally located the widow and found she gave this gun to this man I have in mind. The facts connecting this up, are undiniable and it is too bad that I couldn't have gotten a hold of some inside information and if I had, I could have busted this thing wide open in its early stages.*"

As with so much of Parker's writing, the exact sequence of events is vague and confusing. Who had the gun? To whom did he give it, and how did Parker find out about it? And how could Parker have traced a gun unless he had access to it or somehow knew its serial number? Most importantly, who was "the man I have in mind"? Wendel?

But in spite of his shifting theories of the case, Parker's constant insistence on Hauptmann's innocence continued to carry great weight with the governor.

As was his custom when working on a case and getting close to a solution, Parker did not share his findings with the press. Suspicious reporters still tried to pin Parker down, but Parker ducked them and said nothing about what he was doing. As for what he was thinking, one incident gives some indication. On a trip to New York at this time, Parker's chauffeur, a man named Ray Johnson, later reported the Old Chief stopped in a bookstore and purchased a detective story titled "Convicting the Innocent."

But if Parker was being cautious where reporters were concerned, the governor was not. On December 5, the same day as Parker's letter, a reporter asked Governor Hoffman if he thought some of the evidence in the Hauptmann trial was suspect. Hoffman replied that he thought it was and that Ellis Parker thought so as well. The reporter then asked if Parker was still investigating the case and Hoffman replied he was. The next morning, the headline on the back page of the New York Daily News said

LINDBERGH CASE REOPENED

Following up on the story, a reporter asked Hoffman if he had ever seen Hauptmann. Hoffman casually replied that he had visited Hauptmann in prison six or seven weeks earlier. The next day the story was on the front page of every newspaper in the area. Papers featured the story, showing front-page photos of Hoffman, Hauptmann, and Ellis Parker. Editorials soon followed, almost unanimous in their condemnation of Hoffman's act. Hoffman attempted to backpedal somewhat in the face of this condemnation. He downplayed Parker's investigation as nothing new because former governor A. Harry Moore had actually appointed Parker back when the kidnapping first occurred.

The same day, the Camden Courier-Journal carried a headline on page 1.

PARKER PROBES LINDY CASE WITH HOFFMAN'S KNOWLEDGE

According to the story, Hoffman did not order an inquiry, Parker was inquiring on his own. Mark Kimberling, when asked about rumors Parker had seen Hauptmann in jail said Parker had attempted to, but was turned away because he did not have a court order. Parker, of course, had seen Hauptmann twice, but the governor didn't want that story to get out so tthe loyal Kimberling covered it up. Speculation ran rampant about Hoffman's role. Stories reported Parker had a different suspect in mind, but was keeping the name a secret for now. This rumor, it turned out, was true.

The New York Journal ran a story quoting a "high state official" confirming Hoffman was directing the investigation and quoted the governor saying "Hauptmann may never die in the electric chair."

On December 6, the Philadelphia Bulletin ran a story quoting Hoffman saying Ellis Parker was convinced of Hauptmann's innocence. The article also said Parker had been present at the Lindbergh estate several days after the kidnapping, but had gotten no cooperation and had left. On the same day, the Camden Morning Post carried a headline.

HAUPTMANN CASE REOPENED BY HOFFMAN AND PARKER

The article reported the governor's visit to Hauptmann. "It was just a casual visit, made in my capacity as a member of the Court of Pardons," Hoffman said. Parker's belief in Hauptmann's innocence was also stressed. In case anyone missed the point, the article carried side by side photos of Parker, Hoffman and Haptmann with the caption "Condemned Man and Two Who May Save Him." In his picture, Hauptmann was smiling.

By December 7, the papers were in a frenzy. The Courier-Post reported Parker told the governor the name of the man he suspected as the real kidnapper and speculated there would be a year's reprieve as a result. Parker's theory about Isidore Fisch's involvement was explained, as was Parker's dismissal of the wood evidence. Parker said the state police helped make Lindbergh the victim of a $50,000 hoax by allowing the ransom note to be turned over to underworld figures who circulated it. (He was referring to Mickey Rosner, who copied the note and passed it around.) Parker contrasted this action with Schwarzkopf's refusal to provide him (Parker) a copy of the note when requested. The state police of course had actually resisted Lindbergh's insistence on the presence of Mickey Rosner, and were understandably stung by Parker's statements. An anonymous state police spokesman said "Ellis Parker has talked a lot, but he hasn't said anything yet....He is the greatest ballyhoo man for Ellis Parker that even Ellis Parker could want." But Parker's most inflammatory quote was "Give me the evidence the state was afraid to use at the trial and I will bring in the murderer." Parker was not only going out on a limb, he was handing his enemies a saw.

Wilentz reacted as well. He fed a story to the Philadelphia Evening Bulletin through Assistant Attorney General Robert Peacock about the December 1934 meeting when Parker expressed belief in Hauptmann's guilt. The occasion was a meeting of state officials in the Attorney General's office. In the same article, the Bulletin reported former governor A. Harry Moore, now a U.S. Senator, denied he ever employed Parker to investigate the Lindbergh case or to act as his representative. Technically, this was true, but no one claimed he officially employed Parker. Moore went out of his way to disassociate himself from Parker, saying, "Soon after the child's disappearance, I called a conference of the leading police officials of the county (He probably means 'country'), which included the head of the United States Department of Justice, in an effort to solve the crime. Parker was not among those present at the conference....What work Parker has done on this case, if any, has been done as a freelance investigator."

In view of the fact Moore wrote to Parker asking him to look into the Lindbergh matter, this statement was misleading, as it was no doubt intended to be. Senator Moore obviously did not want to be associated with anyone attempting to save Hauptmann.

The story of the new investigation was now being picked up further afield and inquiries came in to Mt. Holly from around the country and even England and Greece. Parker, meanwhile, was on a duck hunting expedition on the New Jersey coast, and could not be reached for comment. County Prosecutor of Pleas Howard Eastwood, however, said he was not aware Parker was working on the Lindbergh case. This was a remarkable statement considering Eastwood was Parker's boss.

In spite of the storm of speculation about his activities, Parker still gave the reporters little encouragement. In a written statement on December 9, Parker said he had not discovered or turned over any new evidence in the case.

The same day, the Supreme Court announced it would not review the Hauptmann case. Four days later, Judge Trenchard set the date of Hauptmann's execution for the week of January 13, 1936.

Lloyd Fisher filed Hauptmann's appeal with the Court of Pardons on December 23. When the Supreme Court refused to consider the case, this became the last formal chance to overturn or nullify the conviction. The case was heard on January 11, and unlike the Court of Errors and Appeals, the Court of Pardons deliberated and gave their decision the same day. The eight judges denied the appeal by a vote of seven to one. The lone dissent was Governor Harold Hoffman. Now there was nothing standing between Hauptmann and his January 17 appointment with the electric chair.

Lloyd Fisher still had a few meager legal options left. On January 14, after being refused a request for a writ of *habeus corpus* from the U.S. Circuit Court of Appeals, he petitioned the Supreme Court for permission to file for a similar writ. It was an act of legal desperation, but it was the only chance left as the date of execution got ever closer.

Frustrated, Hoffman felt he had no more room to maneuver. He still believed Hauptmann might be innocent, or at least had accomplices he could name, but in only a few hours, that chance would be gone forever. Harold Hoffman's political future might be gone as well, for he had done just enough to place himself on the side of Hauptmann in the public eye without actually convincing anyone of Hauptmann's possible innocence or his own good intentions. Harold Hoffman had always taken the position he had no opinion on Hauptmann's guilt or innocence. He said he only wanted to make sure justice was done to everyone's satisfaction and possibly find the names of any accomplices as well. Unfortunately, he had not been able to convince the public of his professed noble intentions and had been condemned as a meddler who was either politically opportunistic or hopelessly naïve. He was now further boxed in by the press. The articles bolstered the public's expectation Hoffman and Parker held evidence that would soon clear up the case once and for all. Now if he didn't produce that evidence, he would be labeled a liar as well. Like a gambler who keeps betting long shots to try to recoup what he has already lost, Hoffman had to make another try to gain a long shot victory.

On January 16th the Supreme Court refused Lloyd Fisher's request for a writ of *habeus corpus*, and Hoffman knew he could wait no longer. He must decide and he must decide now.

The governor met with Ellis Parker who assured him he knew the identity of the real culprit and could produce both the killer and his confession if he had a little more time. Newspapers were rife with speculation Parker had disclosed the real killer's name to Hoffman, and they may have been right. Certainly such assurances from Parker would have been a far more powerful motive for a delay than simply hoping something would turn up, especially considering the political risks involved. Hoffman couldn't have been seriously expecting Hauptmann to confess since every delay made such a confession less likely. One thing is certain; without Parker and his input, Hoffman would never have risked his political career for Bruno Hauptmann. Whatever the reason, the governor decided to roll the dice one more time.

Hoffman called a meeting with David Wilentz and Hunterdon County Prosecutor Anthony Hauck and told them he was ordering a 30 day reprieve to allow time to clear up problems in the case to ease both his own mind and the public's. Under the law, the new execution date had to be at least four weeks from the date of the judge's new order. That would place the new execution date around the end of March.

Predictably, a storm of criticism greeted the announcement. The public clearly felt Hauptmann had been given more than enough delays and second chances, and that Hoffman was once more interfering with the course of justice. The Newark Star Eagle was particularly brutal, featuring a composite photo on the front page showing Hoffman standing next to a smiling Bruno Hauptmann and patting him on the back. The caption read *"The Murderer and His Friend: Publicity for Hoffman, Shame for New Jersey."*

At the center of the storm, Hoffman continued to publicly insist he was doing the courageous and unpopular thing to assure justice. Privately, he hoped Ellis Parker would somehow come through with a confession from the real kidnapper. If he did, both Parker and Hoffman would be heroes. If he didn't, they would both go down in flames.

As part of his efforts to resolve the question of Hauptmann's guilt, Governor Hoffman unofficially assembled an assorted group of investigators to supplement Ellis Parker's efforts. Dr. Erastus Hudson, a fingerprint expert who had searched in vain for Hauptmann's prints on the ladder was among the members, as was Robert Hicks, a Washington lawyer knowledgeable about ballistics, and Samuel Small, a handwriting expert. Three private detectives, William Pelletreau, George

Foster, and Harold Keeves were also part of the governor's team. The team was of little real value since it consisted of people predisposed to believe in Hauptmann's innocence. Bill Pelletreau, the Jersey City private investigator studied the ransom notes and became convinced the notes had not been written by Hauptmann, but by a Russian con man named J. Nosovisky. Furthermore, Pelletreau claimed, J. Nosovisky was the author of an anonymous letter Governor Hoffman received proclaiming Hauptmann's innocence. Pelletreau also believed J. Nosovisky was the mysterious J.J.Faulkner who made a large exchange of ransom money gold certificates at a bank, then disappeared. Unfortunately, Pelletreau could produce little evidence to support these assertions.

At the end of January, 1936, Hoffman ordered Schwarzkopf to continue his investigation. In his letter, Hoffman asked a dozen questions about areas of the case that were questionable. Some of the questions were more like accusations, since they involved actions and positions of the state police investigation. Schwarzkopf was furious, seeing the order and the questions as a vote of no confidence in his ability and his integrity. In Schwarzkopf's view, he was being asked to disprove his own findings. Not surprisingly, Schwarzkopf failed to find any evidence to contradict his earlier conclusions.

Sensing his investigation was going nowhere, Hoffman zeroed in on the wood evidence. Several people, including Ellis Parker himself, questioned Koehler's wood matching and matching the attic board with the kidnap ladder. A member of Hoffman's team, Robert Hicks, rented Hauptmann's house and brought another wood expert, Arch Loney to question whether the notorious rail 16 was really from the attic of Hauptmann's house. Hoffman arranged a meeting at the house with Loney, Koehler, Prosecutor Anthony Hauk, State Police Lieutenant Bornmann, and David Wilentz. The meeting lasted five hours, several times degenerating into a shouting confrontation with Bornmann referring to Hoffman as a son of a bitch. When the smoke cleared however, even Hoffman was convinced the board was genuine.

With all hope of being able to salvage his reputation from the fiasco fading rapidly, Hoffman felt tired and depressed. He decided he would not continue his efforts to save Hauptmann. He just didn't have the ammunition. The only thing that could save the day would be if Ellis Parker could somehow pull off a miracle.

Chapter 12-
The Second Lindbergh Kidnapping-
1936

Ellis Parker sat in his office staring at the spot on the wall and slowly filling the room with smoke from his ever-present pipe. A close observer might have noticed the beginnings of teeth marks on the stem of the pipe, evidence of the tension, pressure and frustration Parker was feeling.

Ellis Parker was running out of time, and he knew it. Wendel was still living in New York. Parker had a suspect he was convinced was guilty, but there was no confession forthcoming and no way to entice the man to go someplace where he could be arrested. Sensing the Court of Pardons would turn down Hauptmann's appeal and with the January 17 execution date looming, Ellis Parker sent a telegram to Paul Wendel on January 10 indirectly urging him to come forward. In the telegram, Parker said "Time is short.....he is innocent but will soon be dead."

Wendel had not risen to the bait. Instead, he sent Parker a letter on January 14 reporting on his progress investigating the

Lindbergh case. In the letter, Wendel claimed he had identified Cemetery John as the notorious Dutch Schmidt of Chicago's Touhey Gang, one of many scraps of unsubstantiated and ultimately useless information Wendel supplied. Wendel remained in New York, and with the warrants waiting for him in New Jersey, it seemed unlikely he would ever return.

Parker cursed. Of all the dumb luck. By fleeing a few small time embezzlement warrants, Paul Wendel was literally getting away with murder. This could go on for months, but Parker didn't have months. Hauptmann had been convicted and had exhausted all his appeals.

The governor's stay of execution expired and Judge Trenchard set a new and final execution date of March 31, 1936. There would be no more delays. Parker knew if Wendel's confession was not obtained by then, Hauptmann would die and he would have failed in the greatest case in his career. A confession from Wendel would solve everything . The press and the country would hail Ellis Parker as a hero. How could it be done? Parker thought of his options, and of the people he could call on to help him. One of the first people he thought of was Murray Bleefeld.

In his efforts to corral Paul Wendel, Ellis Parker had used his vast network of police, politicians, informers, ex-criminals, and others. One of these contacts was Murray Bleefeld, an obscure, small time criminal. With his underworld contacts and unquestioning willingness to perform any assignment, Murray Bleefeld was someone Parker felt could come in handy if there was any unusual job to be done -

especially a job that was not strictly according to the law. Although based in Trenton, Bleefeld had a lot of contacts in New York, and Parker thought these contacts could be put to good use in apprehending Paul Wendel.

Ellis Parker had first met Murray Bleefeld just a few months earlier. Murray Bleefeld's brother David, also known as Jeff Taylor, had been involved in an organization of cleaners and dyers. In 1934 a vicious price war broke out among the cleaners and dyers in the Trenton area, with fires, bombings and occasional murder. The violence was from organized crime pushing the cleaners and dyers for protection money. Just how deeply David Bleefeld was involved in the protection racket is uncertain, but he appears to have been a low-level enforcer, available to do mischief or violence on behalf of the higher ups. In 1935, he was tried and convicted of malicious mischief for putting molasses in the crankcase of a truck from a company that refused to go along. In October of the same year, David Bleefeld began serving a two year sentence at Trenton State Prison. He was still wanted in Philadelphia for the arson of a laundry plant on Germantown Avenue.

Soon after David Bleefeld arrived at Trenton State Prison, John "Jay" Arbitel contacted Murray Bleefeld and told him he knew a man who could help his brother. Arbitel, a former bootlegger, was currently proprietor of the American House Bar in Trenton. Like many other local people on both sides of the law, Arbitel knew Ellis Parker and knew he was someone always willing to do a favor.

Some time in December, the two men met with Ellis Parker at Parker's unofficial second office, the Mt. Holly Elks Club. In the high-ceilinged Victorian parlor, with a massive mounted elk's head on the wall looking on, Parker listened to Murray's story about his brother David and agreed to see what he could do to make things easier.

In early January, 1936, Parker got David Bleefeld transferred from Trenton State Prison to the Bordentown Prison Farm, a much better and easier facility. Both David and Murray Bleefeld were now firmly in Parker's debt. When Parker asked Murray Bleefeld to work for him on the Lindbergh investigation, there was never any question what the response would be. Parker explained the importance of making sure the right person was punished and deputized Bleefeld on the spot.

Bleefeld, accompanied by Herman Bading, was sent to observe the comings and goings of Paul Wendel, now living in the Hotel Stanford on 32nd Street in Manhattan. They got a room in the adjoining Hotel Martinique and set to work, but soon found there was not much to watch. Detective work, Bleefeld thought, was unexpectedly dull.

The surveillance of Wendel yielded nothing new, but did enable Parker to keep tabs on his suspect's whereabouts. In Mt. Holly, Parker pondered the situation. Wendel wouldn't return to New Jersey with the outstanding warrants against him, and Parker couldn't arrest him in New York without the knowledge and cooperation of the New York authorities. Even if the New York police did believe him and help, they would either botch it or worse, take the credit. The more he pondered his problem, the more convinced he became that only some drastic action on his part could get the case off dead center and on its way to a satisfactory conclusion. If he had more time, he could continue to gently pressure and out think his suspect as he had done with so many others. But time was in short supply. The execution of Bruno Hauptmann was drawing ever closer, the public was clamoring for the governor to either name a new suspect or stop interfering, and the state Republican Committee had just stripped Hoffman of his position of party leader, an unprecedented move in New Jersey. Everything seemed to be coming to a head.

And still Wendel wouldn't budge, and Ellis Parker felt increasingly pressured and frustrated. He had to find some way to bring Wendel to justice in time, but how? This time, in the biggest case of his career, the usual methods wouldn't work. Something extraordinary was called for. Parker turned towards the office door.

"Anna, get Ellis Jr. on the phone. Tell him I need to see him and to bring his car. We're going to New York to talk to Murray Bleefeld."

Parker decided he could wait no longer. Just as he claimed to have done in the Honest John Brunen case, he would force events. He would get that long overdue confession. Without any authority, he would have Paul Wendel picked up and held until he confessed. He would have him kidnapped. Now he had to line up some help to pull it off.

His first contact was his son. Ellis Jr. officially worked for the State Motor Fuel Tax Department, but was able to devote time to helping his father when needed. He believed in his father and was ready to do whatever Ellis Sr. said needed to be done. Ellis Jr. was well acquainted with his father's theory of the case, and was involved in some of his early investigation. At times, Ellis Jr., Ellis Sr. and Paul Wendel almost seemed to be working as a team. Ellis Jr. had even driven with Paul Wendel to visit Hopewell. The apparently detailed knowledge of the crime Wendel displayed on that occasion had helped solidify Ellis Sr.'s certainly of Wendel's guilt. When his father revealed his plan to him, Ellis Jr. was eager to put it in motion. They went over the details on the way to New York. Ellis Jr. would be in charge of the others and would be his father's go-between. The others had to be people who had New York connections but were not known to the public and were not closely connected to Ellis Parker. Parker's plan to reveal the real kidnapper was finally under way.

When Parker and his son met with Murray Bleefeld, Parker explained they were carrying out an important secret plan to get Wendel to confess and prevent a terrible miscarriage of justice. As deputies in this important investigation, Ellis Jr. and Murray Bleefeld would indulge in a little play-acting to get this confession. They were to "arrest" Wendel, isolate and confine him. They would pretend they were police to get Wendel off the street and into a car. Once they had him someplace they could confine him, they would claim they were with the New York mob and demand his confession because of all the police attention coming down on their operations. His confession would supposedly allow them to get back to business as usual. When they had the confession, they were to send it secretly to Ellis

Parker, then bring Wendel back to New Jersey so Parker could take him into custody.

On the face of it, the cover story was unconvincing. Someone had already been arrested, tried, convicted and was waiting to be executed for the crime so what sort of police scrutiny could have been going on and what could they have been looking for? The cover story really didn't need to be airtight; its real purpose was to shake a confession loose and then to drive Wendel into the arms of his friend Ellis Parker for protection. Parker's protection would involve reinforcing the confession "for Wendel's own good." Ellis Parker would get his long-awaited confession, get Wendel back to New Jersey, and stop the execution of Hauptmann all in one bold stroke.

Perhaps in an effort to support Governor Hoffman, and because he now saw a way clear to break the case open at last, Parker gave an interview to Phillip Kinsley of the Chicago Tribune about this time. The February 7 article that resulted gives a rare insight into Parker's mindset and view of the case, assuming Parker was sincere in what he said. Although Parker was lucid, he kept diverting the conversation into stories of his past cases and his past glories. This was not unusual when Parker talked to reporters, but might also indicate his mind was not quite as focused as it had been.

To Phillips, Parker seemed in remarkably good spirits, laughing and joking. Although Phillips couldn't know it, these good spirits might have been the result of Parker knowing he had now set the wheels in motion.

"Hauptmann is as innocent as you are of that kidnapping and murder," Parker insisted. "He got in on the ransom money. That is all."

After stating that Hauptmann did not write the ransom notes because they do not match his style, Parker teed off on the official investigation.

"If I had my way, Colonel Lindbergh and his lawyer, Colonel Henry Breckenridge never would have been allowed to run things their way and go after the case with a brass band. I don't care who they are. It would be in justice (?) to solve this right. An egotistical fellow and a corporation lawyer who don't know anything about crime detection. The case was bungled from the start. The identifications are no good. Some of the evidence was framed. I regard the finding of Dr. Condon's address and phone number on a panel in Hauptmann's house as framed evidence."

When Phillips asked Parker if he expected to get any new evidence in the case, Parker laughed and said "If I did, I wouldn't tell you. It's a cold trail now. I like cold trails, however. I don't know what we can do. I feel sure the kidnapping and extortion are two separate jobs."

Parker further said that circumstantial evidence is the only kind that counts because memory can go wrong, but facts don't lie. This was a strange view for Parker to hold in light of the fact that the case against Hauptmann had been heavily circumstantial, with weak eyewitness testimony and virtually no direct evidence such as fingerprints, fiber samples, etc.

Murray Bleefeld was surprised when Parker told him about the plan to kidnap Paul Wendel, but soon got in the spirit, offering to recruit others for the project. In a few days he recruited his brother-in-law Martin Schlossman, and a Brooklyn cab driver named Harry Weiss. Such was Murray Bleefeld's enthusiasm, he even recruited his own father, Harry, and got him to let them use his home in Brooklyn for the place of detention.

Murray Bleefeld, Harry Schlossman, and Harry Weiss
(Photo from the New York Evening Journal)

Ellis Parker, along with Ellis Jr. met with the team at Childs Restaurant at 31st Street and Sixth Avenue in New York a few nights later and deputized them. Parker did not fill in the others on the details of the plan, leaving that to his son and Murray Bleefeld. For Harry Weiss, the cab driver, and Martin Schlossman, part owner of a dry cleaning business, this was a glamorous and exciting adventure in a noble cause. In the depths of the Great Depression, fate had given them a once in a lifetime chance to rise from the mind-numbing obscurity of their daily lives and become heroes. With all the thousands of people who had searched for the Lindbergh kidnapper, they would be the ones who would bring him to justice.

The unlikely conspirators were now assembled and fully prepared to do bad things for a good cause. What's more, because Parker had deputized them they believed they were acting legally.

By the night of February 13, everything was in place. Snow was falling in New York as Ellis Jr. handed out fake badges and toy guns to the others. In the Sheepshead Bay section of Brooklyn, a newly built basement room in Harry Bleefeld's house awaited its occupant, and in Mt. Holly, Ellis Parker puffed nervously on his pipe, anxious for his plan to unfold. Fewer than 50 days remained until the scheduled execution of Bruno Hauptmann.

Valentine's Day, February 14, 1936 dawned as the sun struggled to appear through a frigid gray sky. New York was in the grip of a cold winter. Two inches of snow fell during the night to add to the packed snow and ice the city's weary public works crews hadn't yet been able to remove from the previous storm. The temperatures hovered in the 20s during the day, and dropped into the teens at night, so little of the snow had melted. A few bundled-up pedestrians scurried by, their feet crunching on the hard ice.

Ellis Parker's actor-deputies took their places near the Hotel Stanford. Murray Bleefeld, Martin Schlossman, and Harry Weiss sat waiting in a car fingering their badges and guns, and running over the plan in their minds. Martin Schlossman was behind the wheel. Ellis Jr., wearing a false mustache, waited in a nearby doorway, nervously shifting and stamping his feet to keep warm during the vigil. The cold had driven many people indoors, so there would be few witnesses. The men carefully scanned the red faces passing by, looking for their quarry.

The Hotel Stanford in New York
(Author photo)

Finally around noon, Paul Wendel emerged from the subway stop on 32nd Street and walked toward his hotel. Ellis Jr. signaled to the parked car and Murray Bleefeld and Harry Weiss got out and came up behind Wendel like a scene from a bad detective movie.

"Hello, Paul. DeLouie wants to see you down at headquarters."

James DeLouie was a detective with the Trenton Police Department. The plan was to lure Wendel into the car by making him think he was to be questioned on the outstanding warrants for embezzlement and bad checks. It was a transparent deception, since the Trenton Police had no jurisdiction in New York. Wendel obviously would have known this since he was staying in New York to avoid the New Jersey warrants in the first place.

Surprised, Wendel spun around towards the sound of the voice and saw the two men. Wendel hesitated, sizing up these two strangers who had accosted him. For a few seconds, the three stood on the cold street looking at each other silently, their breath forming frigid clouds that hung in the air.

"You are Paul Wendel of Trenton, aren't you?"

Wendel nodded. "Of course."

"Jimmy told me to pick you up," Bleefeld continued. "He only wants to question you for a little while."

Still Wendel hesitated. For a moment he seemed to be considering calling for help, but Bleefeld placed a gun in Wendel's ribs to emphasize the request. The gun was only a toy, so Wendel could have simply walked away at that point. It would have been far better for Ellis Parker if he had.

He didn't. As they stood there, the car pulled up to the curb next to them.

"Hank," Bleefeld said to Weiss "get in the car." He turned to Wendel.

"You too - and be quick about it."

Weiss opened the door and Wendel reluctantly got in after him. Bleefeld and Weiss were now in the back seat with Wendel, one on each side. Wendel squirmed and looked as if we were about to try to break away.

"Take it easy, Doc."

"How do you know I am a doctor?" Wendel asked suspiciously.

"You were pointed out to us."

The car started up, proceeded south on Broadway. Ellis Jr. watched them pull away, then followed at a discrete distance in his own car. When they passed Police headquarters on Centre Street, Wendel accused the men of lying to him about being police.

"We're federal officers," was the reply. "We're headed for Floyd Bennett Flying Field to meet another federal man."

They crossed the East River on the Manhattan Bridge and soon Wendel and his mysterious abductors were in Brooklyn. As he noted the tangle of streets they were passing, Wendel recovered somewhat from his initial confusion and started to keep track of their location. By several landmarks, he realized they were in the Sheepshead Bay section of the borough. He thought of trying to break free when they stopped at lights, but the guns stopped him. As the car got closer to their destination, Wendel was handcuffed and pushed to the floor. Finally, the car turned down an alley towards the open door of a garage under a house.

The house at 3041 Voorhies Avenue, belonged to Murray Bleefeld's father Harry, and was selected to give the required privacy and isolation. A modest two story row house of reddish-brown brick near the end of the block, Harry Bleefeld's home featured a narrow garage underneath that opened on to the alley behind. The place was perfect for visitors, both voluntary and otherwise, to come and go undetected.

The car pulled into the garage and the door was carefully closed behind it before Wendel was taken from the back seat. He was moved to the adjacent basement still handcuffed and locked in a room that was to be his home for the next week. The narrow windows were boarded so that only a few shafts of daylight showed through the cracks.

Now the play-acting began in earnest. The three abductors, Murray Bleefeld, alias Moe Taylor or sometimes Bill, Harry Weiss, alias Hank Spindellio, and Martin Schlossman, alias Jack sat Wendel down on a bench in the basement room and surrounded him menacingly. Wendel looked up at his captors.

"Why am I here? What do you want?"

Murray Bleefeld supplied the answer.

"If Bruno burns, so do you. You kidnapped the Lindbergh baby and you're going to confess."

Wendel denied he had anything to do with the Lindbergh kidnapping and demanded to be released. The men then tied Wendel's legs to the legs of the bench and pinned his arms with a leather strap around his chest. Wendel noticed the legs of the bench had been securely fastened to the floor. Without another word, the men left and the room was plunged into darkness. Wendel called out until one of the men returned and threatened to shoot him if he made another sound.

Ellis Parker Jr. arrived about 15 minutes later. He called Mt. Holly to report back to Ellis Sr. that everything was going according to plan so far. All they had to do was to keep the pressure on for a day or so and Wendel would come forth with the confession Ellis Parker was sure he was itching to make. There was nothing to do now but continue with the masquerade and wait for Wendel to crack.

About six that night, Murray Bleefeld returned to put cotton in Wendel's ears, though Wendel was able to work the cotton out a little later. Harry Weiss looked in on him about eight the same night and told him he would be held until he talked. All the rest of that night, Wendel was left alone, strapped to the bench in darkness. He could hear movement outside occasionally, and the sound of low talking. The light was turned on at irregular intervals, then switched off again. He was given no food or water, and in the cold room, Wendel felt the first pangs of hunger. Who were these people, he wondered? Did they really expect him to confess to a crime for which another man had already been tried and convicted? It seemed so bizarre, but then again, Wendel had enough past contacts with underworld figures to realize that it was possible that a group of them was acting independently. Maybe these men really were gangsters.

They left Wendel alone to think about his predicament. The next day around noon Harry Weiss came in to the room and told Wendel Bill would be arriving soon so Wendel had better do as he was told. Wendel protested his treatment, but Weiss brushed it aside. Soon Murray Bleefeld appeared and put it to Wendel plainly.

"Doc, you're going to confess to kidnapping the Lindbergh baby. Think it over."

Over the next three days Wendel's captors appeared and disappeared frequently trying to get Wendel to sign a confession.

During these exchanges, Bleefeld was called from the room several times to confer with Ellis Parker Jr. who remained out of Wendel's sight. Bleefeld and Weiss conducted most of the questioning, alternating between threats and promises of money to be made if a confession was forthcoming. On one occasion, Bleefeld said he was working for "a high police power," and Weiss added "Someone in Jersey put the finger on you, Doc." Wendel still did not make the connection to Ellis Parker.

Meanwhile, rumors began circulating in the press that the great Ellis Parker, who had been loudly proclaiming Hauptmann's innocence, had another suspect in mind. A few accounts said Parker actually had the mysterious suspect in custody in an undisclosed location. All this speculation heightened the pressure on Parker and made Wendel's confession even more critical.

By February 19, the situation was a standoff. Wendel, weakened by the cold, lack of food, and the psychological pressure looked haggard and worn out. His clothes were wrinkled and dirty and his unshaven face looked like a derelict's. In spite of his condition, he still maintained his innocence and refused to sign a confession. Five days after Wendel was snatched off the street, the players settled into a predictable routine of threats, pressure and denials. There seemed little reason the game could not continue this way indefinitely.

Back in Mt. Holly, Ellis Parker was feeling the pressure as much as Wendel. The approaching execution, coupled with the press speculation pushed Ellis Parker harder and harder as each day passed. Whenever the phone rang, Ellis expected word the breakthrough had come at last and Wendel had finally confessed, but each time his son reported no progress. Parker's suspect, the man he was convinced was the real Lindbergh killer, stubbornly refused to let justice take its course and in doing so was condemning Bruno Hauptmann to the electric chair. In his frustration, Parker knew he had to somehow speed up the vital confession he knew was just on the horizon. He had a further conversation with Ellis Jr. who then told Bleefeld, Weiss and Schlossman new methods would have to be used. Deprivation and pressure were not enough; Wendel would have to be tortured.

That Ellis Parker would direct, or even be party to physical mistreatment is a matter that has been debated ever since, and it was a measure of his desperation and pressure that he even considered such tactics. Ellis Parker, though he sometimes used methods that went somewhat beyond what the law allowed, had no history of violence or physical coercion. Even in an earlier age, when the "third degree" was standard police procedure, Ellis Parker was using his brains and cunning to obtain confessions and convictions. Again and again in his cases, Parker dug deeper and tied up any loose ends even after the case was essentially solved, in order to obtain sufficient evidence that would stand up in court. He never used force to gain a conviction. It was one of the cornerstones of his reputation and his legend. But never before had he been involved in a case that was so notorious, or carried such a severe time limit. And no other case in his long career held the prospect of such rewards for success and such disgrace for failure. Exactly how much of what followed was a result of Ellis Parker's specific instructions will never be known, but it seems likely he was at least aware of what was being done in his name.

Now the actor-deputies began an all-out effort to force the reluctant Wendel to confess. They tied his wrists to an overhead pole while they spread his legs and tied a weight to his head to pull his body into a spread eagle position over a wooden plank. With a rope attached to the pole, Wendel's captors subjected him to stretching as if on the rack. This was uncomfortable enough, but then they started beating him with fists, feet, and even a rubber hose. One blow of the hose caused a bleeding cut on Wendels ear. Bleefeld, Weiss and Schlossman then got more creative and burned Wendel's face with a hot light bulb and threatened to blind him with a lighted cigarette. Still Wendel refused to confess.

In spite of his pain and distress, several things his captors said made Wendel wonder for whom they were worked. They seemed to know things about him that only close acquaintances knew. What's more, they were frequently in conference with a mysterious fourth man who seemed to be the intermediary to someone bigger. Wendel had enough experience with criminals to know that his captors, for all their big talk, were just small time thugs. They were obviously doing someone else's bidding, but whose?

For the next two days a routine of torture, rest, verbal threats and more torture continued. Wendel was given some food and some coffee, but was still famished and weak. Through it all, Wendel still resisted, even when Bleefeld, Weiss and Schlossman threatened to go after his family. As the days passed, the weary Wendel began to believe he might never get out of his prison alive, and eventually came to the inevitable conclusion: the only way out was to confess then recant the first chance he got. Of course, if he could only confess the right way, he could more easily disprove it later. He still didn't know who his captors were, but they plainly were not Rhodes scholars. With his legal training, Wendel felt he should be able to craft a confession in such a way that any court in the land would reject it.

Wendel finally agreed to sign a confession. His captors were pleased and instantly became friendly. They first took a verbal confession and made notes, then told him to write it out. Wendel had a hard time at first with his sore hands, but managed to put together a brief, noncommittal sort of a document. Bleefeld took it away and conferred with Ellis Jr. who carefully read it and pronounced it unsatisfactory. Wendel was told to do it again. This was repeated several times, with more detail being added each time until a fairly lengthy document was produced. In it, Wendel included a personal reference that would be easily disproved if anyone should use the confession against him. He mentioned staying with his sister when he knew he could prove he hadn't visited his sister in years. Murray Bleefeld coaxed him through it, then took it away to confer with Ellis Jr. and Ellis, Sr.

From his long acquaintance with Paul Wendel, Parker recognized the personal reference and said it had to come out. Bleefeld took the confession back to Wendel and told him the "big boss" said some more changes had to be made. Wendel wondered how the "big boss", whoever he was, could have recognized the personal reference. Finally, after some more revisions, the confession was accepted. There in black and white was what Ellis Parker had relentlessly sought for almost four years; Paul Wendel had finally confessed to kidnapping the Lindbergh baby.

"Now, what are we going to do with you, Doc?" Bleefeld asked. "You need to go someplace for your own protection."

Wendel immediately thought of his old friend and protector, Ellis Parker. Ellis would get him out of this. Ellis would know what to do. With Ellis on his side, he would get out of this terrible predicament. So he asked to contact Ellis Parker. Bleefeld readily agreed.

"First we have to send it off to him so he'll know what it's about," Murray Bleefeld said. "Address the envelope in your own writing. And we are going to deliver you, too."

"Why deliver me anywhere? I can call Ellis Parker." Wendel was still not anxious to return to New Jersey.

"Bosses orders."

Wendel knew better than to argue. After all, he was almost free.

Wendel addressed the envelope and provided a short cover letter. One of his captors asked Wendel if he needed anything.

"I've been wearing this same suit since you picked me up" he replied. "Could you have it cleaned? I'd sure hate to have Ellis Parker see me like this."

They agreed and Wendel was left alone once again, wearing only his overcoat. The suit was taken to Fromberg's Cleaners at 1610 Sheepshead Bay Road, about a mile away. David Fromberg noticed a bloodstain on one shoulder, almost as if the owner had a bad cut on his ear.

The next day, Wendel's suit came back from the cleaners. He went through it until he found what he had hoped for - a green dry cleaning tag marked 907-3 XV. Leaving the tag was an incredible blunder by the kidnappers, especially Bleefeld and Schlossman, who were closely associated with the cleaning business and should have known better. Wendel memorized the number and hid the tag.

Murray Bleefeld and the others cleaned Wendel up and prepared him for the trip to Mt. Holly, promising him he would make a lot of money from the confession and could use it to set himself up in a law practice again. How the confessed killer in the most notorious crime in America could expect to set up a law practice and go about his life as if nothing had happened was not explained.

Wendel, meanwhile memorized every detail of the room where he was kept and the bathroom where he was made ready. Now that his captors were more relaxed, Wendel took the opportunity to scratch his initials into the wooden door. He wasn't sure what was going to happen next, but he was relieved to finally get out of that room.

The next day Wendel was blindfolded and bundled into the car again, ready to be delivered to Ellis Parker. Almost as soon as the car left, Harry Bleefeld began repainting and renovating the basement so there would be no trace of the prison from which Paul Wendel had just been released. Even in the unlikely event Wendel ever found his way back, he would never be able to identify the place. As he painted, Harry Bleefeld failed to notice the initials PHW freshly scratched on the wooden door.

.

Chapter 13
Confessions
1936

Back in Mt. Holly, Parker could hardly contain his glee. He had done it. He had found the real Lindbergh kidnapper and had gotten him to confess in time to save the man who was wrongfully accused. He would show up all the doubters, and would be hailed as the one man able to bring justice in the most famous case in the nation.

On February 22, 1936, the confession was sent to Ellis Parker with a note from Wendel.

Dear Ellis:

Inclosed(sic) find a copy of my story that speaks for itself.

I'll be down in a few days to give myself up to you, personally.

Doc,

Paul H. Wendel

As luck would have it, Russell "Hop" Stoddard, a reporter with the Camden Evening Courier, and an old friend of Parker's was nearby when the document was delivered to Parker's office. Years later, Stoddard remembered how Parker was so happy he danced with elation all around the office.

"He starter carrying on like a crazy man, jumping up and down for joy," he recalled.

Like any good reporter, Stoddard was naturally curious to find out what was in the mysterious package that had the Old Chief capering like a schoolboy, but Parker wasn't ready to disclose what he had received just yet. Parker retired to the privacy of his office to study the document. Of course, he already had a good idea what was in it, since he had directed a revision by telephone already, but there was something immensely satisfying in seeing it in print. Parker was so happy he probably didn't read it as critically as he should have.

The confession was a curious document, and in retrospect, it is hard to see how anyone, let alone someone with the shrewdness and experience of Ellis Parker, could have taken it seriously. It ran 25 legal pages and started with a detailed recitation of Wendel's early history and hard luck. Wendel comes across as a law-abiding, even idealistic citizen with an incredible string of bad breaks from an uncaring world. He even claims he suffered because he turned down a bribe.

Nowhere in this somewhat tedious chronicle is there any indication of a history of violent crime, or in fact, any crime at all. Wendel sounds more like an Eagle Scout than the kidnapper of the Eaglet. He is only concerned with being a good citizen and caring for his family, but is constantly foiled by fate and the resentments of lesser men. Still, he bravely goes on his way as best he can. Then, out of thin air, comes the Lindbergh kidnapping. The kidnapping idea springs full-grown out of nothing in a paragraph that has to be read at least twice to grasp its full meaning.

In the fall of 1930, I spoke to my wife, we needed money, that we would have to do something drastic for getting money. I thought of several things so I decided to do something with money in it and that the kidnapping of Charles H. Lindbergh, Jr. would be a good job, with plenty of money and this I decided to do...

This decision, coming after no previous admitted criminal activity, and no thought of starting with a simpler and pettier crime such as robbery is against all common sense. It is as if Wendel said his car had a flat tire, so he decided to steal an airplane.

He goes on to describe building the ladder, scouting the Lindbergh home, and generally making preparations. Buried in this straightforward and obvious account Wendel provides one tantalizing detail. He explained where the unusual "signature" symbol of the red spot and the interlocking circles on the ransom notes came from.

During the preparation of the matter I examined many books for symbols also had an Atlantic Reporter on my shelf which showed symbols with a red center. I decided to use the old circle of chemical symbols with the one of the Atlantic Reporter symbol.

This explanation doesn't ring true either. The Atlantic Reporter, published to summarize cases decided in the various courts of the Middle Atlantic States is a reference work lawyers use to research precedents. It is constantly updated with new volumes. But the Atlantic Reporter didn't use a red circle symbol, it used a key, symbolizing the organization of the cases. Some law libraries used various color dots on the books' bindings as inventory marks, but this practice was not universal. As for chemical symbols, the only type that resembles what was on the ransom notes is the parentheses used to differentiate different parts of more complex chemical compounds. No explanation was given for the three holes.

Although this part of the document does not really explain the symbols, it does indicate that Wendel was actively participating in the preparation of the confession. In spite of Wendel's later claim that the confession was virtually dictated to him, neither Parker nor any of the other conspirators were likely to be familiar enough with the Atlantic Reporter or chemical symbols to invent that explanation without the help of Wendel himself. This does not necessarily indicate Wendel's guilt. He may have simply included something that seemed authentic to his captors, but could be easily disproved later. In effect, Wendel was leading them on, just as he had led Ellis Parker on from the beginning.

Finally, on March 1, 1932, according to the confession, Wendel came downstairs to dinner, than calmly left on his kidnapping mission. No mention is made of how he knew that the Lindberghs would be at home on that Tuesday night when they had never been home on a Tuesday night before, a fact he should have known if he had scouted the place as he said he did.

Wendel then says he came to the estate wearing heavy canvas gloves, put up the ladder, then took off his shoes before climbing. Why would he take off his shoes? He doesn't say. Apparently still wearing the heavy gloves, but not the shoes, he climbed the ladder, reached in the window and felt a vase on the windowsill. He moved the vase to one side and climbed in the window, fixing the ransom note to the windowsill with a thumbtack. Aside from the difficulty of feeling a vase in the dark while wearing canvas gloves, this story has several other implausibilities. For one, where did he carry the thumbtack when he went up the ladder, how did he get it in his clumsy canvas-gloved hands, and how did he stick it in the windowsill without dropping it? There is an even more basic problem with this story: the actual note found on the window sill was <u>not</u> thumb tacked. There is another minor inconsistency. Wendel says that after he moved the vase to one side and got in the room, he put the vase back. Why would he need to put the vase back? So the Lindberghs would not notice someone had been there? It would seem that when they noticed the baby was missing they would know someone had been there regardless of where the vase was resting. One more minor point: there was no vase on the windowsill; it was a beer stein.

Then the story gets even less believable. Wendel says he put the baby in a laundry bag, and took him down the front stairway. (Presumably in his stocking feet.) The front door of the Lindbergh house is not directly at the base of the stairs, but is at the end of a hallway that passes by the living room and the study. To get down the front stairway in the Lindbergh house and out the front door requires walking down the first floor hallway and passing directly in front of the doors of the living room where the family was sitting, and directly in front of the door of the study where Colonel Lindbergh was sitting after 10:00. Wendel would have had to pass within 20 feet of the family without being seen or heard. The Lindbergh house at Hopewell is surprisingly small on the inside, and anyone coming down the steps would be in plain view. In addition, anyone making it out the front door unseen would then have to backtrack around the corner of the house in front of at least five windows to get back to the place where the ladder had been erected. Needless to say, no muddy sock prints were ever found on the stairs.

Wendel says he then took the baby around the corner of the house to where the ladder and his shoes were left, then, with the baby still in a laundry bag tied around his neck, took the time to put his shoes back on. He took down the ladder but decided to leave it when he saw lights coming.

Wendel then says he returned with the baby to his Trenton home and took care of it with his wife and children. Then he makes another leap in the narrative.

Finally, after doing all we could for the baby, it died a natural death, so later I took it up to Mt Rose Road near the orphanage and buried it. I will give you a complete story covering everything when I see you.

Now that I have told my story, my conscience is eased.

Paul H. Wendel

How confessing to kidnapping and causing the death of a 20-month-old child could ease anyone's conscience is not explained. Also unexplained was exactly what kind of a natural death could have come to a 20 month old being fed and cared for. Nor did the confession touch on other basic questions, such as why a native born, college educated man would write the misspelled, clumsy Germanic type language found in the ransom notes. In addition to all these other problems, the confession sets out a scenario that does not fit any of Ellis Parker's theories of the crime. Parker claimed the baby on Mt. Rose Heights was not the Lindbergh baby - the confession said it was. Parker claimed the extortion was done by a different party than the kidnapper - the confession implies it was all done by the same man. Parker believed a letter to the Trenton Chief of Police established the kidnapping was done by a gang - the confession said it was done by Paul Wendel alone. Also unexplained is what became of the ransom. Isadore Fisch is never mentioned even though Parker theorized that Fisch had cheated Wendel out of the ransom. To believe the confession is to believe that Ellis Parker somehow identified the right man even though almost all of his theories about the case were wrong.

But for all its many faults, inconsistencies and illogic, the document was the long sought signed confession to the Lindbergh kidnapping by the man Ellis Parker suspected. Now it was time to get Wendel down to Mt. Holly so Parker could coax him into refining and honing the confession into something that wouldn't get laughed out of court.

On February 24, Murray Bleefeld and the others bundled Wendel into a car and brought him back to Manhattan, then to Mt. Holly. In doing so, they crossed the state line between New York and New Jersey, making the abduction of Paul Wendel a federal offense.

At approximately 7:30 that evening, a black sedan pulled up across High Street from Parker's house and Wendel was told to go up to the front door and ring the bell. Wendel crossed the street, mounted the wide ornamental front steps and, nervously looking over his shoulder, rang the bell. A few seconds later, Ellis Jr. answered.

"Doc," he said, "We didn't expect to see you until the middle of next week. Ellis is in the library."

At this point, the accounts conflict once again. Ellis Jr. in his later testimony before the Mercer County Grand Jury claimed Wendel was in cheerful good spirits, slapping him on the back and kidding him about married life. Wendel claims he immediately asked for Ellis Sr., told him about his ordeal, and said the men who abducted and tortured him were still outside, but that Parker refused to help.

"I don't want to get my damned head blown off," was Parker's response according to Wendel.

In his trial testimony, Parker claimed that Wendel never mentioned kidnapping or torture, but only asked him (Parker) if he had received the confession, When Parker said he had, Wendel asked what he was going to do and Parker said he was going to arrest him. Wendel then requested that he not be arrested right away, but put into some sort of protective custody, apparently because of the supposed organized crime involvement. Parker decided the Mt. Holly jail wouldn't do; it was too public a place. Besides, Wendel wasn't really under arrest. So Parker called Dr. Jones of the New Lisbon State Hospital for the Insane and Epileptic (also called the Four Mile Colony) and arranged for Wendel to stay there for a few nights, supposedly for his own protection against the "gangsters".

In this case, it is Parker's statements that do not ring true. Anyone, guilty or not, who had just been released to an old friend after being abducted and held prisoner for 11 days would have blurted out his story immediately. It is also hard to imagine Wendel casually accepting the confession and the guilt that went with it when it had taken Murray Bleefeld and the others over a week to get him to sign that confession in the first place. It is more likely that Wendel would have demanded an investigation of his abduction and clearing his name.

Parker, wishing to verify the confession and perhaps fine tune it, wanted to delay formally arresting Wendel. At the same time, however, he needed to keep Wendel someplace handy so he wouldn't slip away. Parker told Wendel he would be convicted based on the confession and that his only hope was for Parker to investigate and help get him out of this predicament. The governor had received a copy of the confession, but had agreed to keep it confidential until Parker could investigate. Then there was the matter of the gang that had abducted him. In the meantime, Wendel had to keep out of sight to give Parker enough time to make his investigation and report to the governor. After a quick meal at Parker's house, Wendel was taken to the Four Mile Colony. He first signed a letter agreeing to remain in custody while Parker completed his investigation. Anna Bading had arrived by this time, and witnessed Wendel write a letter addressed directly to Ellis Parker.

Dear Sir:

I am willing to stay in your custody until the investigation is concluded.

P.H.Wendel

Of course, if Wendel had been legally under arrest at this point, no letter would have been necessary. But then, if he had been legally under arrest, he wouldn't have been on his way to the Four Mile Colony.

At this point, Wendel thought Parker's investigation was aimed at getting to the bottom of his kidnapping and at disproving his confession. Parker's intention, however, was to strengthen the confession of the man he believed to be guilty. While he was waiting for the final arrangements, Wendel tried to show Anna Bading some bruises on his leg, but she declined to look for reasons of delicacy. She did notice, however, a sore, or cut on his ear. Up until this time, Anna Bading appears to have been left out of the Wendel kidnap scheme, probably another example of Parker protecting her.

Parker, Ellis Jr., Anna Bading and Wendel arrived at the Four Mile Colony just before 11:00 that night, followed by Gus Lockwood, the investigator on loan from the DMV and the Governor's Office. When they arrived at Four Mile Colony, Parker talked to the superintendent, Dr. Carroll Jones, and his assistant, Scott Atkinson who were waiting for them. Jones wanted a note from Wendel other than the one Wendel had given Parker. Parker went back to the car and conferred with Wendel. Jones, standing nearby, heard Wendel say "What do you want me to write?" A few minutes later, Parker presented Jones with a signed note from Wendel voluntarily committing himself to custody.

Wendel was taken to a modest but comfortable apartment over a garage near the superintendent's house. Gus Lockwood stayed with him, supposedly to protect him from any return of his kidnappers. Herman Bading and Walter Yoos (Anna Badings's younger brother) also took turns watching Wendel, as did a man named Theodore Kass. Kass was from Brooklyn and had been recruited by Harry Weiss, a fact that would come back to haunt Parker later.

The next day, in the early afternoon, Parker appeared with a letter he had received from the governor saying he had read the confession and the detailed route described checked out.

The letter might have been a forgery designed to prod Wendel, but authentic or not, it was effective. The letter concluded,

....My advice to you is to lock up the entire family and put them in jail.

Harold G. Hoffman, Governor

Parker was sympathetic; the old friend looking out for Wendel's best interests.

"I think maybe you'd better rewrite the confession and leave out the part about the whole family helping to care for the baby. There's no sense getting them involved." Parker said.

Wendel did not want to dictate any confession that would appear voluntary, but wanted to protect his family, so he agreed to redraft the confession with his wife's role downplayed. He agreed to do this on the condition that he be allowed to dictate a repudiation at the same time. Parker agreed, but somehow the revised confession got transcribed, but not the repudiation. Parker also suggested that Wendel write to his wife, asking her to go along with whatever Parker said. Wendel wrote the note, thinking that it would alert her that something was wrong. The revised confession started as a question and answer format, with Parker telling Wendel his rights and then asking if he wished to make a statement of his own free will about the events of March 1, 1932. Wendel's answer is yes, then the confession follows.

The revised confession of February 25, 1936 is in some ways less believable than the first. The unbelievable details from the first confession such as climbing the ladder without shoes, and thumb-tacking the ransom note are still there, but Wendel added some ludicrous dialogue to describe his arrival back home with the Lindbergh baby.

.........went in the house with the child and my wife said, "What have you got there?" and I said "I have a baby" and she said "No fooling?" I said "Look at it".

There are many responses a wife might have if a husband were to walk in with an unexpected and unexplained baby one night, but "No fooling?" is probably far down the list. Expressions of shock and incredulity would be much more likely. Mrs. Wendel acts as if her husband had walked in with a new hat, or a bottle of milk.

Wendel then goes on to describe his family's objections to the presence of the baby and states they had no part in caring for it. Wendel also added a statement to the effect that he didn't want legal counsel and intended to plead *Non Vult* to the kidnapping. This is the same as a plea of *Nolo Contendre*, or no contest. It means the defendant is not going to defend against the charge and will accept full punishment. The plea is used primarily for minor offenses when the accused is reasonably sure he would lose and wants to avoid a conviction on his record. This would hardly be an appropriate plea in a felony kidnap-murder case, and Wendel knew it. He added the plea to further undermine the credibility of his confession.

The next morning, February 26, Ellis Jr. was back with Anna Bading and the transcribed version of the confession Wendel had dictated. A few revisions had to be made, including the omission of the *Non Vult* plea. Wendel signed.

In addition to the omission of the *Non Vult* plea, several other changes were made to what was to be the final confession. The reference to thumbtacking the ransom note was deleted, and this version claims the baby was placed on a bed in the attic room of Wendel's house. This also seems implausible. Wendel's house on Greenwood Avenue was a duplex shared with another family, so any crying from a baby might have easily been heard. Besides, the attic is small and unlikely to be adequately insulated or heated to house a sick baby in freezing weather. Nevertheless, the confession claims the baby was left alone and died by falling off the bed where it had been placed and hitting its head on the wooden floor.

Paul Wendel's house today
(Author photo)

Both the non-thumbtacked ransom note and the baby's death by a blow to the head are much closer to the actual facts of the case than the earlier versions of the confession. There is little doubt Parker was responsible for at least suggesting these revisions, if not actually adding them. Parker apparently never stopped to ask himself how the real kidnapper could have gotten these basic details wrong. Just to make sure there was no problem with Wendel being in his custody, and no implication of Wendel's family, Parker added a final paragraph;

Now that I have told you all about this affair, I am willing and want to remain in your custody until you get through. My family had nothing whatsoever to do with this and knew nothing about it.

Original read and signed by Paul H. Wendel in the presence of Ellis Parker Jr and Anna E. Bading on February 26, 1936.

So the final confession was signed and witnessed. It was somewhat more believable than the first version, but still would have been suspect even if Wendel stood behind it and insisted every word was true.

This, however, he had no intention of doing.

Now it was time for Parker to get corroborating statements to nail the door shut on Wendel. As soon as the confession was signed, Ellis Jr. headed for Trenton. He arrived a little after 11:00 and located Wendel's son, Paul Jr. Ellis Jr. asked him to go to Mt. Holly with him to help out Paul Sr. who was in trouble. On the way, Ellis Jr. asked questions about the Lindbergh case and asked Paul Jr. if he thought his father could have made a ladder. Paul Jr. replied that his father couldn't even drive a nail straight.

At the house on High Street, the senior Parker showed Paul Jr. the first hand-written confession, and Paul Jr. recognized his father's handwriting. He remarked that his father must have been crazy to say something like that.

"Did you participate in the crime?" Parker asked.

"No."

"Do you believe your father committed this crime?"

"No."

"Well, if you don't want to see your father burned, you and the rest of the family can help to save him," Parker told him. "What you have to do is sign statements corroborating the confession."

Parker assured Paul Jr. that his statement would be only for the governor and Judge Trenchard, and would not be made public. In the statement Wendel repeated much of the substance of his father's confession. Parker helped him get the details right.

They planned a trip to Wendel Sr.'s New York hotel for the next day, February 27th to get his law books and other possessions before the police confiscated them. Paul Jr. didn't have the stomach to break the news to his mother and sister, so Anna Bading was given the job. By 7:00 that night the statement had been prepared and signed. On the drive back to Trenton, Paul Jr. claimed that Ellis Jr. talked about how the state police were going to look bad and how the Wendels would ultimately make money selling their story to newspapers, magazines, and radio. Ellis Jr. claimed people would soon forget, calling the affair a "seven-day wonder." How this unlikely development would have squared with the Wendels making millions by telling their story wasn't explained.

Paul Jr. wasn't convinced the public would forget so easily, and said he would have to change his name. Ellis Jr. later claimed that Paul. Jr. said. "I always knew they would get my father for this." Paul Jr. appears to have been amazingly naïve or amazingly trusting to believe any criminal could be helped by substantiating his confession, but he went along anyway, so great was his trust in his father's old friend, Ellis Parker.

The next morning, February 27th, Ellis Jr. and Anna Bading arrived at the Wendel house in Trenton. Possibly as a result of Paul's financial troubles, the Wendels were now living at 349 Walnut Avenue, a much more modest house than the Greenwood Avenue residence they occupied at the time of the Lindbergh kidnapping. Paul Jr. and Ellis Jr. went off to New York to retrieve Paul Sr.'s possessions from the hotel room, while Anna Bading visited with Mrs. Wendel and her daughter, Dorothy. Parker had been to Wendel's house before, and Anna Bading was well acquainted with the family. They talked of minor matters for a half hour or so, then Anna Bading gave Mrs. Wendel the letter her husband had written asking her to go along with what Parker said and to help him.

Anna Bading told them Paul Wendel was in custody and had confessed to everything. At first, Mrs. Wendel thought she was talking about the bad check and embezzlement charges. When she learned it was the Lindbergh kidnapping her husband had confessed to, she was aghast. Anna Bading added Wendel asked the family to help him by backing up his confession.

"Well, I don't see how it can be possible," Dorothy said.

"We've always backed him up when he has been in trouble, but for this we won't stand," said Mrs. Wendel.

"Paul Jr. has given a statement backing up everything in the confession," Anna Bading added.

Mrs. Wendel was not convinced. "I don't see how the boy can say a thing like that. I don't believe he was home at the time."

Dorothy then asked to be taken to Mt. Holly to see the confession and to see Ellis Parker. When Ellis Jr. returned from New York, they all got in the car and headed for Mt. Holly. Dorothy told Ellis Jr. that she could not make a statement that was not true, and that she never saw any baby in the house, or heard anything about it. Ellis Jr. said that she must know something about it otherwise it wouldn't have said so in the confession. Dorothy's answer was to the point.

"I don't care what was in the confession. I don't know anything about the Lindbergh baby either being in my home or being kidnapped."

It must have been a long ride to Mt. Holly.

When Ellis Parker came into the parlor to meet his guests, he said "You could have knocked me over with a feather when your father walked in here on Monday night."

When she read the first confession, she said her father must be crazy to write anything like that. When Parker mentioned the ladder, Dorothy repeated her brother's claim that Wendel was so unhandy the Wendel children had to do all the repairs and maintenance around the house.

By now the quick corroboration he had expected to get from the family was obviously not forthcoming, and Parker should have started to reconsider the validity of the confession. But Parker did not easily let go of a bone once he had it in his teeth. He questioned Dorothy about the upstairs room and what was kept there. Parker suggested that Wendel had committed the crime in a fit of temporary insanity, and that if the family would go along, they would make things easier on Paul Wendel and make money besides. Dorothy still refused to write or sign any false statements. Parker once again assured her of his friendship and promised to do everything he could for her father and for the family. She thanked Parker and left without signing anything. On the way back to Trenton, Ellis Jr. repeated the idea of the leniency of Wendel's sentence and the money to be made if the family would go along.

When she returned to Trenton, she wasted no time in finding her brother and loudly condemning him for signing the statement. Her brother said he only did it to help their father. Dorothy called him a fool.

On March 11, Ellis Parker Jr. again picked up Paul Wendel Jr. and took him to Mt. Holly to make another statement and to be fingerprinted. His sister's bawling out had apparently had limited effect.

Meanwhile, Paul H. Wendel remained at the Four Mile Colony. He was treated well, but not allowed any contact with the outside world. Parker assured him this was on orders from the governor to give Parker a chance to work without interruption to prove his innocence. Wendel claims that the Parkers actively pressured him to take responsibility for the confession, assuring him that he would get off lightly with a temporary insanity plea and reap riches for telling his story. Wendel says the Parkers threatened, bluffed, and cajoled in an effort to get him to stand behind his confession. Other than the actual confinement, however, Wendel claimed no physical duress.

By now, Parker must have realized Wendel was not going to take the rap for the Lindbergh kidnapping willingly. He must also have realized that, outside of his very questionable confession, Wendel was not even a likely suspect. Whether Parker ever had any doubts about his conclusion or not, he didn't act as though he did. In fact, Parker acted as though he had the main truth about Wendel's guilt, and only had to clean up some of the details. He pushed to fine tune the confessions and the statements and shifted his theory to fit the new facts. (The body he long insisted was not the Lindbergh baby suddenly seemed to be the Lindbergh baby after all.) Nor did anyone around Parker ever seem to question the basic premise of Wendel's guilt. Such was Parker's reputation that everyone thought if they didn't see what Ellis Parker saw, they must be the ones that were wrong.

Parker continued on his difficult, and ultimately doomed quest to find sufficient evidence to back up Wendel's confession. All the while, the clock ticked ever closer to Hauptmann's scheduled execution on March 31, 1936. Parker's time was running out just as fast as Hauptmann's.

On March 26, 1936, with less than six days to go before the execution, Ellis Parker made a last attempt to get a signed corroborating statement from Dorothy Wendel. Ellis Jr. showed up at Dorothy's apartment and said Ellis Sr. was waiting for her in the car. When Dorothy got to the car, she found Ellis Sr., with Anna Bading and her trusty steno notebook. Ellis Sr. said he wanted to get a statement and Dorothy said she would give a statement, but it must be the truth. He asked her to relay the family's history prior to 1932. As she recounted all the reverses her father experienced, Parker said that was why he kidnapped the Lindbergh baby; to get even with the world for all it had done to him. Parker then repeated his opinion that Wendel had temporarily gone out of his mind.

Parker told Dorothy to make no statement to the press should they come asking. It is a measure of just how highly the Wendels regarded Ellis Parker that they hadn't screamed bloody murder to the press already, but Dorothy agreed.

Parker reluctantly decided he had all the evidence he was likely to get. The execution was just days away. At this point, he should have realized his attempt to get Wendel to stand by his confession was doomed and dropped the whole project, but he was convinced he had the right man and he had to save Hauptmann. Besides, he had already mailed envelopes with copies of the final confession to the Governor and the State Board of Pardons, and expected them to arrive the next morning. The point of no return had been passed and the long awaited storm was about to break.

John Reisinger

Chapter 14
The Storm
1936

Gus Lockwood was bored out of his mind. He was a trusted investigator, but now he felt like a combination prison guard and nanny. Sitting day after day at the Four Mile Colony playing cards with Paul Wendel was getting on his nerves. Wendel had taught him the card game Hassenpfeffer, but how many times could you play it and still keep your sanity? Lockwood believed in Ellis Parker and was anxious to do his part, but there were limits. He had been complaining for the past week so, on the night of March 25, 1936, he was relieved for a few hours. With a feeling of relief, Lockwood headed for nearby Trenton and his favorite bar. After a few drinks he felt better; he felt good. As he looked around the bar, he chuckled to himself. All those people around him were going about their business without a hint that he, Gus Lockwood, was guarding the real Lindbergh kidnapper practically under their noses.

The man next to him started complaining about the police to no one in particular. He said that if the state police had spent less time chasing harmless motorists and handing out speeding tickets, they would have captured the Lindbergh kidnapper a lot sooner than they had. Lockwood laughed.

"I got news for you, pal," Lockwood blurted out, "They still haven't got him. Hauptmann didn't do it. I've been guarding the real killer for a month. Ellis Parker found him. And I'll tell you something else. We got a signed confession!"

A little further down the bar, a reporter for the Trenton Labor News turned his head, wondering if he had heard correctly. He moved a little closer. He could hardly believe his ears. A confession from another man? What's more, the man had been apprehended by Ellis Parker himself! The rumors were true. The reporter paid for his drinks and quietly slipped out of the bar.

The next morning, the Trenton Labor News carried a story that said Ellis Parker had a new suspect in the Lindbergh case and the suspect had confessed to everything. The mystery suspect was being held and guarded at an undisclosed location. The paper was full of praise for both Parker and Hoffman, saying they had carried on a courageous fight and had been completely vindicated by this new development.

The same morning, envelopes were delivered to the members of the Board of Pardons. There was no cover letter, just a copy of Wendel's latest confession. As each member read the contents of the envelopes they received, they called each other, and then the governor and David Wilentz. It was incredible. Ellis Parker must have sent it, since the first page said it was taken in his presence. Everybody had heard the rumors of Parker closing in on a different suspect, and everyone had heard Parker publicly voicing his doubts about Hauptmann's guilt, but no one expected this.

Later the same morning, after Wendel's name leaked out, a reporter from the Trenton Times appeared at the Wendel home asking for comment on the story in the Labor News. As Parker had instructed, Dorothy said she didn't know anything about it and the reporter left. A little later, Dorothy was visited by Detective Joseph O'Malley and Sergeant Zapolsky of the state police. She said she had to take care of her baby, but promised to set up a time to be questioned. After the state police left, Dorothy immediately placed a call to Mt. Holly and told Anna Bading that the story was out.

When David Wilentz got a copy of the confession he found it full of inconsistencies and outright inaccuracies. If it had come from anyone other than Ellis Parker, he would have laughed at it, but he knew it was never smart to bet against Parker where criminals were concerned. Wilentz was irritated at both the document and its timing. It was just like Parker to pull something like this, he thought, something that was both awkward and embarrassing. With only four days until Hauptmann's execution Wilentz knew he had to check into this confession and do it quickly.

He called Schwarzkopf to discuss the situation, then sent a telegram to Parker demanding he turn his prisoner over to state authorities or to an officer of Mercer County.

Ellis Parker had been expecting the telegram. He knew he couldn't hold Wendel once the word got out, but he was damned if he'd turn him over directly to Schwarzkopf or Wilentz. So Parker called his friend Sheriff Bradley in Trenton, but couldn't reach him and then called Chief Detective James Kirkham of Mercer County instead.

"Jim," Parker said, "I've got a prisoner to turn over to you tonight; a fellow named Paul Wendel." Parker didn't mention what Wendel had done, and Kirkham didn't know about the confession.

When Kirkham mentioned the call to the Mercer County Prosecutor, Erwin Marshall, Marshall remembered Wendel's name and the embezzlement warrants that were still unserved. He told Kirkham to get the old warrants from the Sheriff and serve them on Wendel when he picked him up.

By this time it was night. Parker got Wendel from his apartment at the Four Mile Colony and drove him to White Horse, a small crossroads town southeast of Trenton near the Mercer County line. Parker had chosen White Horse as a place where Wendel could be turned over with a minimum of fuss and no questions asked. For once, Parker didn't want to be the focal point of events; he counted on the confession to do the talking. On the way, Parker made one last attempt to get Wendel to stick to his confession as the only way to save himself, but Wendel replied he wanted to talk to David Wilentz.

"You'll be charged with murder before you ever get to see him," Parker warned, but Wendel was not persuaded. As if in a spy movie, the two men waited by an old hotel in the darkness. Outside, the occasional car drove past, its driver unaware of the drama unfolding on the quiet street. Finally, a car pulled up alongside.

When Kirkham appeared, Parker still didn't mention why he had Wendel, but merely turned him over and gave Kirkham some papers to go with him. With a last glance at Wendel, Ellis Parker drove away in the darkness. When Kirkham had a chance to read the papers Parker had given him, he couldn't believe his eyes. Was this for real? Could this ordinary looking middle-aged man really be the infamous Lindbergh kidnapper? How was it possible when they had already convicted Bruno Hauptmann? Kirkham thought he had better play it safe and get Wendel charged with the crime immediately. He took Wendel to Charles Mulford, a Justice of the Peace and had his prisoner arraigned on a charge of murder. The charge said;

"Paul H. Wendel did willfully, and with malice aforethought, murder one Charles Augustus Lindbergh, Jr. And give him mortal wounds, of which said mortal wounds he languished a short time and died."

Kirkham then took Wendel to the Mercer County Jail and turned him over to Sheriff Bradley. Incredibly, Kirkham then forgot to give the sheriff the signed confession and the murder complaint he had just sworn out, so the sheriff put Wendel in jail not on a charge of murder, but on the outstanding embezzlement charges. In spite of this oversight, though, Wendel was finally in official custody and away from Ellis Parker.

Sheriff Bradley had been told to inform David Wilentz as soon as Wendel appeared. Wilentz was waiting anxiously along with Schwarzkopf and several others, in the lounge of the Stacy Trent Hotel in Trenton. The sheriff must have wondered why so many high powered officials were so interested in a small-time embezzler, but dutifully made the call to the Stacy Trent well after midnight.

At a little before one in the morning, Wilentz, Schwarzkopf and several state police arrived at the Mercer County Jail and found it an island in a sea of people. The word that a new Lindbergh suspect had been arrested had somehow gotten out, and a surging crowd of reporters, photographers, and curious onlookers threatened to get out of control.

Wilentz and the others elbowed their way through the crowd as flashbulbs exploded around them. In the jail they saw a very average looking middle aged man sitting by himself quietly and calmly. He regarded Wilentz and the others a moment then smiled and extended his hand.

"Gee, but I'm glad to see you," he said. "I'm Paul Wendel."

Back in Mt. Holly, Ellis Parker was tired. He had tried his best, but still didn't know what Wendel would say. He hoped that, once he had the world's attention, Wendel would finally seize the opportunity to brag about what he had done. But why had he been so reluctant up until now? Well, there was nothing more to be done. Hauptmann would probably get another stay of execution, but that was temporary. Everything depended on Wendel, and Wendel was anything but dependable. Parker sighed. It was early in the morning. The sun wouldn't appear for several more hours. Everything was peaceful and calm, but he knew it was just the calm before the storm.

Wilentz still did not know what to make of Wendel. He looked so ordinary, but he had signed a confession. So the attorney asked the crucial question. "Mr. Wendel, this statement you signed; is it true or false?"

Wendel didn't hesitate. "It's false, of course. I don't know a thing about the kidnapping and I certainly didn't have any part in it. I was kidnapped and forced to confess."

Wilentz raised his eyebrows. "Did you say forced?" he asked, hoping the answer was yes.

"That's right ... forced. Look at this." Wendel rolled up a trouser lag and revealed several bruises.

Wilentz felt both relieved and curious. "We want to hear the story from the beginning."

Wendel smiled. "Sure. I've been waiting a long time to tell it."

When Wendel finished his story, his audience couldn't decide which was more fantastic; the confession, or the story of his captivity. Was it possible the man was deranged? He seemed normal enough, but you never really knew with some people. The only thing they all were sure of was that Paul H. Wendel might be an embezzler, he might be a thief, and he might be a liar, but he almost certainly was not a kidnapper.

Wilentz asked Wendel to give a statement summarizing what he had just said, and Wendel readily agreed, commenting he had had a lot of practice in signing statements in the past weeks. He wrote and signed a statement denying any involvement in the kidnapping and telling of his imprisonment and of being forced to confess. It was almost 3:00 AM when Wilentz and the others left.

By now, the crowd outside had grown even bigger, so Wilentz felt compelled to make a statement. He summarized what had happened and assured the crowd that the murder charge had no substance and would soon be straightened out by the Mercer County Prosecutor, Erwin Marshall. At that moment, however, Marshall was home in bed, completely unaware that the embezzlement suspect might actually be the Lindbergh kidnapper. He found out what happened when he sat down to breakfast the next morning and opened the Sunday paper. The headline read,

PAUL WENDEL CHARGED WITH MURDER OF LINDBERGH BABY

Marshall was on the phone to Kirkham in a few seconds and at the jail in a few minutes. He called Wilentz and Schwarzkopf and they arrived soon after. Wendel told his story again, this time in more detail and to a stenographer. They were all convinced he was innocent, but the fact remained he was charged with murder and the charge would have to go before a grand jury. The biggest problem was that the Court of Pardons would hear Hauptmann's final plea for clemency the next day, and having someone else formally charged with the same crime would complicate things immensely.

The press started nipping at Governor Hoffman's heels in earnest, suggesting Wendel might have been framed the way the governor had hinted Hauptmann was. Hoffman's denials were strenuous and indignant. The reporters descended on Ellis Parker as well. Parker stood behind the confession, saying Wendel's accusations of coercion were nonsense and hinting they were another symptom of the temporary insanity and mental instability that had led Wendel to kidnap the Lindbergh baby.

To add to the surreal atmosphere, the New York Times announced that Gaston Means, now in prison for extorting $100,000 from wealthy socialite Evalyn Walsh McLean to get the Lindbergh baby back, had also signed a confession. According to Means, he and an unnamed woman had been paid to kidnap and kill the baby by a Lindbergh relative. Means was known as a man who would never tell the truth when a lie would do, and his confession was officially discounted the following day.

The next day, March 30, 1936, Mercer County Detective Leedom and Captain Lamb of the State police interviewed Paul Wendel Jr., and Dorothy Wendel in the presence of Wendel's attorney, Richard Kafes. Kafes had been Paul Sr.'s mentor and associate years before. They told the whole story of how the Parkers tried to convince them to corroborate their father's confession and assured them it was for everyone's benefit.

The same day, the New Jersey Court of Pardons heard Hauptmann's final plea, presented by Lloyd Fisher. In the afternoon, the court rejected the plea, clearing the path to execution once more. Lloyd Fisher asked Judge Trenchard for a stay of execution to allow the Mercer County Grand Jury to finish its investigation. Wilentz, frustrated by the delays and by the circumstances under which the confession had apparently been obtained reminded the judge that no evidence had been found to connect Wendel with the crime, and there was every reason to suspect Ellis Parker helped frame an innocent man.

"We have had enough time to determine this is the most vile fraud ever perpetrated on New Jersey," Wilentz declared.

Judge Trenchard decided not to grant a stay. Now it was up to Mark Kimberling.

No one wanted to take responsibility for extending the execution yet again, but everyone was aware if Hauptmann was executed and the Mercer County Grand Jury returned an indictment against Wendel afterwards, there would be hell to pay. Outside the Trenton State Prison, the crowds gathered in the cold, waiting for word of the execution while Kimberling waited in vain for guidance. Just before the time scheduled for the execution, Kimberling telephoned Marshall of the Mercer County Grand Jury. They were still deliberating. A few minutes later, the time of execution almost to the minute, Kimberling's phone rang. Allyne Freeman, foreman of the Mercer County Grand Jury requested the execution be postponed for 48 hours to allow the jury time to complete its work and make its decision. Although it carried no weight legally, Kimberling now had an official request and decided to postpone the execution. Kimberling's order from the court said the execution was to be the week of March 30 with the warden deciding the exact date and time, so Kimberling felt he was within his authority to push the date back to April 3.

About this time, yet another bizarre incident occurred. The Lindberghs had donated their Hopewell estate to the State of New Jersey fairly early in the case. They specified that the estate be used for a child welfare institution, but at the moment, the place was deserted with the exception of Joseph Lyons, a lone caretaker. On April 1, a car with five men inside showed up at the estate. When challenged by Lyons, the men in the car did not give their names, but claimed they were there for the governor. Lyons claimed that when he still refused admittance, an altercation ensued involving shoving and an attempt to get him out of the way by pushing him with the slow-moving car. Finally, the car and its occupants sped away.

The car was traced and found to be a state-owned vehicle. Governor Hoffman downplayed the incident, claiming the men were simply there to take some measurements. The car was driven by Frank Holmes, chairman of the State Board for the Cleaning and Dyeing Trade, and a close ally of Harold Hoffman. With him was private detective Leo Meade, former state trooper William Lewis, and Willam Saunders, investigator for Hauptmann attorney C. Lloyd Fisher. The fifth man was not identified. There was no altercation, the men claimed, just a disagreement when Lyons tried to prevent them from leaving. Just what they were there to measure, what the measurements were expected to accomplish, and why it took five men to make the measurements was never explained.

That same day, the Mercer County Grand Jury met again to decide whether to return an indictment of murder on Paul Wendel. Ellis Parker testified. In his testimony, Ellis Parker said things that came back to haunt him later. By this time, Parker realized Wendel had denied everything, and his exasperation showed. Parker complained of Wendel's constantly shifting stories and the wild goose chases and false leads he had supplied. He said Wendel was crazy and almost made him crazy as well. He evaded a question about a remarkable earlier statement he made that he didn't believe Wendel had a "God damned thing to do with the kidnapping". Most importantly, Parker claimed he had no idea how Wendel got to his door the night he showed up, and never indicated he had any involvement other than to help untangle the confusing situation.

By this testimony, Parker painted himself into a corner from which he never escaped. Now he had to stick by his claim of non-involvement in the Wendel kidnapping regardless of events, or be charged with perjury. This was a fatal mistake on Parker's part. David Wilentz, the Trenton Times and many others were already speculating on the possibility that Parker had framed Wendel, and Parker should have seen the tide was turning against him. He would have been far better off admitting what he had done and explaining he took extraordinary measures to save an innocent man from the electric chair. He would have gotten a lot more public sympathy and might have gotten off with a fine or suspended sentence, if he went to trial at all. But he could not bring himself to admit he was wrong in a case on which he had staked so much of his reputation. Perhaps he didn't want to give his rivals and detractors the satisfaction. It must have seemed a safe bet at the time. No one could prove any real connection between Parker and the Wendel kidnapping, and there seemed no way the New York police would ever find out who was involved in Brooklyn. In fact, it must have seemed unlikely anyone would even find out Wendel had been taken to Brooklyn at all. New York was a big city and Wendel had been grabbed in Manhattan. To Parker, it must have seemed his secret was safe. He forgot that most of the criminals he had tracked down and apprehended over the years had thought exactly the same thing.

During the grand jury sessions, perhaps as an insurance measure or a way to enhance his image nationwide, Parker had given an interview to the Chicago Tribune in which he related his proud record of crime fighting success. (And provided a completely different account of the Ivy Giberson case than the one he had related to author Fletcher Pratt just two years earlier. In this version, Parker caught Ivy Giberson by finding she had bought a new widow's outfit in advance of the crime!) On April 3, the glowing article appeared in the Chicago Tribune. The title was "Detective Parker Convicts 288 Criminals in 42 Years."

While Parker felt secure in his reputation in New Jersey, however, developments were taking place on the other side of the Hudson River. New York Police Commissioner Lewis Valentine, along with Kings County (Brooklyn) District Attorney William F.X. Geoghan announced they were investigating the alleged kidnapping of Paul Wendel, since it occurred within their jurisdiction. The Department of Justice said it too was looking into the incident as a possible violation of the Lindbergh Law since Wendel claimed he had been taken across a state line.

For Brooklyn District Attorney William F.X. Geoghan, the Wendel kidnapping was like a gift from heaven when he needed it most. He had had a stormy time as District Attorney. Several of his men had been indicted; he had been investigated for corruption, and an investigation was looking into charges Geoghan made some vital records in the Druckman murder case disappear. In that case, his office had failed to secure a grand jury indictment even though the blood-splattered killers had been arrested on the scene. A special prosecutor appointed later secured the indictment with no problem.

Geoghan felt besieged. He seemed to be getting publicity for all the wrong reasons. Just a few years before, he made a big show of publicly burning a plot of marijuana his men had seized, growing in the backyard of a row house. After soaking the yard with gasoline, Geoghan marched over to light it as scores of reporters and onlookers watched. As he applied the torch, the gasoline erupted in an explosive fireball that singed his eyebrows like a cartoon character, and he ran for his life. His moment of triumph turned to a moment of humiliation.

Now he was under public scrutiny again, and the public wasn't happy with what it saw. New York Mayor LaGuardia, running for reelection, publicly questioned Geoghan's record on racketeers. A Special Grand Jury recommended Geoghan's dismissal, and Geoghan's political life hung in the balance. He needed a distraction, preferably one that would polish up his tarnished image at the same time. This Wendel business was perfect. With one stroke Geoghan could show he was tough on kidnapping and associate himself with the Lindbergh case as well. He decided to give Paul Wendel his full attention. He sent his trusted aide, William McGuiness to Trenton for a three-hour interview with Wendel. McGuiness had an incentive to help with the distraction as well; he had just been indicted for taking bribes.

Whatever his other shortcomings, Wendel was an intelligent man. He had kept his wits when he was kidnapped, and made note of his surroundings as much as he could. From landmarks he was able to see and remember, he thought he was taken to Brooklyn, probably to the Sheepshead Bay section. He also knew what the house looked like, at least from the inside, and had counted the steps from the basement to the first floor. If he could only trace the house, he could prove his presence there by the initials he had scratched in the basement door. Best of all, he still had the dry cleaning tag and had given it to Wilentz. Wendel had observed several local landmarks as well. He particularly remembered a tall yellow smokestack that looked like it was from a factory.

With the information supplied by Wendel, Geoghan's men embarked on a feat of detection that would have done justice to some of the cases of Ellis Parker himself. This time, however, Parker was the hidden culprit and the man he thought a criminal was helping the detectives.

Back in Geoghan's office, McGuiness reported his interview with Wendel. They soon realized that the yellow smokestack was the engineering plant of the Coney Island Hospital; just above Brighton Beach and within a mile of Sheepshead Bay. If he could see it from where they took him, the place must be within maybe a two mile radius.

McGuiness smiled. He noted the green laundry ticket with the number 907 3XV printed on it. "We'll have the police check out every laundry within two miles of the Coney Island Hospital. If we can find the laundry, we can find the kidnappers."

By late the next day, Geoghan and Police Commissioner Valentine had placed 22 detectives on the case and the police had a list of four laundries in the search area that used the type of tag Wendel had saved. They were getting closer.

The Mercer County Grand Jury finished hearing testimony from Wilentz and Governor Hoffman and decided there was nothing to the confession, certainly nothing that would require any action on their part. They adjourned without making a decision. Officially, they "discontinued" the investigation. This meant that Wendel would not be prosecuted, but remained charged with murder because the Grand Jury had not voted the necessary "no bill" of indictment to get the charge dropped. When asked why the Grand Jury had taken this action, the foreman explained they could not vote a "no bill" because no actual written charges had been presented. No one could find the original warrant. After more confusion and head scratching, an embarrassed Chief of Detectives James Kirkham finally produced the missing warrant. The document was still in his pocket from the night he had placed it there and forgotten about it!

Lloyd Fisher was not giving up on his quest to save Hauptmann from the electric chair. The next morning he sent a wire to Governor Hoffman asking for another reprieve, and one to Hunterdon County Prosecutor Anthony Hauk demanding the Hunterdon County Grand Jury consider indicting Paul Wendel for kidnapping based on his confession. Hauk replied the grand jury could not investigate unless he could present it with a signed complaint and he had not received one. Fisher immediately sent his secretary to pick up Anna Hauptmann at the Stacy Trent Hotel in Trenton and get her up to Flemington. Soon, in yet another bizarre twist to the case, the wife of the man condemned for the kidnapping signed a complaint against Wendel for the same crime. Fisher wired Hauk telling him the complaint he needed had been delivered.

In Trenton, a frustrated Mark Kimberling could not believe he was heading for the same dilemma he faced on March 31. Hauptmann was due to be executed tonight and the grand jury at Mercer County had still not formally made a decision. Not only that, now there was a possibility the Hunterdon County Grand Jury would take up the case as well. Now what should he do? Determined not to get caught in the middle again, Kimberling called Marshall in Mercer County and was told the Grand Jury had not gotten a formal complaint in time, (because James Kirkham still had it in his pocket) and it could not make a formal decision. This was no help at all, so Kimberling wrote a letter to Wilentz seeking guidance and sent it by messenger. Wilentz replied by the middle of the afternoon. His letter told Kimberling the sentence was to be carried out on schedule unless there was a reprieve by the governor, a stay of execution by the court, or a commutation of sentence. He did not mention any of the Grand Jury actions. Now Kimberling knew what had to be done. He looked out his window and saw the crowds gathering and the lines of state police keeping them orderly. This time, the people would not be disappointed.

Bruno Hauptmann was executed that night, four years, one month and two days after the kidnapping. Hauk sent a reply to Fisher saying he would be glad to submit the complaint against Paul Wendel to the Hunterdon County Grand Jury ... at their next regularly scheduled session.

In Brooklyn, one of the four Brooklyn laundry owners checked his records and said the man who brought in the suit gave his address as Emmonds Avenue. It turned out to be a dead end. Geoghan was impatient, but believed they were getting closer. He sent William McGuiness and Francis Madden to New Jersey and questioned Wendel further. Then they went to Mt. Holly and questioned Ellis Parker, Ellis Parker Jr., Anna Bading, and Dr. Jones, the superintendent of the Four Mile Colony Mental Hospital. Parker stuck to his story of noninvolvement, but Geoghan's men were suspicious. Back in Brooklyn, police questioned David Fromberg of Fromberg's Cleaners. He remembered mending Wendel's suit when it was brought in for cleaning. He remembered because there were several bloodstains.

On April 10, Geoghan's men brought a "Rogue's Gallery" photo album of local criminals to Wendel in his cell in the Mercer

County Jail. Wendel flipped through the pages then stopped. He recognized one of his kidnappers. The name under the picture was Murray Bleefeld. He turned some more pages and found Harry Weiss as well. Acting on this information, the police soon found Bleefeld's father lived at 3041 Voorhies Avenue, right in the area they were searching. They took pictures of the house and found Harry Bleefeld's son-in-law Martin Schlossman lived there as well. They took a picture of Martin Schlossman to Wendel who promptly identified Schlossman as another one of the kidnappers; the driver of the car. The police showed Wendel a picture of the Voorhies Avenue house, but Wendel couldn't identify it for sure. He was more familiar with the inside.

A few days later, the Mercer County Grand Jury finally cleared Wendel of the murder charge and he was released on $10,000 bail. (He was still charged with the embezzlements.) Wendel was promptly taken to Brooklyn as Geoghan's guest and put up in a comfortable suite on the tenth floor of the St George Towers Hotel at Brooklyn Heights. It was the same suite Governor Hoffman used on one of his previous visits to Brooklyn. Soon the police and Wendel were at 3041 Voorhies Avenue, which the police had kept under surveillance. Once inside, Wendel still wasn't sure. The house had been altered since he had been there and looked different. A partition had been removed and there was fresh paint. Even the concrete floor looked new. But soon Wendel found the initials he had scratched in the basement door. Now he was sure; this was the house.

The police, meanwhile, rounded up about 20 suspects at the local Parkville station as a sort of crude line up. Wendel scanned the people and picked out Martin Schlossman. Afterwards, Wendel posed for newsreel cameras with Geoghan.

Schlossman denied any involvement at first, but changed his mind when he saw the evidence against him. He promptly named the other participants, including Ellis Parker and Ellis Parker Jr. When Geoghan confirmed the Parkers were involved, he was ecstatic. The case had gotten even better. Now he could show he was a man who was firm with kidnappers and police officers who abused their authority. Since that was pretty much what he had been accused of doing himself, Geoghan saw a great opportunity to redeem himself and save his political career. Murray Bleefeld and Harry Weiss were still at large. Parker had given Bleefeld $200 to get himself lost and Bleefeld promptly headed for Florida. Acting on a tip Bleefeld was in Detroit, Geoghan dispatched several men but they returned empty handed.

In the relatively short time since the Wendel kidnapping story surfaced, the New York police made remarkable progress, especially compared to how far the New Jersey State Police progressed in the first few months of the Lindbergh kidnapping. They didn't have all the suspects in custody, but they had their names and they had the house where Wendel had been held. The owner of the house, of course, was Harry Bleefeld, Murray's father Murray, currently ailing from both rheumatism and heart problems. Geoghan had the elder Bleefeld arrested on April 22, but released back to his family that night because of his condition. The strain, coupled with his declining health proved too much and Harry Bleefeld's condition worsened.

The King's County Grand Jury was convened and heard from numerous witnesses, including Harry Fromberg, owner of the dry cleaners where Wendel's suit was cleaned, and Romeo Pelzer, a small contractor hired to alter Harry Bleefeld's basement room after the abduction so that Wendel would not recognize it should he ever find it agin. On April 23, the Kings County Grand Jury indicted Martin Schlossman, Harry Bleefeld, Murray Bleefeld, Harry Weiss, and Ellis Parker Jr. for kidnapping and assault. Martin Schlossman's contact had been with Ellis, Jr, and in spite of his suspicions, could not definitely tie the elder Parker to the plot. Ellis Jr. was nowhere to be found. Geoghan's men questioned Parker Sr., but he claimed to have no knowledge of his son's whereabouts.

Geoghan immediately put out an eight-state alarm and had men checking passenger trains and steamship lines, but there was no sign of Ellis Jr. He sent men to question Ellis Sr, and to make not-so-subtle threats. Parker stuck to his story and had a few threats of his own.

"If my son goes to jail," he shouted, "a lot of people are going to go with him!"

Geoghan turned up the heat. He held a press conference in which he revealed that Ellis Jr.'s house on Mill Street in Mt. Holly had been under surveillance by four New Jersey State Troopers, but Ellis Jr. had given them the slip after toying with them for several days.

"He's got a brand new Buick," Geoghan fumed, "and he's been taking it out at night and driving it around at 80 miles an hour just to lead the state police on."

313

When one of the reporters asked why the police hadn't given Jr. a ticket for all this speeding, Geoghan said he'd been "just joking" about the 80 miles an hour part.

On April 28, Ellis Jr. was still missing, but Harry Weiss was arrested. He had fled when he heard of a possible death penalty for kidnapping and had been hiding in a boarding house in Youngstown, Ohio. His wife and her attorney led police to Harry because she feared he was in danger. Weiss also accused Ellis Parker and Ellis Jr., and filled in more of the details. Ellis Jr., he said, supplied the kidnappers with toy pistols and fake badges for their deception, and supervised the operation while wearing a false mustache and glasses. The whole business was sounding more clumsy and amateur all the time.

In yet another twist, police turned up a letter Weiss wrote on April 6 claiming Wendel planned his own kidnapping to cover up the fact he actually was the Lindbergh kidnapper. Weiss claimed Wendel told him all this a few days before the actual kidnapping while in Weiss's taxicab. Weiss was vague when questioned about the letter, and police dismissed it as an attempt to provide himself with an alibi if he got caught. But Weiss's behavior became even more erratic. The day after he was arrested, Harry Weiss tried to hang himself with his necktie in his cell in the Brooklyn City Prison, but guards spotted him and cut him down in time. He was placed on a suicide watch.

Harold Hoffman was fending off unwelcome attention as well. Former Representative Frankin Foyt publicly questioned Hoffman's right to serve as a delegate to the upcoming

Republican convention and demanded that Hoffman pressure Ellis Parker to produce his missing son. Hoffman retorted,

"Please congratulate Mr. Foyt on his renewed interest in his party and in the affairs of New Jersey. Tell him I will be very glad to call upon him any time I feel I need his advice."

The dominos continued to fall. On May 1 Murray Bleefeld heard about his father's condition, and acting through an intermediary, turned himself in at Albany, New York. He was taken to Geoghan's Brooklyn office and questioned. Bleefeld also identified Ellis Parker Sr. as the moving force behind the kidnapping, but unlike Schlossman and Weiss, he had been in direct contact with Parker when the kidnapping was planned. Bleefeld even placed Parker in Brooklyn, saying the Old Chief had reviewed each revision of Wendel's confession while waiting outside the Voorhies Avenue house in a car. Geoghan was delighted. Now he could get the biggest fish of all. He persuaded Bleefeld to plead guilty in the upcoming trial, promising he would serve no jail time as long as he told the whole story in court. Bleefeld agreed.

A few days after Murray Bleefeld appeared, Theodore Kass and his attorney came forward in Brooklyn. Kass said he was recruited by Harry Weiss, but worked for the Parkers guarding Wendel at the New Jersey Four Mile Colony. Now Geoghan had another direct connection between the Parkers and the Brooklyn kidnappers.

Determined to pull out all the stops getting convictions for the Parkers and the others, Geoghan requested a budget appropriation of $20,000 to cover the investigation and trial, proposing a revenue bond to raise the money. His request was granted.

Ellis Parker Jr. continued to elude Geoghan and his men. A bill was introduced in the New Jersey legislature authorizing a $1,000 reward for Ellis Jr.'s capture. Rumors about Ellis Jr.'s whereabouts spread, especially in Mt. Holly. He was "sighted" at various locations, and one rumor had him hiding disguised as a woman. The truth was that Ellis Jr. never went any farther than Ellis Sr.'s rambling house on High Street in Mt. Holly. Ellis Parker had now added harboring a fugitive to his list of offenses.

With the new evidence from Bleefeld, Geoghan asked the Kings County Grand Jury for a new indictment to supersede the old one and to include Ellis Parker Sr. Meanwhile, he attempted to bring Anna Bading to Brooklyn for questioning. Approaching a New Jersey Circuit Court, he obtained an order for Anna Bading to appear, but attorney James Mercer Davis intervened at Parker's request and found a state law forbidding a citizen from New Jersey being summoned to another state against his will unless extradited. To do so, Davis argued, would constitute "banishment." Anna Bading stayed in Mt. Holly.

On June 2, the Kings County Grand Jury handed down the new secret indictment that included Ellis Parker Sr. Geoghan wasted no time; he sent William Madden and two detectives to Mt. Holly to get local Justice of the Peace William O'Grady to issue a fugitive warrant for Ellis Parker. The job of arresting

Parker fell to Lt. Lewis Bornmann, the same man who had found the matching attic board at Hauptmann's house.

At 8:30 that night, a relaxed Ellis Parker was just finishing up a card game at the Mt. Holly Elks. He bid his friends good night and stepped out the front door onto High Street. Lt. Bornmann and the others were waiting. Ellis Parker, the Chief Detective of Burlington County was arrested on the steps of the Elks Club in sight of his office, the jail, and his house. Parker was calm, asking to make a phone call to his attorney, James Mercer Davis. The next step was for Parker to request bail in front of a Justice of the Peace, but Davis insisted Parker not appear before the same Justice that had issued the fugitive warrant. The parties agreed to a substitute and Parker arranged for his old friend John Throckmorton to hear his request. Throckmorton soon arrived and held a hearing in the downstairs reception room of the Elks Club. There, under the watchful eye of about 50 Elks members and a huge mounted elk head on the wall, Justice of the Peace Throckmorton ignored Madden's request for $7,500 bail and set bail for just $500 pending the outcome of extradition hearings.

After the dust settled, Parker held court on the porch of the Elks Club. His arrest, he said was "just spitework" designed to embarrass Governor Hoffman for his failure to reappoint H. Norman Schwarzkopf as head of the state police. Hoffman's old friend and ally Mark Kimberling now held the job.

"They couldn't get my secretary," Parker said, "so they came after me. Well, I will fight extradition to the end. I'd be a fool not to do so. I have friends here and when you have friends you don't have to worry about other fellow."

The Mt Holly Elks Club
(Author photo)

Back in Brooklyn, Geoghan was disgusted at the low bail. "Here is Jersey justice," he said. "If this is the way things are done there, I wonder why Junior had been hiding so long."

Now he would have to get Parker extradited to Brooklyn to stand trial, but a month earlier, Parker's friend Governor Hoffman had publicly questioned the validity of Geoghan's investigation and hinted he would oppose extradition. When a reporter reminded Geoghan of Hoffman's words, Geoghan's reply showed just how tenacious he was about the case.

"Governor Hoffman will not always be governor of New Jersey and this indictment will always hold good."

On July 7, Governor Hoffman announced he would not grant the extradition of either Ellis Parker or Ellis Jr. to New York. In his official statement, Hoffman said Wendel was unworthy of belief. He accused the New York authorities of coddling Wendel, pointing out that Wendel was released to them with the promise he would remain only 15 days and had so far been kept in comfort and luxury by New York authorities for three months. In Hoffman's view, Wendel was making a mockery of the New Jersey courts and New York was helping him. But Hoffman's case for refusal of extradition was best summed up in the following sentence;

> *"Placing the forty-two years of devoted and zealous service of Ellis Parker Sr. against the mendacity and criminality of Wendel, I could not in decency and honor have done anything but deny extradition."*

Hoffman claimed denial of extradition was a common occurrence and cited instances of several previous governors refusing extradition. One example was the "I Was a Fugitive From a Chain Gang" Robert Burns case in 1930. Hoffman's predecessor, Governor Moore had refused extradition back to Georgia in that case. The difference was that Robert Burns had already been convicted and punished severely. In addition, that extradition refusal was widely popular because it was seen as a way to see justice done rather than justice thwarted. This governor would not be so fortunate.

A spokesman for the Kings County Grand Jury deplored the "indifference, not to say interference of the New Jersey authorities." Several New Jersey newspapers felt the same way and charged the governor was, once again, meddling to thwart the course of justice. Later, when authorities in New Jersey pressed Geoghan to return Wendel to face the old embezzlement and bad check charges. Geoghan said he would send Wendel to New Jersey as soon as New Jersey sent the Parkers to Brooklyn. Wendel remained in the Towers Hotel as a guest of the taxpayers of New York.

The day after Hoffman denied extradition, Ellis Jr. reappeared after being a fugitive for over three months. Ellis Sr. telephoned Mark Kimberling to ask him to have a trooper with the proper warrants wait at Ellis Jr.'s house for his return. Ellis Jr. reappeared and said he had disappeared because he knew he was innocent but was afraid of being "hijacked" to embarrass his father and Governor Hoffman. Ellis Jr.'s bail was also set at $500 and he was back home in time for his daughter's birthday. The governor let it be known he intended to refuse extradition of Ellis Jr. as well.

The Parkers achieved a stalemate in the interstate chess game waged for their freedom. On the same day, Joseph Goldstein, a former magistrate acting on behalf of Harry Weiss and Martin Schlossman contacted U.S. Attorney General Homer S. Cummings and demanded the Parkers be tried in federal court for violation of the Lindbergh Law.

This began another round of maneuvers between those determined to prosecute the Parkers and those who wanted no part of it. The Federal Grand Jury let it be known it would go forward on the Parker case if the Attorney General decided it had jurisdiction. Not wanting to be involved, Cummings refused to advise, but left it to a subordinate, U. S. Attorney John J. Quinn to render an opinion. On July 24, Quinn advised the Federal Grand Jury they were empowered to act and their inquiry began immediately.

While the Federal Grand Jury began to grind out justice, Geoghan and the New York authorities were not standing idly by. Geoghan still hoped to drag the Parkers to Brooklyn, but was determined to try Bleefeld, Weiss, and Schlossman if he couldn't. He decided to hedge his bets to assure a conviction and, in the presence of defense attorney Harry Leibowitz, promised both Schlossman and Weiss they would not get any jail time if they testified and pled guilty. He had earlier made the same promise to Murray Bleefeld. New York Governor Lehman had also been active in the cause, requesting Hoffman reconsider his refusal to extradite the Parkers. Hoffman, announced he would hold a public hearing on the matter. A short and acrimonious public hearing was held in Trenton on August 7. To no one's surprise, Hoffman said nothing new had arisen to change his mind, and demanded Wendel be returned to New Jersey. Kings County Assistant District Attorney William Madden, the man who arrested Ellis Parker at the Elks Club, only to have him walk away on only $500 bail, represented Geoghan so he had probably reached a point of high frustration and exasperation by this time. When Hoffman remarked on the state of confusion in Kings County, Madden replied;

"It ill becomes your Excellency to make such remarks."

"Well," replied Hoffman, quoting Will Rogers, "I only know what I read in the papers."

"Well, your Excellency," Madden replied, "after your experience here in New Jersey, you shouldn't believe it all."

"Well, a hundred thousand people in New York believe what they read about Kings County," Hoffman retorted.

"And two hundred thousand people in New Jersey believe what they read about you," Madden replied.

Further discussion was drowned out by the loud applause.

Only two months earlier, Ellis Parker sat on the porch of the Elks Club puffing on his pipe and telling people "when a man has friends, he doesn't have to worry about the other fellow." Whether he began to realize it or not, "the other fellow" was now the federal government, and no amount of friends sitting around the Elks Club could protect the Old Chief. Parker's web of friends and contacts could keep the New York authorities at bay, but once the Federal Grand Jury took up the case the American Sherlock Holmes was heading for his last bow.

In Newark, the Federal Grand Jury went over the familiar ground covered by previous inquiries, but more information had been uncovered and Parker's denials of involvement were even less credible. Wendel told his story again, as did the kidnappers, and all roads seemed to lead back to Ellis Parker. As if to underline how badly the investigation was going for Ellis Parker's cause, Anna Bading and Clint Zeller were arrested for perjury by a Federal Marshall right outside the jury room on October 5. They testified they were not in New York on February 6, 1936, when the Grand Jury had reason to believe they were. After three hours in the Hudson County jail, they were released on $10,000 bail each. Not only was the Grand Jury skeptical about Ellis Parker, they didn't believe his trusted subordinates either.

On October 20, the Federal Grand Jury handed down indictments. Ellis Parker Sr. and Jr. were named, along with Murray Bleefeld, Martin Schlossman, and Harry Weiss for the crime of kidnapping in violation of 18 U.S.C.A. sections 408a and 408c, better known as the Lindbergh Law. In handing down this indictment, the Grand Jury crossed into a controversial area. Prior to passage of the Lindbergh Law, kidnapping was almost entirely a state issue. Only when a kidnapping clearly crossed state lines did the federal government get involved, and then only when invited by the states. The Lindbergh Law, passed only a few months after the kidnapping of the Lindbergh baby and a little more than one month after the baby was found murdered, made kidnapping a federal offense and carried the death penalty if the victim was harmed. What made the Federal Grand Jury's action controversial was the original intent of the law was to combat the kind of kidnapping for ransom the Lindbergh case represented. Such cases were especially troubling because of the implied and too often real danger of murder unless a ransom was paid.

The Parker/Wendel affair, though it could technically be considered a kidnapping, was obviously far from the type of crime the law was intended to combat. Not only was Paul Wendel a long way from being an infant, but there was never any threat or ransom demands made to his family. His family didn't even know he had been taken until he was in Ellis Parker's custody, a custody that was to some extent consensual. Wendel was certainly taken into custody against his will and imprisoned under false pretenses by someone who had no legal authority to do so. Still, Ellis Parker was an officer of the law working through men he had deputized for the purpose. There was never any question of ransom; the motive was clearly to further the investigation of a crime. So why apply a law designed to fight kidnapping infants for ransom to the extralegal arrest and detention of a crime suspect?

The answer has to do with how the law was written and how it was construed by those responsible for its enforcement. The original law was broadly written. It was not limited to the kidnapping of infants, and was even broad about ransom demands, talking about kidnapping for "ransom or reward." Under that definition, Parker might never have gone to trial. Two years later, however, congress amended the Lindbergh Law by adding the words "or otherwise" to the phrase "for ransom or reward." Now the law covered the kidnapping of anyone for any purpose whatever, and that was the wording of the law when Wendel was kidnapped. Under the law, it didn't matter what Parker's reasons were, or whether he expected ransom, or even whether Wendel's family was aware of it; the fact that Wendel was taken and held against his will was sufficient grounds for an indictment.

Charging Parker with kidnapping for actions taken while investigating a kidnapping was unusual enough, but what made it even stranger was the fact that Bruno Richard Hauptmann himself had not been charged with kidnapping. Under state law kidnapping itself was not punishable by death, so the prosecutors charged and tried Hauptmann for felony murder. The man executed for the Lindbergh kidnapping was never tried for kidnapping, but the detective who tried to solve the case was. Unfortunately for Ellis Parker, irony was not a valid defense.

The first action taken by Parker's attorney, James Mercer Davis was to file a motion to void the indictments, on the interesting contention that the jury had been improperly constituted due to its "lack of Negroes". In a similar brief, Davis contended the arrest of Anna Bading and Clint Zeller was an improper extension of the jury's powers, especially in view of the jury's racial makeup. Ellis Parker was not going to go down without a fight. The plea was unsuccessful, but was not decided until February 2, 1937. Meanwhile, the Parkers remained free

From November 1936 to January 1937, Paul Wendel wrote a series of articles about his abduction for Liberty Magazine presenting himself as a wronged innocent who only wanted to help. He also made himself the center of attention. In his view, the kidnapping, the murdered baby, and Bruno Hauptmann himself were only supporting players to the great Paul Wendel saga.

"I was the reason that the world had to wait to hear that Hauptmann was dead!" he wrote, indicating that, whatever faults he might have, insufficient ego was not one of them.

Wendel then went on to paint a picture of himself as a man who in no way resembles a convicted perjurer under seven indictments for fraud, embezzlement, and passing bad checks.

"Little had I thought as I went on my quiet, simple, peace-loving way-first as a chemist and then as a lawyer, then again as a chemist-that I would become the focal figure in such a breath-taking crisis."

To increase the dramatic impact of the articles, Wendel posed for photographs in which he recreated the more sensational parts of his ordeal. The articles read like a cliff-hanger serial, with the innocent and virtuous Wendel as the beleaguered hero.

Liberty Magazine sent a letter to ex-Governor Hoffman indicating the Wendel articles would soon appear, and asking if he wanted to review them and comment. Hoffman's private reaction can be imagined. What he actually wrote in reply was that Wendel had been only a distraction and an impediment to the Lindbergh case and had contributed nothing positive. Hoffman concluded by saying that he doubted that anything Wendel wrote would have any value.

In spite of their self-serving and melodramatic tone, however, Wendel's Liberty Magazine articles, especially the photos, encouraged an unfavorable image of Parker in the public mind. With a trial becoming a real possibility, the timing couldn't have been worse for Parker's chances.

On February 9, 1937, the Parkers along with Anna Bading pleaded not guilty at their arraignment in Newark. On the same day, the trial of Bleefeld, Schlossman, and Weiss began in Brooklyn. Geoghan personally prosecuted the three, and though he was disappointed by his inability to reach the Parkers, there was still a lot of good press to be gained. Bleefeld had already agreed to plead guilty and freely testify against the Parkers on Geoghan's promise to spare him any jail time. Weiss and Schlossman had a slightly different deal; they would plead guilty to the lesser crime of assault in exchange for their testimony on the kidnapping. The kidnapping charge against them would then be dropped and they would get suspended sentences for the assault. This would cement the case against the Parkers if and when Geoghan could get his hands on them.

Apparently, though, someone had neglected to tell Judge Fitzgerald about the deals, because he dismissed the assault charges and made the trial exclusively on the more serious kidnapping charge that carried a mandatory twenty year sentence. Burton Turkus, attorney for Schlossman and Weiss was furious and accused Geoghan of "the most reprehensible form of trickery."

"He apparently never intended to keep his promises," Turkus said. "A confession obtained by the District Attorney by such means should be just as ineffective and is, if anything, more vile and contemptible than a confession beaten out of a defendant in the back room of a police station."

Turkus resigned from the case in protest while Geoghan claimed there had never been any deal. Possibly as a result of the turmoil, the jury, after deliberating for 20 hours, hung up at 9 to 3 for conviction, saying they couldn't decide if Wendel had gone willingly. On February 14, Judge Fitzgerald declared a mistrial. Less than a month later, after a second trial, Schlossman and Weiss were convicted. In the second trial, Schlossman's former attorney Samuel Liebowitz testified he had been present when Geoghan had offered his leniency deal to Schlossman and Weiss. The protest was to no avail. Schlossman and Weiss were sentenced to 20 years in Sing Sing.

A few days after Schlossman and Weiss were sentenced, Federal Judge Thompson granted a temporary injunction preventing U.S. Attorney J. J. Quinn from bringing the Parkers to trial in federal court. A few days later, another federal judge overruled the injunction. Finally, on March 22, Judge Clark overruled a previously filed demurrer to the indictment of the Parkers, clearing the way at last for a trial in the federal court in Newark. Parker and his attorneys fought fiercely to avoid a trial, taking advantage of every avenue the law allowed, but the delays and roadblocks they had produced had finally run out.

The long battle had taken its toll on Ellis Parker. Instead of fighting crime, his days were now spent fighting for his own survival. He lost 40 pounds and was complaining of kidney and bladder trouble. Understandably, Parker wanted to avoid traveling to the federal court in Newark each day. Although it would not delay the trial, Parker's attorneys filed an application for Change of Venue and a motion for a Bill of Particulars, legal language for a request to hold the trial closer to Mt. Holly and a claim that the indictment was too vague. These efforts were later turned down as well. Ellis Parker, the Old Chief, the American Sherlock Holmes, the Country Detective with the World Wide

Reputation, the Most Borrowed Detective in America, the Bald Eagle of the Pine Barrens would stand trial in federal court in Newark for kidnapping.

John Reisinger

Chapter 15- The Trial of Ellis Parker -
The Prosecution-
1937

One of the Ellis Parker legends is that he was the first person tried for violation of the Lindbergh Law. This statement, however rich in irony it might be, is not even close to the truth. At the time of Parker's trial, there had already been 29 such cases tried, and 69 defendants convicted. Among the sentences were two death sentences, 16 life imprisonments, and other jail terms averaging 23 years each. Of course none of these defendants were sentenced for kidnapping in the pursuit of solving another kidnapping. In that regard, Ellis Parker was the first.

The federal courthouse in Newark was an imposing gray stone building occupying the better part of a city block. An attempt had been made to soften the brutal appearance of the face of the structure by placing multi-story columns along one side and entrance porticoes along the other, but the place still looked like the secret police headquarters of a totalitarian country. On rainy days, when the wet and gloom made dark streaks appear on the gray stone, it would be hard to think of a more depressing place to be. Inside, cavernous halls echoed with footsteps and the anxious conversations of lawyers and

331

witnesses. Bright, glaring fluorescent lights failed to significantly lighten the somber atmosphere. Ellis Parker was no stranger to courtrooms, but as he, Ellis Jr. and his attorneys walked into the building, it was like entering another, more sinister world. This was not the human scaled, almost folksy county courthouse in Mt Holly; this was federal district court and the building reflected all the overwhelming and impersonal power it represented.

Martin Schlossman and Harry Weiss had been transferred to the Hudson County Jail in Jersey City to be available to testify, even though Murray Bleefeld was still free on bail awaiting sentencing. In yet another bit of confusion, William Pelletreau, the Jersey City detective who worked with Parker on Governor Hoffman's last minute Lindbergh investigation, submitted an affidavit to Hunterdon County Prosecutor Anthony Hauck. The affidavit, signed by a prisoner in the Bronx County jail, claimed he had been invited to take part in the Lindbergh kidnapping in 1932 by an "international spy" who was the real culprit. Hauck promised to investigate further.

Judge William Clark was 46, and was appointed to the federal bench when he was only 34. With his close cropped dark hair, Clark somewhat resembled David Wilentz. A Harvard graduate and an army veteran of the Great War, he was familiar with the case, and decided several of the preliminary motions.

It soon became apparent the trial of Ellis Parker would be as hard-fought as the preliminary maneuvers had been. James Mercer Davis battled with the prosecution about jury selection and which parties got the most challenges. The final jury consisted of four men and eight women. United States v. Parker, et al became the first major case in New Jersey federal court in which women served as jurors.

James Mercer Davis moved for a severance of the Parkers' trial from those of the co-defendants, a move which could negate the evidence in all the previous confessions. He was particularly anxious to eliminate Bleefeld, calling him a "stalking horse for the government." His motions were denied. (Those who put stock in omens may have noted actor William Gillette, famous for playing Sherlock Holmes, died the same day.)

In addition to Davis, the defense team for the Parkers included former governor George S. Silzer, rumored to be in line for a vacant Supreme Court berth; Harry Green, who would prove to be the Parkers' most tenacious supporter; and, Harry Weinberger. Governor Harold Hoffman was active in recruiting and partially paying for the defense team.

In the weeks leading up to the trial, the defense team planned their strategy. Outside attorneys informally polled by Hoffman's attorney, William S. Conklin recommended a defense based on "truth and justification". This would admit the kidnapping but explain Parker's reasons. It was useless to deny Parker's role in the kidnapping, argued Conklin, because there was too much proof to the contrary. There were several potential problems with this approach, however. The judge might consider the mitigating testimony a "virtual retrial of the Lindbergh case" and not allow it, leaving Parker with an admission of guilt but little to show for it. In addition, Parker had denied participating in the kidnapping in his grand jury testimony and was likely to resist admitting it now to avoid charges of perjury.

Exactly which of these factors was decisive is not clear, but the defense team finally decided to reject the "truth and justification" defense and deny everything, hoping the unsavoriness of the prosecution witnesses and the great reputation of Ellis Parker would carry the day. It would prove a fatal error.

John J. Quinn, the federal attorney whose opinion had opened the door for a federal Grand Jury investigation was the prosecutor, assisted by Hubert Harrington.

Although the prosecution had more witnesses and evidence to back up its case than the defense, each side worried that its star witness might prove a liability. Wendel testified well in the Grand Jury hearings, but he had an unsavory past and a reputation for lying that could undermine his credibility. Murray Bleefeld, with his shady associations, wasn't much better.

For the defense, on the other hand, Ellis Parker would seem to be a powerful witness. He had a distinguished past and was well regarded in the community and by his peers. But James Mercer Davis had known Parker long enough to know that Parker wasn't accustomed to being questioned and could be testy and defiant if cornered. Parker's testimony so far was a concern. He was vague and evasive where he should have been forthright and stubbornly insistent even when the evidence pointed the other way. Outwardly Ellis Parker appeared calm, but he looked old and tired, as if the trial and his health problems had been chipping away at him for the past months. Instead of the air of confident authority he usually carried in court he seemed to waver between detachment and defiance. Davis only hoped he could keep Parker under control long enough to get him acquitted.

Testimony got under way on May 3 with Bleefeld, Schlossman, and Weiss all pleading guilty, leaving the Parkers to face the charges alone. At his point, it should have been apparent the Parkers had no chance of convincing a jury of their innocence in the face of three confessions by their former co-conspirators. Despite of the odds against them, the defense decided to stick with the previous claims of non-involvement. Whether this tactic was at Parker's insistence or his attorneys, it would prove disastrous because it would undermine Parker's strongest asset: his sincerity.

The government took the position Parker cynically plotted the kidnapping to force an innocent man to confess and take the rap for the Lindbergh crime in the hope of promotion and profit. Prosecuting U.S. Attorney John J. Quinn made the government's case clear with his opening statement.

"We will show you that the Parkers, Sr. and Jr., attempted to commercialize on the death of the little Lindbergh baby," Quinn began. "We will show you that Parker. Sr., over a period of years, had created an ego complex that he was the greatest detective alive. ....We will show that Wendel actually worked with Parker on the Lindbergh case. Then Parker got this great idea. He thought he could convince Wendel to confess to the crime and then get him out of jail later. Parker actually thought he could convince Paul Wendel to go to prison and confess the Lindbergh crime. He hoped to create the condition that the people of the country would rise up and prevent the electrocution of Hauptmann. Parker told Bleefeld he would take J. Edgar Hoover's place as head of the FBI. He told him Mark Kimberling would become head of the state police. The latter has happened. Parker was counting on telling the true story of the Lindbergh baby in countless magazines and periodicals to make money."

The weakness in the prosecution's case was its insistence that Parker had knowingly tried to get an innocent man to confess. This would be extremely difficult to prove. Throughout Parker's long career, no one had known him to attempt to frame an innocent suspect. If the defense could convince the jury that Parker had honestly believed Wendel to be the kidnapper, and that Wendel himself had given Parker reason for that belief, they might convince the jury the matter was simply an arrest made without the proper procedure by a well-meaning but overzealous officer. With any luck, they might even convince the jury that Wendel was an accessory to his own kidnapping.

The first few prosecution witnesses placed Ellis Jr. in New York and Ellis Sr. at the Four Mile Colony. Anna Bading was called as a prosecution witness and questioned about her shorthand notes taken during Wendel's Four Mile Colony stay. Among the notes was Wendel's repudiation of his confession. It had never been transcribed.

Finally, Quinn called Paul Wendel to the stand. Davis objected, pointing out Wendel's conviction for perjury in 1920. Judge Clark noted Wendel's pardon in 1924 and allowed the testimony. The arguments also disclosed another bizarre fact; both Judge Clark and Parker defense attorney George Silzer were members of the Court of Pardons that pardoned Wendel in 1924.

Wendel took the stand dressed in a dark suit, looking like a respectable doctor or lawyer, and the last person anyone would ever suspect of being a kidnapper. Under Quinn's questioning, Wendel repeated his story, adding details of Parker's cajoling and claims of political influence. He also testified that Parker discussed the Lindbergh kidnapping with him as early as March 12, when Parker asked him to contact his underworld friends. Wendel recounted his kidnapping and torture once again, filling in the sensational details along with the story of his forced confessions and his repudiation.

At the defense table, Ellis Sr. watched impassively while Ellis Jr. took notes. To compensate for the absence of his usual pipe, Ellis Sr. chewed gum and during breaks smoked a cigar in the corridors. James Mercer Davis watched intently; he had to destroy Wendel's testimony to secure an acquittal for the Parkers.

When Quinn finished, Davis rose to cross-examine Wendel on the changes he made to his confessions and whether the changes were in his handwriting and bore his signature. Davis then hammered at discrepancies in dates to discredit Wendel's testimony and to show he had gone to Parker about the Lindbergh case earlier than he had admitted. Davis produced letters from Wendel to Anna Bading as late as January 1936 in which Wendel made coded references to still hunting for the Lindbergh baby.

Davis's strategy was to portray Wendel as an early and active participant in the Lindbergh case who continually provided Ellis Parker with statements and information pointing to his possible guilt as the kidnapper. If this could be established, Quinn's contention that Parker knowingly framed an innocent man would fall to the ground. The jury would see Parker was simply acting on leads like any good law enforcement man. They would also see Wendel, with his checkered history and hints of inside connections led Parker astray. The kidnapping could then be portrayed as an almost inevitable consequence of Wendel's actions.

After going over discrepancies, Davis abruptly shifted to Wendel's Liberty Magazine articles, the ones containing lurid photographic reenactments of the alleged torture. Under Davis's questioning, Wendel reluctantly admitted he was paid for the articles. The prosecution's contention that Parker sought personal profit was now turned against their star witness. Maybe Wendel was the one seeking profit; he had certainly been the only one finding it.

Davis then took Wendel through the confessions line by line trying to show inside knowledge of the crime.

Hours later, when the cross examination was finally through, Davis scored a few points by catching Wendel in some inconsistencies and planting the idea Wendel actively participated in actions that aroused Parker's suspicions. Still, he had not shaken the evidence that Wendel, whatever his personal foibles and shortcomings, was taken against his will.

The trial of Ellis Parker was front page news in the Trenton Evening Times and even the New York Times on many days, but during the Wendel cross examination, the story was pushed off the front pages by another sensational New Jersey event. The German airship Hindenburg crashed and burned at Lakehurst Naval Air Station, the same place Ellis Parker had solved the murder of two sailors seven years earlier.

Anna Bading was called to the stand again and testified Wendel was willing to plead *Non Vult* to the kidnapping, even after he dictated a repudiation. She also testified she saw no marks on Wendel other than a scab on his ear. He had asked her to look at bruises on his legs, but she hadn't. Knowing the bruises would help verify the torture claim, Quinn wasn't about to give up easily. A series of questions and answers followed that must have been frustrating to Quinn.

Quinn: When he said, "Anna Bading, I show you the bruises on my legs," did you look?

Bading: No. There was no occasion to, Mr. Quinn.

Quinn: When he said "Look, they are black and blue," did you look?

Bading: No, I did not. He was sitting in a chair.

Quinn: When Wendel called on you to look at his legs, why didn't you?

Bading: After all, I am a woman and he and I were in a room together.

In his cross-examination, Davis brought up a previous occasion when Wendel reportedly tied himself up and falsely reported his pharmacy robbed. This was a plus for the defense because it not only underscored Wendel's untrustworthiness, it showed he had a history of falsely claiming to be a crime victim.

Quinn introduced telephone records and questioned various telephone operators to establish the series of calls between Ellis Parker's home and Harry Bleefeld's house in Brooklyn. Parker was being tied to the kidnappers step by step.

A very nervous Gus Lockwood was next to testify for the prosecution. Quinn quickly established Lockwood's status as an employee of the governor. Lockwood was questioned about his relationship with Parker and his involvement with Wendel's stay at the Four Mile Colony. He admitted guarding Wendel and said Wendel had even been invited out with him several times. He too said he saw no bruises, but that Wendel's shoes had been taken away at one point because Wendel was hitting himself on the legs with them. Lockwood spoke of bizarre behavior on the part of Wendel. At one point, Wendel held seances to commune with the spirits. At this point, Judge Clark could not resist interposing. "What would Wendel say; let me have the next trance?"

The courtroom exploded in laughter.

But in spite of the laughter and the general feeling both Anna Bading and Gus Lockwood helped Parker's case, Lockwood did provide one piece of information that damaged the defense's theory that Wendel encouraged Parker's suspicion of Wendel's guilt. Although he said Parker was not told about it, Lockwood said Wendel paced up and down and raved occasionally.

Quinn: What did you do about his ravings?

Lockwood: I just sat there and played solitaire.

Quinn: How would he rave?

Lockwood: He would pace up and down and he would talk to himself.

Quinn: What would he say?

Lockwood: He kept saying he did not kidnap the Lindbergh baby.

This was not the behavior of a man trying to con people into thinking he was guilty. It was precisely the kind of behavior expected of an innocent man pressured to confess to a crime. Lockwood also spoke of the presence of Theodore Kass, another of Wendel's guards, at Four Mile Colony. This too was damaging to the defense, because Theodore Kass was from Brooklyn and was associated with Murray Bleefeld. Theodore Kass was a direct link between Parker and the kidnappers.

Harry Weiss testified about Wendel's kidnapping and torture in great detail. In addition, Weiss identified Ellis Jr. as the man on the scene in Brooklyn and the man who directed the torture.

Murray Bleefeld told a similar story to Weiss', but added several additional sensational details. To the defense, Bleefeld was a dangerous witness because, unlike Weiss, he was actually involved in the planning with Ellis Parker. According to Bleefeld, Parker once told him Wendel claimed he could get the Lindbergh baby back and offered to split the ransom money. If Wendel really made the offer, it certainly would have been good reason for Parker to suspect him. Bleefeld revealed Ellis Jr. and Wendel once drove to the Lindbergh estate and Wendel revealed an intimate knowledge of the details of the crime. In spite of testifying to reasons Parker might have legitimately suspected Wendel, Bleefeld's testimony damaged Parker's case. Not only did Bleefeld bolster Wendel and Weiss's kidnapping and torture testimony, he provided details of Ellis Parker's role.

Meanwhile, the defense team turned up a letter Weiss wrote to Kings County District Attorney Geoghan claiming Wendel told Weiss privately he was indeed the Lindbergh kidnapper and no one would suspect him because he was working on the case with Ellis Parker. Weiss claimed this revelation was what inspired him to beat Wendel in Brooklyn. The prosecution claimed any such story Wendel told was under duress. The letter appears to be an attempt by Weiss to provide himself with a plausible justification for his participation in Wendel's torture. It was written to Geoghan when Weiss thought he would only be charged with assault, so a letter justifying the torture would be a handy thing to have on file.

On cross-examination, Davis hammered away at exact times and dates of meetings to both discredit Bleefeld and set up an alibi for the Parkers. The questioning was detailed to the point of tedium. Davis brought up Bleefeld's underworld connections and shady past, tying him in with people whose credibility was low. Davis hit paydirt when he asked Bleefeld if Wendel ever made a voluntary confession before his written one. Bleefeld replied Wendel confessed and talked freely about the crime for about four hours. Of course, this didn't prove Wendel was actually guilty, but it supported the defense's contention Wendel had given Parker plenty of reason to believe he was.

One of the next witnesses was Theodore Kass, who removed all possible doubt about Parker's involvement in the Brooklyn kidnapping. As others had testified, Kass was one of the men Parker had guarding Wendel at the Four Mile Colony. Kass testified he was recruited for the job in Brooklyn by none other than Harry Weiss. If the Brooklyn kidnappers recruited people to guard Wendel at Four Mile Colony, Ellis Parker was obviously working with them.

Former warden Mark Kimberling, now head of the New Jersey State Police created headlines when he revealed Parker's visits to Hauptmann, but he did not give many details, or even the dates. Quinn attempted to find out just who authorized these visits, but was met with vigorous objections from Parker's attorneys, so no one else was mentioned.

Wendel's wife and a friend who was a plumber testified Wendel was with them on the night of the Lindbergh kidnapping, providing some unintended comic relief. The plumber, Carl Markau, testified he was helping Wendel connect some pipes in his basement laboratory. Davis was suspicious.

"Why didn't you do Wendel's work in the afternoon, rather than wait until night?" Davis demanded.

"That was my business," Markau replied.

"Well it's my business now," Davis snapped back.

Davis then went on to question the increasingly exasperated Markau about what he had done in the afternoon.

"If you knew a little something about plumbing you wouldn't ask them foolish questions," Markau replied to the laughter of the spectators.

Amid the laughter, however, one interesting bit of Markau's testimony went unnoticed. He claimed he and the Wendels heard the news of the kidnapping on the radio about 10:00 PM. Since this was about the time the kidnapping was discovered and the first news bulletin didn't go out until well after 11:00 PM, the claim begged for some good follow-up questions, but the opportunity passed.

David Wilentz testified how Parker had turned down his request to testify at Hauptmann's trial, saying he knew nothing about the case. But Hunterdon Prosecutor Anthony Hauk had the most damaging testimony when he revealed he asked Parker what tied Wendel to the Lindbergh kidnapping. According to Hauk, Parker had answered "I have nothing against him; not a thing."

With that, the prosecution rested its case. Quinn had done most of what he set out to do. He showed the crime had been committed and had tied Ellis Parker to it. He had been less successful establishing Parker's motive as self-gain. Wendel had taken some hits from Davis's cross-examination, but his basic story was unshaken.

Parker's attorneys immediately filed a motion for a directed verdict of dismissal, claiming the Lindbergh Law required the kidnapper must have expected ransom, reward, or other compensations. Parker, they said, did not expect to profit and no evidence had been presented to show otherwise. The only party to profit, claimed Harry Green, was Wendel himself because on cross examination, Wendel admitted being paid for his Liberty Magazine articles.

Judge Clark agreed there was no direct monetary profit motive shown, but the "or otherwise" clause in the Lindbergh Law could apply to Parker if he hoped to profit by enhancing his reputation.

The defense also claimed there was no kidnap across state lines, since Wendel requested he be taken to Parker. His transport, therefore, was voluntary. Parker's attorneys requested all testimony about events subsequent to Wendel being taken to Parker's home be thrown out on the grounds that the Lindbergh Law only pertained to kidnapping across state lines and that act ceased to apply as soon as Wendel was in New Jersey. Finally, they protested the case was being tried in Essex County when the alleged crime had occurred in Burlington County. In all, there were 11 reasons for a directed verdict of acquittal. The motions were all denied and the trial continued.

Ellis Parker's defense team now had to decide how to best fight his case now that the prosecution was concluded. They hoped to damage Wendel's credibility enough to generate a reasonable doubt about the Parkers' guilt, but Wendel stubbornly stuck to his story, despite tripping up on some of the details. Worse still, several other witnesses corroborated at least parts of his testimony. Now that the opportunity to undermine Wendel had been lost, James Mercer Davis knew he had only one good card to play: the reputation and credibility of Ellis Parker himself. In a case that came down to conflicting testimony, Davis believed the word of Ellis Parker would carry more weight than that of Paul Wendel, so he constructed his defense to emphasize Parker's long-standing reputation and his stature as America's greatest detective. No reasonable jury would take the word of an erratic man like Paul Wendel over a solid and well regarded defender of the public such as Ellis Parker.

The troubling question was, would Ellis Parker be up to the task? He was not in the best of health, appearing restive, tired and often cranky. He plainly resented defending his actions. The Old Chief was accustomed to asking the questions, not answering them. Could he do it? If the thoughtful, clever, and professional Ellis Parker came across on the stand, Davis felt they had a chance. If not, the outlook could be grim.

Chapter 16
The Trial of Ellis Parker
The Defense -- The Verdict
1937

James Mercer Davis opened for the defense on May 26. He put forth the theory Wendel gave Parker ample reason to suspect him of the Lindbergh kidnapping and most of the other witnesses lied about Parker's role. Murray Bleefeld, he said, planned the kidnapping on his own, although whether to profit or help his friend Parker was not clear. Wendel led everyone on and ultimately was responsible for whatever happened.

"We will prove," Davis said, "Wendel told Parker he could affect the return of the baby alive. He aroused Parker's suspicions with his constant reports that he could do this." Davis then claimed the defense would show Bleefeld and Weiss had lied in their testimony.

"We will prove," he concluded, "the Parkers could not have been at the various places at the times Bleefeld and Weiss said they were."

The uphill battle to acquit the Parkers began. The defense led off with a move that was, at best, ill advised. To establish Parker's superior credibility by reminding the jury of his great history and reputation, Davis presented a parade of character witnesses, including various Burlington County officials, judges, bank presidents and a state senator. This was certainly a more impressive set of backers than Wendel had been able to produce, but character witnesses, especially "important people" witnesses are of limited value in a trial. Jurors often resent being told what to think of a person before they have even heard any evidence, and most juries realize that a person's good reputation doesn't necessarily prove him innocent. Everyone has friends who will speak well of him, even criminals. In Ellis Parker's case, character witnesses would be particularly ineffective since everyone was familiar with Parker and knew his good reputation already.

The character witnesses' testimony was even less effective because most of them turned out to have little direct knowledge of Parker's methods and tactics, let alone his actions regarding Wendel. Their testimony was mostly generic statements to the effect that Parker's reputation was good and people respected him, something the eight women and four men of the jury already knew. Worse yet, the witnesses gave Quinn the perfect opening to bring up questionable aspects of Parker's past.

In his cross-examination, Quinn asked the character witnesses if they had read *The Cunning Mulatto,* the 1935 book chronicling some of Parker's cases. Almost no one had read it, which did little to boost anyone's credibility with the jury. Quinn had done his homework; he knew about the Honest John Brunen case when Parker had his prime suspect kidnapped to obtain a confession. Quinn grilled each witness about the incident and none were aware of it. Quinn also asked about the Rancocas Creek Rumrunning Scandal of 1925, and the fact Parker had been suspended as a result. None of the character witnesses seemed to be aware of the incident and some were openly surprised to hear about it.

When told about the Honest John Brunen case, one witness didn't believe Parker had ever been involved with anything like kidnapping. "I don't think he would kidnap a puppy dog," he said.

"Stick around and you'll see," snapped Quinn.

Parker was ill served by his well-meaning friends. If they had been better informed about the man they were trying to help they would have known about Parker's suspension, and able to say the suspension was a temporary measure to avoid public criticism and not based on any actual wrongdoing. Also, if they had read *The Cunning Mulatto* all the way through, they would have known the suspect Parker allegedly kidnapped in the Brunen case was guilty of the murder Parker was investigating.

With this line of questioning, Quinn was able to undermine whatever positive effect the witnesses might have had while at the same time reminding the jury repeatedly of things that reflected badly on Parker.

Clifford Cain, one of Parker's detectives, then testified he was with Parker in his office on February 22, 1936, a day Murray Bleefeld claimed Parker was in New York. Two other witnesses said they saw Parker in Mt. Holly at different times on that date.

The defense at this point was trying to prove discrepancies in the testimony of Bleefeld and Weiss in hopes of discrediting their entire stories. It seems to have been a tactic born of desperation. Witnesses getting confused about dates is common; it does not necessarily mean they are lying. Still, if they were to sway the jury the defense had to discredit the testimony of Bleefeld and Weiss.

The opposing attorneys continued to battle. Davis questioned Alfred Mullen, a Burlington County court officer who said he had been with Anna Bading on February 6, 1936, a time Murray Bleefeld claimed she was in New York. Judge Clark reminded Mullen of previous telephone evidence showing a call from a Mrs. Bading in New York to Ellis Parker on that date.

"Does that have any effect on your statement that Mrs. Bading was with you at 4:36 PM on that date?" Judge Clark asked.

"No, sir, not a particle of difference," Mullen replied, "My recollection is very clear. Mrs. Bading was with me at 4:30 that afternoon."

Davis was on his feet a moment later, loudly moving for a mistrial, saying the court's action in reading the testimony was an attempt to intimidate the witness and was highly prejudicial. The motion was denied.

Several more alibi witnesses followed, all claiming they were with Parker on days Bleefleld said Parker was elsewhere. Then Davis attempted to enter documents on the Lindbergh baby autopsy and was refused by Judge Clark. This was not the first time Davis tried to get Lindbergh case information into the record. By doing so he hoped to create doubt about the official finding to support Parker's actions. He also wanted to keep reminding the jury of the overriding importance of the case Parker had been trying to solve. The prosecution was just as anxious to keep the Lindbergh case far in the background.

"All the courts in the land settled the Hauptmann case," Quinn thundered, "and Parker is not bigger than the courts. That case is ended and has no place here."

"It is not finished," retorted Davis. "If it were, we wouldn't be here."

Among the witnesses that followed this exchange was a magazine editor who said he had offered Ellis Parker $1,000 a month as a contribution to his investigation and Parker had refused the money. Former Hauptmann defense attorney C. Lloyd Fisher testified he offered Parker money for helping with the Hauptmann defense on several occasions and Parker refused. Quinn objected to this testimony but was overruled. The defense attempted to counter claims Parker acted partly in hopes of gain in the Wendel kidnapping by showing occasions when he could have profited from the Lindbergh case but hadn't.

Anna Bading appeared again, this time as a witness for the defense, telling how she met with Wendel and he dictated a report about his Lindbergh investigations as late as January 1936. This testimony was to bolster the defense's contention Wendel was actively encouraging Parker to suspect him of involvement right up until Murray Bleefeld and the others kidnapped him.

One problem Parker's attorneys never overcame was

suggesting a credible motive for Murray Bleefeld and the others to kidnap Wendel without any involvement from the Parkers. The attorneys suggested Wendel contributed to it and the kidnapping was a hoax; or, that Murray Bleefeld did it to help Parker without Parker's knowledge; or, did it to sell Wendel's confession to the press, but, they were never able to generate any significant evidence or any theory of the case that was convincing.

By the seventh week of the trial, the defense had scored some points and cast some doubt on previous unfavorable testimony, but the evidence still pointed firmly to the Parkers. There was only one person whose testimony could sway the jury and save the day: Ellis Parker himself. The trial would turn on Ellis Parker's testimony and everyone in the courtroom knew it.

On June 10, Ellis Parker finally took the stand in his own defense. The Old Chief looked gaunt and tired. He had lost weight and looked like a sick man as he took the oath. Since he was a Quaker, he did not swear on the Bible, but simply said "I affirm." Parker then settled himself in the witness chair and leaned forward expectantly. It was a dramatic moment and the courtroom was hushed with anticipation. After all the charges and countercharges, all the rumors and theories, and all the breathless newspaper articles, here was the one man who could explain it all. What would he say?

Realizing the garrulous and prickly nature of his client, Davis asked Parker open ended questions that gave him full reign to answer in his own way. The New York Times described Parker's courtroom manner the next day;

"The detective, whose success in solving crimes according to his own homely method gained him fame far beyond the borders of Burlington County, gave a vivid description of his technique in his own independent investigation of the Lindbergh crime. He tried to tell the story in his own way, with occasional sallies of humor, piquantly turned phrases, and with a stubborn insistence that brought several reprimands from the court. He paid little attention to admonitions of counsel on either side when his explanations went beyond the procedural rules; he became argumentative and a bit testy when anybody interfered with him and he seemed to miss the cigar he customarily smokes when engaged in mental activities. Whenever a recess was called he hurried to the corridor to retrieve a half-smoked Panatela which he kept inconspicuously parked on the top of a bulletin board."

Davis led Parker through his early career up to the Lindbergh case. Parker talked about his earlier statement to the press that police should be withdrawn from the Lindbergh estate. He told about the phone call a day or so later from someone who asked if he had meant what he said. When he said he had, the caller said "Well, I trust you will interest yourself in the case without publicity and I am sure you will have success." It was then, Parker said, he believed he was talking to the Lindbergh kidnapper.

"What did you base that opinion on?" asked a puzzled Judge Clark.

"Well now, when he said 'I trust you will interest yourself in this case without publicity', there was caution," Parker relied, "and 'I am sure you will have success.', which was an assurance. So I had caution and assurance."

The judge was probably still confused with this explanation, but he was no doubt clear about one thing; Ellis Parker was a man who could draw large inferences from very little information.

Parker then testified Wendel showed up at his office the next day offering to work on the Lindbergh case and hinting he was in touch with the kidnappers. Parker testified about the fiasco with Calabrese, and other wild goose chases Wendel led him on, and how he came to suspect Wendel of the crime.

"From the things he told me I knew he either had done it or had something to do with it," Parker insisted. "Soon after the kidnapping, Wendel told me that when the kidnapper was driving on the Lindbergh road, a man in a nearby house, swinging a lantern saw him. He showed my son the house. In it lived David Moore. I took a statement from him. Since no one knew anything about this I figured Wendel was the kidnapper or knew who the kidnapper was."

"Any other reason?"

"Yes," Parker replied. "After the baby's body was found, it would have been a good out for Wendel. He could have said it was a closed book. Instead he swore it was not the body of the Lindbergh child and through him the real child could be returned."

When Parker was asked whether he thought the body

thought to be the Lindbergh baby was correctly identified, Parker said he didn't know what to believe. When pressed, he gave an explanation that confused everyone.

"I thought they said it was the Lindbergh baby because if it had been reported all over the country where it was seen, it was a police trick, a purpose so that if anybody did communicate, they would know it was the actual kidnappers, and I thought it was a police trick and I didn't want to interfere with them. That was my thought."

Parker admitted his meetings with Wendel, saying it was important to keep in touch, but heatedly denied he met Murray Bleefeld in New York or ever met Schlossman or Weiss. If ever there was a place for a witness to be cool and detached, this was it, but Parker wasn't. At one point, while Davis was going over the details of dates and meetings, Parker grew so indignant Davis had to plead with his client to have patience with him.

Parker's testimony went pretty much as expected. He denied any involvement in the Brooklyn kidnapping and continued to claim Wendel was in voluntary custody at Four Mile Colony. He affirmed his belief in Wendel's guilt and some of the reasons Wendel was a suspect. He filled in some of the details of his Lindbergh investigation, his dealings with Bleefeld, his relationship with Wendel, and his actions when Wendel appeared at his home. Although Parker was occasionally cantankerous, it went about as well as Davis had hoped. Davis must have had concerns about the cross-examination to come. If Parker got testy with his own attorney, how would he react to hostile probing by Quinn? Davis would soon find out.

Beginning his cross-examination, Quinn asked Parker if he still believed Wendel was guilty of the Lindbergh kidnapping, When Parker said he did, Quinn asked him to explain and Parker started reading from Wendel's confessions. Quinn protested Parker should not be allowed to simply read whatever he wanted, but should answer direct questions. He was overruled. When Quinn questioned Parker on discrepancies in his Grand Jury testimony on several occasions, Parker claimed the court reporter had transcribed incorrectly and he wasn't responsible for what they wrote down. Parker's combativeness was beginning to show, especially when Quinn asked Parker to tell him about his conversation with Murray and Jeff Bleefeld the first time they met. Parker, apparently thinking the request too vague, refused.

"You ask me questions and I will answer them," Parker grumbled.

"Give me that conversation," Quinn repeated.

"No, I won't. I won't tell you anything unless I am asked a question."

"You have to give me that conversation," Quinn demanded.

Possibly thinking he should intervene before his client was found in contempt, Davis sprang to his feet.

"What will you do to him if he doesn't give it to you?" he asked.

"The court will make him give it," Quinn replied.

"Oh no it won't," Parker insisted. "You ask me a question and I will answer it. Now what do you want to know?"

"I want that conversation."

"Well, I will tell you to the best of my recollection," Parker replied, "but if you interrupt me, I won't tell you anything."

He then related the conversation. The whole exercise seemed to be an attempt by Parker to control the questioning.

The drama continued when Quinn asked Parker about his habit of doing favors
for people, implying Parker had other motives.

Quinn- You are just a kindly old man willing to do favors for strangers?

Parker- Yes, I would do a favor if I could for anybody.

Quinn- Were you a kindly old man when you told the Mercer County Grand Jury you wish you had shot Wendel in the back?

Parker- I was not.

Quinn- What? You now say that you didn't say you wish you had shot Wendel? (Apparently Quinn thought Parker said "I *did* not.")

Parker- I didn't say that. I said I was not in a kindly frame of mind. I might have said that.

Quinn- Then you did say you were sorry you didn't shoot Wendel?

Parker- I don't think I said it. I think I said I wished someone had knocked me in the head for not throwing Wendel in jail the minute I got him.

A few more interesting exchanges followed.

Quinn- Did you talk to Wendel during the time Hauptmann was being tried?

Parker- Yes

Quinn- What did he say?

Parker- He said it was a shame because the German was nothing more than a money passer.

And;

Quinn- Did you tell Wendel if the baby was returned you would be in line to head the state police?

Parker- No. I wouldn't have the job if they handed it to me on a silver platter.

And;

Quinn- Did Wendel deny he had taken the Lindbergh child in this conversation?

Parker- No.

Quinn- Did he admit it?

Parker- Yes.

And;

Quinn- Did you tell him (Wendel) that you ran the country and could do as you pleased?

Parker- Why, he's an educated man and he knows different.

Quinn asked Parker about Theodore Kass, the Four Mile Colony guard recruited by Harry Weiss in Brooklyn. Parker claimed he didn't know Weiss or how he came to be at the Four Mile Colony. Quinn then asked why Parker, having received Wendel's confession, sat on it for 33 days. Parker's answer was the last thing he should have said under the circumstances.

"I don't have to answer to anyone when I investigate a

case."

His attorneys must have winced.

Quinn also got Parker to admit hiding Ellis Jr. at his High Street home.

"Did you not state," demanded Quinn, "you did not know where your son was?"

"If I'd have told anyone," Parker replied, "I'd have been a damn fool for telling."

When the cross-examination finally ended, there were no revelations beyond Parker's claim that Wendel verbally confessed to him. However, Parker did establish he still believed Wendel was guilty and he had reasons for doing so. He also admitted telling Governor Hoffman about the confession before it was made public, and filled in some details about meetings and events. Parker sometimes came across as combative and independent, characteristics that fit all too well with a person who would kidnap a suspect to force a confession regardless of what proper procedure dictated.

Parker's team decided not to put Ellis Jr. on the stand. Davis claimed there was no need because the testimony showed the prosecution witnesses were unworthy of belief. The real reason was probably to deny Quinn another opportunity to find inconsistencies. Ellis Jr. would no doubt have been reduced to making the same flat denials as his father without having his father's prestige to carry it off. Another factor was that in federal court, the prosecution is not allowed to bring a defendant's refusal to testify to the jury's attention, and the jury is instructed to draw no unfavorable inferences.

The move took the prosecution by surprise, but they soon recovered and put on a series of rebuttal witnesses who pecked away at various defense witness statements. The only notable part of this phase was when Quinn accused Parker of winking at his attorneys and Harry Green made another motion for a mistrial on the grounds that Quinn's accusation was "unfair and prejudicial."

Quinn made the closing summation for the prosecution on June 22, repeating the charges he made in the opening statement, and pointing out where the defense had failed to show what they had promised. The defense said it would show Parker asked Bleefeld to find Wendel in New York, and it would show Bleefeld and Weiss tried to sell their story for gain. No such proof had ever been produced, Quinn said. He ridiculed Parker's belief in Wendel's guilt and held Weiss and Schlossman up as victims because they had already been sentenced to 20 years in prison for what they did for Parker.

"No man should be permitted to capitalize on a little life for the sole purpose of making him feel he is the greatest detective of all time and to satisfy a very dangerous ego." Quinn said. "Parker was not a great detective, but a built-up detective, and committed a greater sin than any racketeer in attempting to perpetrate fraud on the courts of this country and on every family in this country by producing Wendel and his ridiculous confession as Hauptmann was about to die." Then in a dramatic moment, Quinn pointed his finger at Parker and said "Mr. Parker, you're never going to clear your conscience for what you've done; never!"

Ex-governor George Silzer led off for the defense in their closing statement, telling the jury, incorrectly, that in order to prove kidnapping, the prosecution had to prove Parker did it for some material gain. This, he said had not been proved. Furthermore, Bleefeld was "an intelligent crook; a smooth individual in a $25 suit, his hair glazed down and his face washed." Such a man could not be believed.

If Hauptmann had not been found, Silzer claimed, Wendel would have been the man tried for the crime. As he said this, a man in the back of the courtroom suddenly shouted his agreement, then ran forward, put his hand on Wendel's shoulder and said "That's the man." Police quickly hustled the man out of the room and into custody. He was Phillip Moses, the taxi driver who claimed he drove three men to the St. Raymond's Cemetery the night the ransom was paid. Moses had testified at the Hauptmann trial.

Harry Green then took over the summation and also attacked the character and reliability of the prosecution witnesses once again. Finally, Davis finished up with the suggestion Bleefeld's testimony was the result of a deal with Geoghan. Possibly wishing to draw attention away from Parker's performance as a witness, and playing to the eight female jury members, Davis compared the shiftiness of the prosecution witnesses with the businesslike demeanor of Anna Bading. Davis compared Bleefeld and Wendel's version of events with Anna Bading's and said he was willing to rest his entire case "on the word of this good little woman."

. The judge, in his charge to the jury, told them for a

finding of guilty, it was necessary to find Wendel was kidnapped, held for ransom, reward or otherwise, and transported against his will to New Jersey. If any element was missing, the Parkers were entitled to an acquittal. Judge Clark reviewed the testimony and commented on some of the issues raised. At 12:45 the jury retired to deliberate and to consider more than 5,500 pages of testimony.

The jury was left with the testimony of three witnesses for the prosecution who were probably less than completely trustworthy and conflicting testimony from one witness for the defense who was well respected and a law enforcement officer of many years. The defense should have had the advantage except for one persistent fact; the version of events put forward by the prosecution made more sense and was more consistent with the evidence than the one put forward by the defense. The evidence fit well with the scenario of Wendel and the others, but not with the picture painted by Parker's attorneys.

The jury deliberated through the afternoon. Whatever they decided, Paul Wendel, the center of the case, would not be there to see it. As he finished lunch, accompanied by a federal marshal, two men accosted him and tried to force him into a car. The marshal stopped them and one of the men claimed he had loaned Wendel $2,000 bail money years before and had forfeited it. He was trying to bring Wendel back to Trenton so he could reclaim his money. People seemed to be standing in line for a chance to kidnap the hapless Wendel, so he was taken back to Brooklyn for his own safety.

At 6:45 PM, the jury sent a message to Judge Clark

asking if it was possible to vote for conviction with a recommendation of leniency. The judge replied that it would, and he would consider such a recommendation carefully. The jury took four ballots, but finally reached a decision. After the nine week trial, the jury had taken six hours and 15 minutes to deliberate. At 7:00 PM the jury filed back into the courtroom.

Ellis Parker sat chewing gum, one hand on the back of a nearby chair and the other shielding his eyes from the glare of the overhead lights. Ellis Jr. bit his nails, and everyone in the courtroom listened with anticipation. Jury foreman Anna Voightlander rose and announced the verdict; guilty with a recommendation of leniency. The Parkers looked at each other for a moment as Ellis Jr.'s wife Katherine cried softly. At the request of Parker's attorneys the jury was polled individually and gave the same verdict. Judge Clark thanked the jury and set June 30 for sentencing.

The newspapers were generally favorable about the guilty verdict and published editorials praising the judge and the jury. The New York Sun quoted extensively from *The Cunning Mulatto* account of Parker's kidnapping in the John Brunen case and dryly concluded;

"In his long career as a detective, Parker may have tried kidnapping on other occasions. The two of which the public knows do not suggest that kidnapping has been one of his most useful instruments."

The Trenton Evening Times, like several other papers

praised the "eight housewives" on the jury, breathlessly jumping to the somewhat premature conclusion that "women are not so easily bamboozled by queer explanations and fancy excuses."

For a few days, there was talk of possibly a fine and suspended sentences for the Parkers, but on June 30, Judge Clark put an end to the speculation. He made a sentencing statement that was a good summary of the case and why it went the way it did.

"I think that the way you met the accusation of the United States was an unwise one," he began. "I do not know whether to hold you or one or more of your counsel responsible for that. However, it is my judgment that in the first place you seemed to be making every effort to take advantage of the technicalities of the law. In the second place, once the trial itself was actually reached, it seemed to me that there again your method of meeting this accusation was an unwise one."

"I think the jury could not help feel that your defense that you had nothing to do with the kidnapping and torture and this holding of Wendel was not a true one. It seemed to me that the jury, whether they believed the witnesses Wendel or Bleefeld, or whether they did not believe Wendel or Bleefeld, could not escape from the overwhelming coincidence of the fact that you, Ellis Parker Jr., were registered in New York; that there were these telephone calls, entirely unexplained; that Theodore Kass was a guard at the New Lisbon Colony (also known as the Four Mile Colony) for Wendel, and that he was a friend and had been produced by Weiss and Bleefeld.

"I am not, of course, going to review the evidence, but it seemed to me that the jury could not avoid those facts as pointing undeniably to the fact that your defense was not a truthful one; and it seemed further to me that in making that defense you weakened the defense that you or your father, Mr. Parker believed that Wendel was actually the kidnapper and murderer of the Lindbergh child.

"I also think that it was difficult for the jury, or for anyone else who heard the evidence to believe your story, Mr. Parker, about the telephone call from this mysterious person whose voice you did not recognize, although you had known Wendel for years; but whether that was difficult for them or not, certainly the fact that you did not frankly say that you had attempted to give what is popularly known as the third degree to Wendel in some belief that he was actually the kidnapper, your lack of frankness in this respect, it seemed to me, influenced, and properly influenced the jury."

By this time, it must have been apparent that no suspended sentence was in the cards. But Judge Clark was not finished.

"I have the impression, Mr. Parker, again I want to say that I say this with no personal criticism or personal judgment; but I have the impression that your life as a law enforcement officer and the position of power that you have reached in the community have given you the feeling that you are above the law, that what you want to do is the right thing to do whether the law permits it or not, and that is the cause of your having made a mockery, because that is what I think the result is, made a mockery of the processes of justice in New Jersey.........Again I say to you Mr. Parker, that I feel that you have been brought to disregard the law by the power that has been given to you in its enforcement. That is a serious thing."

Then Judge Clark sentenced Ellis Parker to six years in the federal penitentiary and Ellis Jr. to three.

Chapter 17
His Last Bow
1937- 1940

The same newspapers that once sang Parker's praises now hailed his conviction. Clearly out of patience with Parker's delays, denials, and attempts to thwart justice, the Newark News said the conviction

"...demonstrated that not all courts and juries are responsive to unseen political pressure....It stripped Mr. Hoffman of every excuse for his refusal to honor Governor Lehman's request for the Parkers' extradition."

The Newark Star Eagle said justice had finally been served, and the Trenton Evening Times criticized the defense strategy of character witnesses and denials. A few papers lamented the tragedy of Parker's downfall, but most showed solid approval. Governor Hoffman had no comment on the conviction except to say the Lindbergh case was still not solved.

Parker's supporters made comparisons to the 1932 kidnapping case of Garett Schenck, a Hopewell fish dealer seized by several private detectives shortly after the Lindbergh kidnapping. The detectives took Schenck to Somerset, Pennsylvania and held him for 76 days while they tried to force a confession from him. Finally, the detectives gave up and released him. Schenck couldn't get anyone to take an interest in his case at first. Federal authorities determined that no violation of federal law had taken place since no ransom was asked. Since Schenck was from New Jersey and the abductors were all from Pennsylvania, there were also jurisdictional issues, so the case languished. Finally Schenck persuaded the Pennsylvania authorities to investigate and arrest the detectives. Eight men were convicted of conspiracy to kidnap. Two of the detectives were fined $500 each, and six were fined $50 each. None of the detectives went to jail.

Of course, the Lindbergh Law only applied to kidnapping for ransom at the time, and the detectives held no official authority to abuse, but the differences in the outcome of the two cases are still startling. Had Ellis Parker handled his part of his case differently, perhaps his sentence would have been almost as light. No one will ever know.

The Parkers were released on bail and returned to Mt. Holly while their attorneys filed the first of several appeals. The wheels of justice turned slowly as the Parkers faced their friends and neighbors as convicted kidnappers.

That December, the Parkers sent a Christmas card to their friends. Underneath a picture of carolers was a poem entitled MY NEW YEAR'S WISH -I'd Rather Have a Friend. Although the card was signed Ellis H. Parker and Family, the poem seemed to be Ellis's answer to the critics who said he had kidnapped Wendel for the money and fame it would bring.

> Some folks I know would rather have
> A million bucks to spend
> But if I had to make my choice
> I'd rather have a friend.
>
> Some people think that fame must be
> Life's greatest dividend
> But if I had to make my choice
> I'd rather have a friend.
>
> For fame is quick to run away
> And leave you high and stranded
> But when you have a real true friend,
> You're never empty handed.
>
> I guess that's why it must be
> At this time of year
> I get to thinking of my friends
> As New Year's Day draws near.
>
> And get a little card perhaps
> Or something just to send
> To the very ones who make me feel
> I'd rather have a friend.

With a federal conviction for kidnapping, and his fate riding on the appeals his lawyers would file, Ellis Parker needed all the friends he could get.

While Ellis Parker fought to stay out of prison, Paul Wendel had gone from a small time wanted man and petty criminal to a celebrity. He had achieved that most valuable moral high ground, victim status, and he was determined to make it pay off. One of the many ironies of the Parker-Wendel affair is for all the talk of how Parker and Hoffman expected to profit from it, the only person who was able to cash in was Wendel himself. He wasted no time doing so.

Soon after Ellis Parker's trial was over, Wendel wrote to Governor Hoffman claiming the $25,000 reward the New Jersey legislature had appropriated for anyone whose efforts led to the conviction of the killer of the Lindbergh baby. Wendel claimed this money because by repudiating his confession, he was backing up the courts that had convicted Bruno Hauptmann. Needless to say, Wendel never collected. The letter, however, is an interesting look into Wendel's thought processes. Even though it had nothing to do with the Lindbergh case, Wendel lists the same string of injustices he had put in the confessions, claiming the state owed him the money to compensate him for all he had suffered at the hands of state officials. Some of his complaints go back to 1919. He even claims his son was laid off from his WPA job in retaliation for his testimony. Wendel is clearly a man with a load of grievances. His efforts were for naught however. The governor announced the award would be shared by 110 people. Wendel was not one of them.

Since he was considered a material witness for the Kings County trial of the Parkers still to come, Geoghan put Wendel up in the Towers Hotel in New York at taxpayers' expense. Wendel remained there until New York's Commissioner of Investigation found evidence Wendel padded or outright forged many of his expense bills. Twenty percent of the $10,000 in expenses were estimated to be fraudulent. Wendel was finally turned out of the hotel late in 1938.

In a further effort to capitalize on his ordeal, Wendel wrote "The Hauptmann-Lindbergh Aftermath", published by Loft Publishing of Brooklyn. His efforts to inflate his importance came to full flower in this book. In the first few pages he actually says his abduction was "the most vicious crime committed in the 20th century", a claim that must have come as a surprise to the Lindberghs.

In keeping with the exaggerated sense of his own importance displayed earlier, Wendel actually ended the book with a thank you to God for his Divine Intervention:

"JUSTICE at last caught up with the Parkers. Almighty God, who created heaven and earth, heard my prayers. He raised up friends to fight the battle for me. Praise be to God!"

But Wendel's efforts to cash in on his experience did not end there. He promoted the book with mailings that brought complaints about using the mails to defraud. The book's sales proved considerably more modest than the author.

In 1938, Wendel sued the governor and the State of New Jersey in federal court, accusing them of complicity in his kidnapping since the Parkers were acting under the governor's authority. He also instituted libel lawsuits against several New York newspapers, including the New York World Telegram, because of some of the unflattering things they had printed about him. The cases were all dismissed. Governor Hoffman referred to Wendel as "that scoundrel."

On January 11, 1938, the New York Court of Appeals set aside the Kings County conviction of Weiss and Schlossman and ordered a new trial. Weiss and Schlossman were not allowed to present evidence they had acted in good faith because they thought they were acting under authority of law. In their original trial, the judge ruled that intentions did not matter and excluded testimony about Parker's assurances. The appeals court ruled the testimony should have been admitted.

Harold Hoffman's term as governor came to an end and former governor A. Harry Moore replaced him. In Brooklyn, District Attorney Geoghan wasted no time renewing his request for extradition of the Parkers to Kings County for trial on state kidnapping charges. As the new governor pondered this political hot potato, a federal Grand Jury in Kings County handed down indictments for the Parkers, along with Bleefeld, Weiss, and Schlossman for violation of the Lindbergh Law in New York. Because of Federal jurisdiction, the governor did not have to agree to extradition and the Federal Court in Newark ordered the Parkers to report for removal proceedings on March 26.

By early March 1938, the Parkers had been convicted in one federal court, indicted and about to be removed for trial in another federal court, and indicted in a New York court all for the same crime. Feeling trapped and persecuted by a system that didn't understand or appreciate him, Ellis was in no mood to cooperate.

The Parkers failed to appear for the removal proceedings on March 26, and the court issued bench warrants for their arrest. For three days police searched for the Parkers until Federal Judge John Boyd Davis, at the request of James Mercer Davis, issued an order on March 29 that allowed the Parkers to turn themselves in to the nearest federal judge. On April 1, the Parkers surrendered to the federal court in Camden.

Parker sorely missed the support he had always gotten from the governor now that Harold Hoffman was out of office. A. Harry Moore had gone out of his way to distance himself from the Parkers when the storm over the Wendel case erupted, but he now sought to help them. He wrote to President Franklin D. Roosevelt asking for a "careful investigation" of the Parkers' case, hinting that executive clemency would be appropriate under the circumstances.

More legal battles followed. The Federal Circuit Court of Appeals denied a petition for a restraining order to prevent the Parkers appearing before Judge Clark at the removal hearing. The Parkers then made an unsuccessful plea based on double jeopardy. Finally in May, the court ordered the Parkers' extradition to Brooklyn to face federal kidnapping charges there. Before the removal hearing could be held, Ellis Jr. was injured in hot water heater gas explosion at his father-in-law's house. The younger Parker burned his face and hands, causing yet another postponement that lasted until the end of the year.

As 1939 began, the Parkers continued to fight against any further trials until the U.S. Circuit Court of Appeals had decided their appeal.

James Mercer Davis, along with Harry Green and George Silzer filed Parker's appeal with the U.S. Court of Appeals for the Third Circuit, listing 483 claims of error in the original trial. During the struggle over who would try the Parkers and where, the coming decision loomed as the Parkers' best hope of escaping imprisonment. The 483 claims of error covered a wide area. The trial should have been held in Burlington County, the judge's charge to the jury was improper, and the judge, in agreeing to the jury's question about whether they could find the defendants guilty with a recommendation of leniency, had encouraged a guilty finding were among the points raised. Finally, on April 11, the three judges issued a ten page decision dismissing the appeal and upholding the conviction. One judge dissented, believing the defendants were entitled to a trial in Mt. Holly rather than Newark.

The only hope left was an appeal to the U.S. Supreme Court. In spite of the money raised, the Parkers were about $2,000 short of what they needed to make the final appeal. During this period, Parker still had the support of many of his friends and most of the citizens of Mt. Holly. Charles Hansbury, who ran the Mt. Holly Herald, organized a Parker Defense Committee to circulate petitions for a presidential pardon, and to raise money for legal expenses. Harry Green encouraged these efforts and made himself available to advise and act as liaison to Ellis Parker. Hansbury's committee raised money, collected thousands of signatures and pushed the cause through newspaper articles. Later, Hansbury bickered with the rival Burlington Herald, and the effort slowed. Not everyone was in Parker's corner, however. Some Mt. Holly residents thought Ellis Parker should stop the delays and serve his sentence.

Somehow, the Parker team raised the money. Their appeal was made on May 10 but the Supreme Court refused to reverse the convictions, or even to hear the case. On the same day, Governor Moore received a reply from President Roosevelt to his request for clemency for the Parkers. Roosevelt regretted he could not help. Executive clemency, he explained, was only considered when the subject became eligible for parole, and a person was only eligible for parole after having served at least 1/3 of his sentence. Now, after all the battles with courts, judges, and appeals, there were no options left. The Parkers would have to go to prison. Sadly, Ellis tied up his affairs as best he could, and told Cora and the children not to worry. He told a stunned neighbor that he wouldn't be seeing them for a while because he had to go to jail, and assigned the ever-faithful Anna Bading to look after his interests while he was away. Late spring in Mt. Holly had always been one of his favorite times of the year, but now the familiar sights, like his former life, seemed like a dying friend he would never see again.

On June 22, 1939, Ellis Parker and his son reported to Pennsylvania's Lewisburg Federal Penitentiary to serve their sentences. Ellis Parker became prisoner number 8735. The former Sherlock Holmes of America became a clerk in the prison library. One of the books in the collection may have been a well-thumbed copy of *The Cunning Mulatto and Other Cases of Ellis Parker, American Detective*. He wrote to his wife and family as often as he was allowed (two letters a week.) He was not allowed to have contact with anyone outside the family or his attorney, thereby preventing him from getting his side of the story out to the ever-friendly press. Since the co-conspirators were also in jail (except for Murray Bleefeld who had not yet been sentenced) the only version of the story the public heard was Wendel's.

In July, Ellis wrote Cora in a letter addressed simply "Dear Wife". He was upbeat and optimistic, even giving advice for his old boss Howard Eastwood in his bid for a seat in Congress. In another letter a few days later, he is still upbeat, but mentions feeling bad and wrenching his knee. He was anxiously awaiting any help from Harry Green.

Green had not been idle. For someone who didn't even know Parker only a few years before, he was tireless in his efforts. He wrote to political figures, newspapers, and anyone he thought could help Parker's case. Harry Green acted as unofficial go-between for Parker and the rest of the family.

Anna Bading had gone from being Parker's indispensable assistant to something of a personal representative. Along with Parker's other secretary, Hanna

Lippincott, she not only continued to see that the office ran smoothly, but became the focal point of the Parkers' defense efforts as well. Harry Green wrote directly to her several times to plead for more money and to report on his dealings with the courts and with Ellis. Clint Zeller was officially the Chief of Detectives, but there was little doubt who ran the office.

Back in King's County, New York, District Attorney Geoghan was still pushing for Parker's extradition in spite of the fact Parker was serving time for the same crime. Harry Green wrote a letter to U.S. Attorney General Frank Murphy accusing Geoghan of persecuting Parker as a smoke screen to divert public attention from problems and corruption in his office. Green pointed out Parker's age, bad health, and the double jeopardy aspects of pursuing Parker further. He also accused a district attorney in Geoghan's office of conspiring with Paul Wendel to use the action to bring pressure to help Wendel's civil suit.

Camden City Clerk Clay Reesman, along with his wife, was one of Parker's early visitors. He found Ellis in good spirits and positive in his outlook.

"I have no bitterness in my heart against anyone," Parker said, "and I still hold my steadfast faith in God."

Ellis didn't dwell upon his present predicament, but talked about his son, and their future plans.

"Once we get out of here, we intend to forget this whole affair and discuss it with no one," Parker told Reesman.

Finally, Reesman rose to leave, but as he and his wife started down the hallway, Ellis called after them. "Be sure and call Mom. Tell her I am all right."

But the Old Chief was not all right. During the first few months of Parker's imprisonment, visitors started noticing a change in his health. Of course, Parker's health had been deteriorating since well before the trial, but incarceration within the stone walls of a federal penitentiary far from home and family accelerated his decline.

After a few months behind bars, and with the threat of further prosecution constantly hanging over him, Ellis Parker continued to deteriorate. On some days, his condition seemed to have affected his mind as well. Harold Hoffman went to Lewisburg to visit Parker in September and was upset to find

"....he seemed to be going out of his mind, he was incoherent, hysterical, and I could hardly talk to him, and he reiterated his innocence and said that he would rather be electrocuted than plead guilty to even assault because he is innocent."

Alarmed, and fearing the King's County indictments hanging over Ellis's head were aggravating his condition, Hoffman arranged a meeting with both Geoghan and Judge Brancato in Brooklyn. Hoffman told them of his visit and of Parker's condition, ending with a plea for Geoghan to withdraw the King's County indictments. Geoghan was noncommittal, but the judge indicated he would consider the request. The result was a postponement of Geoghan's application for removal of the Parkers to Brooklyn to face kidnapping charges. Finally, in December, Geoghan grudgingly announced he would not seek extradition of the Parkers until after they had completed serving their federal sentences.

Cora Parker, meanwhile, had to put the beloved High Street home up for sale to raise money to pay legal debts and keep the wolf from the door. She moved to a much more modest house on Garden Street, a house with absolutely no view of the jail, the courthouse, or the Elks Club. The shore house at Brant Beach, where they had spent so many happy times with children and grandchildren over the years was also sold, as were the several properties Ellis bought at tax sales as an investment. Much of this money went to pay bills sent by James Mercer Davis. Other than Hauptmann, and the Lindbergh family itself, no one paid a heavier price in the Lindbergh kidnapping than the man who tried to solve it.

Because he was allowed limited communication with anyone outside the family, and because his health deteriorated almost from the day he was incarcerated, Parker never got his side of the story out. With so many contacts in the press, he probably could have gotten family members or relatives to give interviews, but he didn't. Perhaps he was just too weary of the whole business and too aware of how the deck was stacked against him. After so many years in Mt. Holly, he was like a plant that had been uprooted and left to die.

Meanwhile, the citizens of Mt. Holly continued to sign petitions for Parker's release. Many believed the Old Chief had been right all along and the politicians silenced him to avoid the embarrassment a Wendel conviction would have caused. There was talk of erecting a statue of Ellis Parker at the courthouse and money was collected for the purpose.

But time was not on his side. In December Hoffman's secretary Bill Conkling wrote to Governor Moore that Ellis Parker's health was failing rapidly. Sensing time might be running out, Harry Green sent a rough draft of an application for a pardon to Lewisburg for Ellis's comments in early January. A few days later, Jane Parker visited her father and wrote an anguished letter to the governor about Ellis's failing health. Everyone worried how much longer Ellis would last. Then Harry Green received a telegram from Ellis Jr.

MY FATHER HAS HAD A SLIGHT STROKE AND IS PARTIALLY PARALYZED PLEASE RUSH THE PAPERS

Late in January, 1940, Ellis Parker was confined to the prison hospital. Although conscious, he was partially paralyzed from his stroke. Suddenly it was clear that what everyone feared might happen was becoming reality: Ellis Parker, America's greatest detective and champion of law enforcement, was probably going to die in prison. Harry Green brought the corrected draft of the pardon application for Ellis to sign, but he must have realized it would probably be too late. Green filed the pardon papers along with the Mt. Holly petition with Daniel M. Lyons, a pardon attorney with the U.S. Department of Justice in Washington. The Mt. Holly petition now had 8,000 names.

Parker, meanwhile, was in the prison hospital slowly recovering from his stroke. An anxious and frustrated Ellis Jr.

was at his side most of the time, trying to coax the Old Chief back to good health. But Ellis was more than sick, he was weary and dispirited. Each night when the iron door to his cell clanked shut behind him, his body ached and his mind wandered back to the life he could no longer enjoy. For a man so long enmeshed in his family, his friends, and his work, the separation was unbearable. Back in Mt. Holly, people were saying what really ailed Ellis was a broken heart. Now the question was whether the pardon or Ellis Parker's failing health would end his prison term first.

On the cold night of February 3, Cora Parker received word her husband Ellis had taken a turn for the worse in the prison hospital. She left for Lewisburg along with the rest of the children in two cars. Edward drove his mother through the frigid and lonely Pennsylvania hills to be at Ellis's side one last time. Everyone had the same thought; after all the years and all the memories, was it really going to end this way; Ellis passing away in a cold gray prison far from home? It was almost 9:00 AM when they pulled up at the forbidding gate of Lewisburg federal prison and rushed to the prison hospital. At Ellis's bedside, Ellis Jr. waited, along with Lieutenant William Hall of the prison guard. When Cora saw the still form of her husband and the look on Ellis Jr.'s face, she fainted. They were too late.

At 3:30 AM on February 4, Ellis Parker died in the prison hospital just hours before his family could arrive at his side. Ellis Parker would never see them or Mt. Holly again. After 40 years, the career of the American Sherlock Holmes had ended in a federal prison.

Harry Green, on hearing the news said he intended to pursue the pardon anyway.

"If there is such a thing as a posthumous pardon," he said in Newark, "I'm going to make every effort to obtain one for Mr. Parker. I want to see the old man vindicated, even if it is too late for him to enjoy the vindication.....I am going to follow through just as if the old man were alive. Furthermore, I am going to make every effort to obtain a pardon for Ellis Parker Jr."

Suddenly, everyone seemed to be sympathetic to Parker. U.S. Attorney J.J. Quinn, who prosecuted Parker agreed the move to obtain a pardon would be carried through, and met with Judge Clark the next day to sign the papers. At the hearing, Quinn assured Harry Green he would recommend the pardon if a legal precedent could be established. Judge Clark said if a legal precedent could be found for a posthumous pardon, he would consider it, and said he had already acted favorably on an application for Parker's parole nearly a month earlier.

"Death is always sad, especially so under these circumstances," Clark said. "Mr. Quinn and I regret it came too soon for our action to help in freeing Mr. Parker to pass his last days at home."

On February 20, U.S. pardons attorney Daniel M. Lyons denied Harry Green's application for a pardon for Ellis Parker.

Ellis Parker Jr. was granted leave to attend the funeral and comfort his mother as best he could. He was accompanied by a guard from the prison. The viewing was held at the house at 509 Garden Street on February 7, 1940. Although the viewing was scheduled for 7:00 PM, people were admitted starting at 4:00, so great was the crowd that had gathered by then. Ellis's wife Cora, having borne so much, could not face her husband's viewing, and remained under a nurse's care in her second floor bedroom. The children, Ellis Jr., Edward, Anthony, Mildred, Helen, Lilyan Sahol, and Charlotte Fullerton were all there to say goodbye. Anna Bading stood with the Parker family, greeting guests. Parker's body was laid out in the modest living room, and a crowd of more than 4000 friends and well-wishers showed up to pay their respects, passing through the house in a line three deep. A private family service would be held the next day, but this night was for the world. People lined up all along Garden Street, their breath making small frosty clouds of vapor that hung in the cold night air. They found it hard to believe Ellis Parker was gone, he had been part of their lives for so long. Everyone could remember the rumpled figure strolling along High Street trailed by puffs of smoke from his pipe, and they could all remember greeting him as simply "Ellis".

Herman Bading, Clint Zeller, now Chief of Detectives, and Cliff Cain were there, along with law enforcement people from all over. Many of them had called on Parker for help on their more difficult cases, and some wondered how they would get by now he was gone. Those who had visited the Parkers at the High Street house were surprised and saddened to see how modestly they were living now.

The Parkers' Garden Street house
(Author photo)

A visibly-moved Harold Hoffman, now out of office, arrived shortly before 9:00 and spoke with Ellis Jr. and Cora. There were tears in his eyes as he approached the casket. Mark Kimberling, former warden of the Trenton State Prison and now head of the New Jersey State Police was present, as was Parker's former boss, Howard Eastwood, now a state senator. Hauptmann's former attorneys Fred Pope and Egbert Rosencanz were present, as was the indefatigable C. Lloyd Fisher, who had fought so hard to save Bruno Hauptmann. As he left, Fisher said to a reporter, "This is a miscarriage of justice; the worst I've ever seen."

James Kirkham, Chief of Detectives of Mercer County and the man to whom Parker had delivered Paul Wendel was there, along with various state and county officials, judges, and politicians. There were some unlikely mourners as well, such as Russell Blackburn, coach of the Philadelphia Athletics, and major league baseball player Tommy Short. Edgar Alcott, a blind boyhood friend of Parker's was led to the casket by his wife. He spoke of how kind Ellis had always been to him.

Among the crowd were dozens of reporters from the newspapers in the Trenton-Camden-Philadelphia-New York area including Russell "Hop" Stoddard, who had been in Parker's office four years earlier when Parker had danced for joy upon receiving Wendel's first confession. Stoddard, along with reporters Joe Campbell, Al Thompson, and Charlie Humes stood quietly outside the house, shivering in the cold, swapping stories of the Old Chief they had all known so well. Depressed, they went to a nearby bar and ordered drinks, specifying new glasses. They drank to the memory of Ellis Parker and when they finished, smashed the glasses so they could never be used again.

Among the mourners was a lone woman who kept to herself but wished to pay her respects. Anna Hauptmann, the widow of Bruno Hauptmann came to Mt. Holly on that cold winter day to say a prayer and to say thank you. She left a floral tribute and stroked Ellis Parker's hand, murmuring simply "Poor Ellis."

Five hundred people attended the funeral the next day. For the funeral procession to Mt. Holly Cemetery, cars lined up for four blocks, and crowds of people stood along the road in respectful silence. On a hill at the Mt. Holly Cemetery on Ridgeway Street, Cora was escorted by son Edward and during the service, leaned on the arm of daughter Helen. Ellis Parker Jr., flanked by his wife Katherine and the prison guard who escorted him from Lewisburg, wept openly at the death of the man he had so admired, as did many of the townspeople. Ellis Parker was laid to rest among the eight children that preceded him. His pink granite headstone was soon buried in floral tributes.

Parker's grave in Mt Holly Cemetery
(Author photo)

As they stood fighting back the tears on that bright and cold hillside that day, the people who had been a part of Ellis Parker's world must have wondered what life would be like without him. Everyone had memories of the Old Chief. Some remembered how he had gotten their stolen property returned and some remembered passing on some gossip that helped him solve a case. Some remembered all the cases he had solved and how proud they had been that their town was home to such a man. A few even remembered how they had gotten in trouble in their youth but had been given a break and put back on the right path by old Ellis. Such people seldom got in trouble again; not out of fear, but because they didn't want to let Ellis down.

As the funeral service concluded, the crowd began to break up and drift away, many speaking in hushed tones and shaking their heads at the sadness of the occasion. Some had also been present at Ellis Parker's testimonial dinner at Medford Lakes six years before and as they made their way home, remembered what he had said on that occasion. After listening to speaker after speaker talk of his ability and his greatness, Ellis responded in a simple and levelheaded fashion, not at all like the ego-driven and ambitious person the papers later made him out to be. He summed up his philosophy in a few words.

"An officer never becomes any bigger than his friends make him...to have the people's confidence is the most valuable asset an officer can have."

Epilogue

Like actors departing after the last act of a long-running play, the principals involved in the second Lindbergh kidnapping dispersed and went in very different directions.

The Lindberghs never returned to the unfinished Hopewell home and moved to England in an attempt to recede from the public eye. Anne Morrow Lindbergh became a respected author. Charles Lindbergh continued his work in aviation, and became a spokesman for the isolationists that opposed America's entry into World War II.

Anna Hauptmann spent the rest of her life believing in her husband's innocence and working for his exoneration, even suing the State of New Jersey for wrongful death in 1985. She died in 1994.

Morris "Mickey" Rosner, the man who became the "intermediary" between the Lindberghs and the criminal world early in the case based on his connections with the underworld was appointed police chief of Long Beach, New York in 1934. The citizens of Long Beach, a town near where JFK Airport stands today, protested this appointment, but to no avail. Two years later, Rosner was dismissed with no reason given.

Warden Mark Kimberling replaced H. Norman Schwarzkopf as head of the New Jersey State Police in 1936.

James Mercer Davis, Parker attorney, died in 1942.

George Silzer, Parker attorney, died in 1940, just a few months after Ellis Parker himself.

Murray Bleefeld, Harry Weiss, and Martin Schlossman each received a sentence of twenty years to life at New York's Sing Sing prison in Ossining, New York. All were paroled a few years later, but soon returned to their old ways. In 1946, Murray Bleefeld and Martin Schlossman were indicted by a federal grand jury for filing false payroll claims in a Brooklyn shipyard of almost $55,000. Murray Bleefeld contacted writer Phillip Scaduto in 1973, promising the "real story" of the Lindbergh kidnapping. Bleefeld told Scaduto Wendel had confessed freely. Ellis Parker, he insisted, had been right all along. Bleefeld explained his earlier, opposite testimony by claiming he had testified as he had on the promise of no jail time. The result was *Scapegoat*, published in 1976.

Judge William Clark was promoted to the Circuit Court of Appeals in 1938 and served in the army in World War II. After the war he became Chief Justice of the Allied Appeals Court at Nuremberg where he considered officials who had abused their offices in a far more terrible way than Ellis Parker ever had.

Colonel H. Norman Schwarzkopf was replaced as head of the New Jersey State Police by Warden Mark Kimberling. For a time, he narrated the popular radio crime show "Gang Busters". He returned to the military in 1940, was promoted to Brigadier General, and later helped to organize and train the Iranian police force. Returning to New Jersey, he became head of the state's Department of Law and Safety. His son is Gulf War commander, "Stormin' Norman" Schwarzkopf. Col. Schwarzkopf died in 1958.

Harold Hoffman never held elective office again, though he was appointed head of the New Jersey Employment Compensation Commission in 1937. According to his daughter Hope, he seldom spoke of Ellis Parker because he found it too painful. In 1954, Governor Meyner received an independent report of mismanagement and possibly theft of state funds in Hoffman's agency. Hoffman was suspended and the new head of the New Jersey Department of Law and Safety, H. Norman Schwarzkopf was asked to investigate. A short time later, Hoffman gave his daughter Ada a letter to be opened only after his death. Two months after that, he was found dead in his hotel room, apparently of a heart attack. The letter to his daughter confessed to a long career of embezzlement. Starting with his efforts to repay a campaign debt in the 1920s, Harold Hoffman had frantically borrowed, transferred, and outright embezzled funds through the various offices he held. In total, Harold Hoffman embezzled more than $300,000.

David Wilentz reentered private law practice. His firm had many well-connected clients, including several casinos in Atlantic City. Wilentz remained active in New Jersey politics until his death in 1988. His son became a justice of the New Jersey Supreme Court. His law firm, Wilentz, Goldman and Spitzer survives. Headquartered in Woodbridge, New Jersey, the firm has over 150 attorneys.

Cora Parker lived in the Garden Street house for another 10 years, then went to live with her daughter until joining Ellis in 1967. She was dependent on her children for support after Burlington County decided she was not eligible to receive any of Ellis's pension. On Christmas each year, she received an unsigned card postmarked Brooklyn, N.Y. and wishing her the best of the season. From the postmark and the handwriting, she was convinced the cards came from Paul Wendel. The cards continued until the 1950s.

Deputy Clint Zeller replaced Ellis Parker as Chief Detective of Burlington County.

Ellis Parker Jr. returned to Lewisburg, fought more court battles, and was even transferred briefly to Brooklyn to stand trial there. He was never retried in King's County or by the New York Federal Court. His Kings County conviction was finally overturned in 1941 and he was paroled from Lewisburg for good behavior in October of that year. On January 30, 1947, he received a presidential pardon from President Truman.

When he returned to Mt. Holly, Ellis Jr. remarried to live a quiet life, and like a battle scared combat veteran, seldom spoke of his experiences. He passed away in 1972 after directing that his father's papers be destroyed upon his death to avoid incriminating the innocent.

Anna Bading continued as the indispensable assistant to Parker's successors until her retirement in 1960. Ever the confidential secretary, she never told her story to the newspapers, never wrote a book, and never disclosed her wealth of inside information. She seldom spoke of the details of the cases she shared with Ellis Parker, even to her sons. She passed away in 1966. When her family went through her effects, they did not find a single document, photograph, or other evidence of her long association with Ellis Parker.

William F.X. Geoghan remained embroiled in scandal and controversy. In 1940, the embarrassed Democratic Party bosses declined to put him up for reelection and nominated William O'Dwyer in his place, thus ending his public career. Geoghan returned to private practice in Brooklyn and represented Paul Wendel against a charge of practicing medicine without a license in 1944. Wendel was convicted.

Paul Wendel enjoyed his brief period of fame, but after his eviction from the Towers Hotel, interest in his case faded. Paul Wendel disappeared from the public eye and resumed his erratic career of unconventional employment. The outstanding warrants were never served, possibly because Wendel remained in Brooklyn at 186 Clinton Street.

About this time, Wendel became associated with another larger than life character in a different field. One of Wendel's father's German friends was a man with the unlikely name of Dr. Benedict Lust. Lust was German immigrant who contracted tuberculosis and been cured by the then-fashionable "natural" methods of Father Sebastian Kniepp, another German who pioneered alternative medicine and what was called natural healing. Lust had been an enthusiastic missionary for natural healing ever since, and became the leading American voice of the movement. He founded the American Naturopathy Society in 1919 and was made its president for life in 1921. He founded a clinic/wellness home in New Jersey called Wellborn, and, some time after the Parker trial, started collaborating with the son of his old friend Reverend Hugo Wendel. With his pharmaceutical background and his flair for non-establishment methods, Paul Wendel soon rose in the movement and in Lust's esteem.

After receiving a certificate as a "Doctor of Metaphysics" from a place called the Church of Divine Metaphysics in 1944, Wendel became a full-fledged practitioner of divine organic healing, and "natural" techniques, or Naturopathy. His mentor, Dr Lust died the next year, but not before naming Wendel as his successor in the movement. Not everyone was impressed with Wendel as Dr. Lust was, however. In 1946, a Kings County Court sentenced Paul Wendel to six months in jail for fraud and practicing medicine without a license, despite (or perhaps because of) his defense attorney, William F.X. Geoghan. The court found that "the tenets of a church must be practiced in good faith and not used as a shield to practice medicine as a business undertaking."

Wendel was not deterred. He self-published several books with such titles as *Bloodless Surgery Technique and Treatment, Magnetic Healing with Hands, Chemistry of Food and Herbs,* and *Father Kneipp's Health Teachings; Instructions in Water Cleansing, Breathing, Food, Herbs, Earth, and Sunshine.*

The title page of *Father Kneipp's Health Teachings,* published in 1947, gives a hint of both Wendel's checkered career and his sense of self-importance. He lists himself as Paul Wendel, N.D., D.C., M.D., D.C., D.D., and lists his qualifications. Among a number of other things, he says he is a *Research Scientist in Naturopathic, Chiropractic, Natural and Divine Healing.*

About the same time, the State of New York decided to license chiropractors. There was a great deal of disagreement over whether or not the practice was actually a profession, but the death of a patient the year before, coupled with pressure from the chiropractors themselves, forced the issue. Wendel, claiming to be a chiropractor along with his other endeavors applied for a license, but it was denied due to his previous conviction. Wendel decided to use his legal training and sue. An article in the New York Times on July 8 of 1948 says;

> *"Paul H. Wendel brought an action in Supreme Court yesterday to compel the State Board of Regents either to*

license him as a chiropractor and a naturopath or to cease interfering with his 'calling.' He characterized the Medical Practices Act that regulates chiropractics as 'monopolistic class legislation.' Mr Wendel was identified by his attorney William Richter as being a figure in the Lindbergh kidnapping case in 1936..."

Wendel continued his rocky path as a naturopath and chiropractor. In 1951, he published *Standardized Naturopathy*, which became a standard reference work among the movement and is still used as a textbook in the several colleges that grant degrees in Naturopathy today. Like Paul Wendel, Naturopathy exists at the fringes of the official world of medicine. But within the narrow confines of this world, Paul Wendel achieved the adulation and respect that eluded him in the traditional world. He died in 1956, his moment of national fame long gone and his name long forgotten by most of the public. Newspapers that once followed his every move did not note his passing.

* * * * *

Almost eighty years have now passed since the kidnapping of the Lindbergh baby. Although the case was called the "Crime of the Century", far greater crimes were to come. During that period, the world has seen horrors that make the kidnapping and murder of a single baby seem insignificant by comparison. A single murder in 1932 should have long since been lost and forgotten in the 20th century's orgy of war, mass killing and violence, but the Lindbergh kidnapping had such a profound and far-reaching effect on so many lives, it continues to resonate today.

At the Lindbergh estate at Hopewell, the Albert Elias Juvenile Facility that now occupies the house gives guided tours upon request because the interest in the Lindbergh case remains so great. The library where Lindbergh sat now has a conference table. The baby's room still contains the tile-faced fireplace, but the room is filled with computer terminals. The adjoining bathroom, where Betty Gow turned on the light so as not to disturb the baby, is now a nurse's office. The shutters have been removed, including the one with the defective latch, and the famous window where the kidnapper entered now holds an air conditioner.

The New Jersey State Police Museum at West Trenton has an entire wall devoted to the Lindbergh case. On display are the ransom notes and the controversial ladder. Researchers constantly access the museum's archives, and its extensive records on the case. According to Mark Falzini, who has been archivist since 1978, the Lindbergh case remains the most popular part of both the museum and the archives. One of the most poignant displays was the baby's sleeping suit, returned by the kidnapper to prove he had possession of the child. This item, along with the flannel undershirt, the thumb guard, and some hair and bone fragments, was returned to the Lindbergh family in 2003 by order of the attorney general and at the request of the

Lindbergh family. Since it came shortly after an attempt to obtain DNA by a reporter from the Orlando Sentinel, this action has encouraged speculation of conspiracy theorists that the whole exercise was intended to remove any possible DNA evidence from public reach.

The Hunterdon County Courthouse at Flemington, New Jersey actually looks better than it did when the Hauptmann trial was held there in 1935. The tangle of overhead wires is gone and the place has been spruced up. The Union Hotel across the street still looks as it did when it was home to both the jurors and the press. Every September, the courthouse is the scene of performances of "The Trial of the Century", a play based on the trial and using actual testimony. The play is usually sold out.

Numerous books and articles are still being written about the Lindbergh case, and an HBO movie based on "The Airman and the Carpenter" by Ludovic Kennedy was made in 1985. A tall slender actor with thick hair portrays the short, bald, and heavyset Ellis Parker in the movie.

At last count, there were over a dozen websites about the kidnapping, including one that postulates that the kidnapping was a hoax. There are also several Internet discussion boards where the Lindbergh case is discussed, argued, and rehashed constantly. Today, Lindbergh is almost as well known for the kidnapping as for flying the Atlantic.

There is only one Internet website devoted to Ellis

Parker and his life. The site is maintained by William Fullerton Jr, Parker's grandson, and the son of daughter Charlotte who so publicly eloped with William Fullerton in 1929.

Another of Ellis Parker's grandsons, Andy Sahol, still lives in the central New Jersey area and keeps a collection of family records and memorabilia. He is presently pursuing a posthumous pardon for his grandfather. Working with several other interested parties, Sahol has worked tirelessly on research that could help his cause. He believes his grandfather was innocent of the crime for which he was convicted and should be not just pardoned, but exonerated. Sahol feels that Parker was the victim of a conspiracy designed to avoid embarrassment to the New Jersey political and legal establishment. Among his research materials, he has obtained medical testimony that the condition that ultimately caused Parker's death also caused his mental facilities to deteriorate and become erratic in the last years of his life, leading him to make errors of judgment he would never have made earlier. Sahol also points to Judge William Clark's history as a member of the Court of Pardons that pardoned Paul Wendel in 1925 as a conflict of interest in Parker's trial. (As stated in this book, Parker attorney George Silzer was a member of that same court.) Sahol has submitted a detailed pardon request to the appropriate federal office, but has received no reply.

Edward Parker, Ellis's last surviving son passed away in Florida in 2006. He was in high school during his father's troubles and seldom discussed the unhappy days in New Jersey. His son Randall Parker runs several popular weblogs such as

Parapundit and Futurepundit.

Ellis Parker was remembered fondly in Mt Holly for a while. Newspaper articles about his exploits were published off and on, and his cartoon likeness even appeared in an issue of Crime Patrol comics, in a highly glamorized version of the Ivy Giberson murder case (the somewhat frumpy Ivy Giberson was depicted as looking like a chorus girl.) The initial drive for a posthumous pardon gradually lost momentum and died, as did a plan to erect a statue of the Old Chief in front of the Mt. Holly courthouse. The years passed by, the memory of Ellis Parker faded, and today the reminders of his life are harder to find, and less well known.

The old courthouse where Parker had his office still stands in Mt. Holly, New Jersey. The courthouse has been renovated and Parker's second floor office is in an inaccessible and seldom used back section. There is no plaque or marker to indicate his office, or even his existence. The present Chief Detective of Burlington County works out of a modern office in the seven-story municipal building.

The old jail, where Parker held and interrogated prisoners, is now the Burlington County Prison Museum. The archives hold a few records of his cases, including a picture of a smiling Parker at the reins of a horse and cart with his wife by his side. Since the first publication of Master Detective, there has been more awareness and interest in Ellis Parker, so the jail now has several displays and holds occasional Ellis Parker related events.

The Elks Club where Parker spent much of his leisure time and where he was arrested still stands just a few yards from the courthouse. The second floor bar where Ellis Parker played cards and held court is locked much of the time since the members use the newer bar on the first floor. In the first floor reception area, the old mounted elk's head still looks down on the room where Parker met with Murray Bleefeld for the first time, and where Parker's friend Justice of the Peace Throckmorton released Parker on $500 bail over the objections of Geoghan's men. In the main hallway hangs a photo of Clint Zeller, past president and former detective under Ellis Parker.

Ellis Parker's house, at 215 High Street, across from the jail still stands. The house has been divided into offices and apartments and is called, appropriately enough, the Parker Building. Once the showplace of Mt Holly, the massive red brick Victorian/gothic structure's front has been obscured by a plain stucco addition that looks as if it was grafted on from another, far less attractive building.

Parker's more modest second house, on Garden Street, has fared better. It was later home to Ellis Parker, Jr, and then to several Parker relatives. Following an unsuccessful attempt to divide the house into two apartments, the owners sold the house to its present occupants in the 1950s. The living room where Parker was laid out after his death in 1940 still has a cozy,

Victorian atmosphere. When they moved into the house, the owners found only one item the Parkers had left behind: a large cardboard box full of neatly folded newspapers. The papers were from the Philadelphia Inquirer, the New York Times, the Camden Courier-Journal, and several others, but they all had one thing in common: every paper covered some aspect of the Lindbergh case.

Paul Wendel's semidetached brick house at 496 Greenwood Avenue in Trenton still stands, but the stately tree in the front is gone and the front porch has been enclosed. The house has a much more lived-in look than it had in the 1930s. From Greenwood Avenue, an observer can still see the window of the third floor room where the kidnapped Lindbergh baby was kept and died, according to Wendel's confession. The much more modest rowhouse on nearby Walnut Avenue where Wendel's family lived in 1936 and which the Parkers and Anna Bading visited repeatedly in an attempt to get corroborating statements still stands as well. Two of Wendel's grandchildren, when contacted for this book declined to discuss their grandfather or provide any information.

Harry Bleefeld's house at 3041 Voorhies Avenue in Brooklyn still stands, and looks pretty much as it did in 1936, except for the addition of some aluminum window awnings. If Paul Wendel's initials are still on the basement door, they have long since been painted over.

And just a few blocks away from the Parker's second house on Garden Street is the Mt. Holly Cemetery. Ellis Parker's grave is near the top of the small hill to the right as a visitor enters. On the pink granite headstone are the names of Ellis Parker, his wife Cora, and their daughter Mildred. If you visit on a quiet afternoon armed with photographs of the funeral, you are transported back to 1940. You can see where Ellis Jr. stood with wife Katherine and a guard from Lewisburg. You can see where Cora stood, supported by her son Eddie and daughter Helen, and where the pallbearers carried the casket. It almost seems as if the crowds of old friends, admirers and well-wishers have just left and the Old Chief has just begun his eternal rest.

Chapter Notes:

Chapter 1 – A Crime in the Next County
-The details of the kidnapping may be found in several sources, including the NewYork Times and the Trenton Evening Times. The description of the house and the surrounding area is from a personal visit.

-The story of the notification of the state police at Trenton was from *The Lindbergh Case* by Jim Fisher.

-Parker's office is described in several newspaper accounts, by retired Chief of Detectives Harry McConnell, and in *The Cunning Mulatto* by Fletcher Pratt.

-The information on the Mt. Holly prison and the gallows are from the Mt. Holly Prison Museum.

-Parker's early involvement in the DMV investigation is from *Lindbergh: The Crime*, by Noel Behn, from the Liberty Magazine articles published by Governor Hoffman, and from the New York Times

-The details of the early stages of the Lindbergh investigation are found in several sources, including *The Lindbergh Case* by Jim Fisher, *Kidnap* by George Waller, *Lindbergh*, by Scott Berg, *Loss of Eden*, by Joyce Milton, and the New York Times.

-A copy of the letters Parker wrote to Wendel are contained in Parker's court documents in the New Jersey State Police Museum, as is the letter Parker wrote back to Governor Moore accepting Moore's request that he get involved in the Lindbergh case.

-Parker's March 6 article criticizing the state police is from the Trenton Evening Times
The substance of the phone call to Parker is from his federal court testimony.

Chapter 2- A Fiddler Becomes a Detective

-The story of Parker's career as a fiddler and his stolen horse and wagon are from the Burlington Times. There are several other versions in a number of shorter articles as well.

-Details of life in the various historical periods are from *This Fabulous Century* series, Time-Life Books.

Chapter 3- Bloody Murder and Burning Barns

-Washington Hunter's condition is a developmental abnormality that affects roughly one person in 25,000. The medical term for it is *Situs Inversus*, and as Parker said, the condition involves a mirror image reversal of the body's asymmetrical organs. Source: www.emedicine.com, and Dr. Leon Sheer.

-The details of this and most other cases are taken from *The Cunning Mulatto*, by Fletcher Pratt, The Burlington County Times, The Trenton Evening Times, The New York Times, The Baltimore Sun, The Chicago Tribune, The Washington Post, True Detective Magazine, and New Age Magazine. As with so many of Parker's cases, details vary from one source to the next. In one version of the Washington Hunter case, for instance, Parker goes undercover in New York's Hell's Kitchen to track the killers and happens to overhear someone talking about it. He then uses that information to track down the killers.

-The names and birth dates of Parker's children are contained in Ellis Parker's will, on file with the Burlington County Surrogate's Office, and were verified by William Fullerton, Parker's grandson. William Fullerton also researched the information on the Parkers' boarders.

-The diary Parker kept from 1901 to 1904 is in the possession of William Fullerton, Parker's grandson.

-The information of the federal and local efforts to set up a central fingerprint file is from the FBI's website www.FBI.gov.

-The details of the "Cranberry King" murder were supplied by Robert Congleton, Rider University Library archivist.

-The story of the reformed thief Parker took under his roof is from William Fullerton and Andrew Sahol, Parker's grandsons.

Chapter 4- Bootleggers, a Pickled Corpse, and 175 Suspects

-The details of most cases are taken from *The Cunning Mulatto*, by Fletcher Pratt, The Burlington County Times, The Trenton Evening Times, The New York Times, The Baltimore Sun, The Chicago Tribune, The Washington Post, True Detective Magazine, and New Age Magazine

-The background of the evolution of crime is from *Public Enemies* by William Helmer

-The story of Izzy and Moe is from American History Illustrated Magazine.

-The descriptions of the 1920s are from *The Lawless Decade* by Paul Saun, and *Only Yesterday* by Frederick Lewis Allen.

-There are several different accounts of how Parker found the body of Matilda Russo, including one story where he heard the little girl calling to him in a dream. The version presented here is from Parker's own words in *The Cunning Mulatto* and from the New York Times article.

-The story of Ellis Parker protecting Anna Bading and forbidding swearing (by others) in her presence was from Anna Bading's son, Herman M. Bading.
-Information indicating there might have been no kidnapping in the John Brunen case after all was discovered by Lindbergh case researcher Michael Melsky.

Chapter 5- Two Weddings and a Scandal

-The description of Herman Bading is from Harry McConnell.

-The information on Parker's real estate holdings is from William Fullerton, Parker's grandson.

-Anna Bading's low opinion of Paul Wendel was revealed to the author by her son, Herman M. Bading.

-Paul Wendel's appointment as attorney representing the accused head of the Mercer County Workhouse is from a front-page story in the Trenton Evening Times.

-Information on the Rancocas Creek Rumrunning Scandal and Parker's suspension are from the Trenton Evening Times and the New York Times

-Information on Parker's daughter's elopement were taken from newspaper accounts on the website of Bill Fullerton, Parker's grandson, www.fullerton1.com/ellis/html

-Additional information on the Wilson-Roberts case was provided by Dr. John Santaspirt of Moorestown, New Jersey. A tour of the Wilson house was given by the present owners.

Chapter 6- Depression Crimes
-The story of Robert Burns is from www.capitolcity.com

-Background on gangsters is from *The Thirties: America and the Great Depression* by Fon Boardman, Jr., and *Public Enemies* by William Helmer.

-Details of Parker's cases are from *The Cunning Mulatto*, by Fletcher Pratt, magazine articles of the time, , The Baltimore Sun, The Chicago Tribune, and The Washington Post.

Chapter 7- Crime of the Century-Case of a Lifetime
Chapter 8- A Semi Official Investigation
-The story of Harold Hoffman setting up roadblocks is from *Hysteria*, by Andrew Dutch

-The information on the Lindbergh case is from several sources including *The Lindbergh Case* by Jim Fisher, *Kidnap* by George Waller, *Lindbergh*, by Scott Berg, the New York Times, the Trenton Evening Times, the FBI report on the case, and documents in the archives of the New Jersey State Police Museum in West Trenton.

-The story of J. Edgar Hoover's attempts to take over the Lindbergh investigation is from *The Bureau* by Ronald Kessler, and *J.Edgar Hoover: The Man and His Secrets* by Curt Gentry.

-Details of the activities at the Lindbergh estate are from *Lindbergh*, by A. Scott Berg, and *Loss of Eden*, by Joyce Milton.

Chapter 9-Bradway Brown and an International Fugitive
-The story of the Bradway Brown case is from *The Cunning Mulatto*, by Fletcher Pratt, and from contemporary newspaper accounts in the Burlington County Times and the Trenton Evening Times. The fugitive case is from *The Cunning Mulatto*.

-Ellis Parker's letter to J. Edgar Hoover is on file at the New Jersey State Police Museum.

Chapter 10- The Most Hated Man in America
-The information on the Lindbergh case is from several sources including *The Lindbergh Case* by Jim Fisher, *Kidnap* by George Waller, newspaper accounts, and documents in the archives of the New Jersey State Police Museum in West Trenton.

-The information about Wilentz's meeting with Parker and Parker's denial of having any evidence in the Lindbergh case is from the Philadelphia Evening Bulletin of December 7, 1935. The state police representative was not identified.

Chapter 11- Second Opinions, Second Guesses
-The story of Hoffman's reluctance to get involved in the case is from Hoffman's Liberty magazine articles.

-Most of the material on Parker's public statements are from the New York Times, and a collection of local newspapers found in the attic of Parker's Garden Street residence by the new owners in 1949.

Chapter 12- The Second Lindbergh Kidnapping

-The details of the role of Murray Bleefeld and the events leading up to the kidnapping of Wendel are from *Scapegoat* by Scaduto, a series of Liberty Magazine articles, the New York Times, the Trenton Evening Times, and from records in the New Jersey State Police Museum.

-Bleefeld told two versions of how he came to meet Parker. In his Grand Jury testimony, he claimed his brother had introduced him, but when interviewed by Anthony Scaduto in 1976, he claimed it was Arbitel. The Arbitel story seems more likely as it appears David Bleefeld was in prison at the time of the claimed meeting, and Murray might have wanted to protect Arbitel from involvement.

-Parker denied there had been any torture of Paul Wendel. Murray Bleefeld also denied any mistreatment when interviewed for Anthony Scaduto's 1976 book, *Scapegoat*. Even so, it seems certain Wendel actually was tortured. The torture was admitted independently by Schlossman, Weiss and Bleefeld at the time, when they were apprehended, at their grand jury testimony, and at their trial. Their stories were identical in the details. Finally, there was the statement of the tailor who mended Wendel's suit and noticed bloodstains. Ellis Parker's role in this treatment, if any, is less clear, since he wasn't at the Voorhies Avenue house himself. It is likely he was at least aware of the existence, if not the degree of physical coercion being used because Ellis Jr. was reporting to him regularly.

Chapter 13- Confessions

-Copies of all three versions of Wendel's confession are contained in Parker's trial documents on file in the New Jersey State Police Museum.

-The story of Parker's attempts to get corroborating statements from Wendel's children is from statements they later gave to police. These statements are on file at the New Jersey State Police Museum. Wendel's son and daughter's claims that Parker spoke of financial advantages and a quick temporary insanity acquittal before a friendly judge, and the claim Parker said he could guarantee protection because of political connections seem credible because they were consistent with statements made by Wendel even though they were given independently while Wendel was still in jail and had not spoken to his children.

Chapter 14- The Storm

-The story of Wendel being turned over to Mercer County is from *Kidnap*, by George Waller, articles in Liberty magazine by Wendel and by Fred Allhoff, and from additional material from files at the New Jersey State Police Museum.

-The statements of Wendel's children are on file at the New Jersey State Police Museum.

-The information that Ellis, Jr. was hiding in Ellis, Sr.'s High Street home is from William Fullerton, Parker, Sr.'s grandson, and from Parker's trial testimony.

-The details of the detection and capture of Schlossman, Weiss, and Bleefeld are from The New York Times.

-Information on Geoghan and his troubles is from the New York Times. Geoghan's motivation in pursuing Parker is inferred from Geoghan's determination to try Parker in Brooklyn even after Parker had been convicted and incarcerated by a Federal court. Geoghan's was virtually the only voice demanding this trial after the federal conviction.
Parker's arrest outside the Elks Club, and the details of the impromptu bail hearing are from the New York Times.

-The description of the Elks Club is from a personal visit.

Chapter 15, 16- The Trial of Ellis Parker

-The details of the trail are from accounts in the Camden Courier-Journal, the Trenton Evening Times, the New York Times, and documents at the New Jersey State Police Museum.

-Some of the testimony, as well as the excerpts from newspaper editorials are from *The Lindbergh-Hauptmann Aftermath*, by Paul Wendel

Chapter 17- His Last Bow

-The story of the kidnapping of Garrett Schenck is from *Hysteria*, by Andrew Dutch, and was also mentioned in Harold Hoffman's Liberty magazine articles.

-A 1937 Christmas card from the Parkers is in the files of the Prison Museum in Mt. Holly.

-The original manuscript of Wendel's book is in the files of the New Jersey State Police Museum in West Trenton.

-Letters from Parker at Lewisburg are on file at the New Jersey State Police Museum, as is the original manuscript of Wendel's book and several petitions on Parker's behalf.

-Transcripts of Parker's testimony before the grand jury are in the Hoffman collection in the New Jersey State Police Archives.

-The story of how Cora Parker was forced to sell the house on High Street and move to Garden Street is from William Fullerton, Parker's grandson.

-The substance and results of the legal appeals are from case summaries in the Atlantic Reporter for the Kings County Trials, and the Federal Reporter and Federal Supplement for the federal trial in Newark.

-The description of the viewing and funeral are from newspaper accounts in the Burlington County Times, the Camden Courier Journal, and the Trenton Evening Times. The story of the reporters reminiscing and drinking to Parker's memory is from a 1949 Camden Courier Post column by reporter Charley Humes.

-Anna Bading's lack of any memorabilia or documents concerning her long employment with Ellis Parker was told to the author by her son, Herman M. Bading.

-The description of the Garden Street house and the living room is from a personal visit, as is the description of the cemetery and the headstone.

-Depending on the source, Parker's cause of death is described as either a brain tumor, a brain aneurism, or heart failure. His overall ill health no doubt contributed and made a final determination unclear.

Bibliography:

Books

Behn, Noel *Lindbergh: the Crime* (Atlantic Monthly Press: 1995)

Berg, A. Scott *Lindbergh* (G.P.Putnam and Sons: 1998)

Boardman, Fon, Jr. *The Thirties: America and the Great Depression* (Henry Z. Walk, Inc.:1967)

Bourgeau, Art *The Mystery Lover's Companion* (Crown Books, 1986)

Collins, Max Allen *Stolen Away* (Bantam: 1991)

Douglas, John and Mark Olshaker *The Cases That Haunt Us* (Scribner: 2000)

Dutch, Andrew *Hysteria: The Lindbergh Kidnap Case* (Dorrance and Company: 1975)

Evans, Colin *The Casebook of Forensic Detection* (Wiley: 1996)

Fisher, Jim *The Lindbergh Case* (Rutgers University Press: 1987)

Fisher, Jim *The Ghosts of Hopewell* (Southern Illinois University Press: 1998)

Geis, Gilbert and Bienen, Leigh *Crimes of the Century* (Northeastern University Press 1998)

Kennedy, Ludovic *The Airman and the Carpenter, Crime of the Century* (Harper Collins: 1985)

Kessler, Ronald *The Bureau: The Secret History of the FBI* (St. Martin's Press: 2002)

Lee, Dr Henry and Dr Jerry Labriola *Famous Crimes Revisited* (Strong Books: 2001)

Lindbergh, Anne Morrow *Hour of Gold, Hour of Lead* (Harcourt Brace Jovanovich: 1973)

Lindbergh, Anne Morrow *Locked Rooms and Open Doors* (Harcourt Brace Jovanovich: 1974)

Milton, Joyce *Loss of Eden* (Harper Collins: 1993)

Perrett, Geoffrey *America in the Twenties, A History* (Simon and Schuster: 1982)

Pratt, Fletcher *The Cunning Mulatto, and other cases of Ellis Parker, American Detective* (Harrison Smith and Robert Haas:1935)

Repetto, Thomas *American Mafia* (Henry Holt: 2004)

411

Reynolds, Quentin *Courtroom: The Story of Samuel S. Liebowitz* (Wolff: 1950)

Saun, Paul *The Lawless Decade* (Crown Books 1957)

Scaduto, Anthony *Scapegoat: The Lonesome Death of Bruno Hauptmann* (G.P.Putnam's Sons: 1976)

Waller, George *Kidnap: The Story of the Lindbergh* Case (Dial Press: 1961)

Wright, Theon *In Search of the Lindbergh Baby* (Tower Publications:1981)

Articles, Magazines

New Age Magazine, 1927

>*A County Detective With a World-Wide Reputation*

American Magazine, December 1930

>*Smart Criminals Spring Their Own Traps*

Real Detective Magazine, June, 1933

>*The "Hick" Detective of Mt Holly*

Literary Digest, August 4, 1934

>*They Stood Out From the Crowd*

Liberty Magazine, November 28, 1936-January 9, 1937

>*Wendel Tells All*

Liberty Magazine, June 25, 1938

>*What Happened to Ellis Parker?*

Liberty Magazine, 1936

>*Hoffman: What Was Wrong with the Hauptmann Case?*

True Detective Magazine, June 1940

>*The Hidden Truth Behind the Ellis Parker Death Mystery*

Crime Patrol, Number 8, 1947

>*The Alibi*

CPSIA information can be obtained
at www.ICGtesting.com
Printed in the USA
BVHW090544301220
596440BV00006B/826